Encountering
Artificial Intelligence:
Ethical and Anthropological
Investigations

Encountering Artificial Intelligence: Ethical and Anthropological Investigations

AI Research Group
for the
Centre for Digital Culture
of the
Dicastery for Culture and Education
of the
Holy See

Edited by
Matthew J. Gaudet
Noreen Herzfeld
Paul Scherz
Jordan J. Wales

☙PICKWICK *Publications* · Eugene, Oregon

ENCOUNTERING ARTIFICIAL INTELLIGENCE:
ETHICAL AND ANTHROPOLOGICAL INVESTIGATIONS

Copyright © 2024 Dicastery for Culture and Education of the Holy See. All rights reserved.

Except for brief quotations in critical publications or reviews, no part of this book may be reproduced in any manner without prior written permission from the author and the publisher. Write: Permissions, Wipf and Stock Publishers, 199 W. 8th Ave., Suite 3, Eugene, OR 97401.

Pickwick Publications
An Imprint of Wipf and Stock Publishers
199 W. 8th Ave., Suite 3
Eugene, OR 97401

www.wipfandstock.com

SOFTCOVER ISBN: 979-8-3852-1028-2
HARDCOVER ISBN: 979-8-3852-1029-9
EBOOK ISBN: 979-8-3852-1030-5

THEOLOGICAL INVESTIGATIONS
of
ARTIFICIAL INTELLIGENCE
BOOK SERIES

Series Editors
Matthew J. Gaudet, Santa Clara University
Jason King, St. Mary's University—San Antonio, TX
M. Therese Lysaught, Loyola University Chicago

Society has crossed the threshold of massive upheavals due to the advancement and proliferation of artificial intelligence and other technologies. The Theological Investigations of Artificial Intelligence book series offers reflections on this technological revolution and its consequences from the tradition of Catholic social, economic, and ethical thought.

The series is published in collaboration between the AI Research Group for the Centre for Digital Culture, which is part of the Holy See's Dicastery for Culture and Education, and the *Journal of Moral Theology*. It advances the *Journal of Moral Theology*'s mission of fostering scholarship deeply rooted in traditions of inquiry about the moral life, engaged with contemporary issues, and exploring the interface of Catholic moral theology, philosophy, economics, political theory, psychology, and more.

Online versions of the volumes in the Theological Investigations of Artificial Intelligence series are available for free download as chapters at jmt.scholasticahq.com. Paper copies may be purchased from Wipf & Stock. This dual approach reflects the *Journal of Moral Theology*'s commitment to the common good, as it makes the scholarship of Catholic theological ethicists broadly available, especially across borders. Additionally, you can find the series listed on the website of the Dicastery for Culture and Education at: http://www.cultura.va/content/cultura/en.html.

The AI Research Group is a group of North American theologians, philosophers, and ethicists who have come together at the invitation of the Vatican Centre for Digital Culture, under the auspices of the Dicastery for Culture and Education of the Holy See, to discuss the current and future issues that the continued development of artificial intelligence poses for life and society as we know it. This book is the result of the collaborative efforts of these scholars from 2020 to 2023. The lead authors for this volume were Matthew J. Gaudet, Noreen Herzfeld, Paul Scherz, and Jordan Wales, and the contributing authors were Nathan Colaner, Jeremiah Coogan, Mariele Courtois, Brian Cutter, David E. DeCosse, Justin Charles Gable, OP, Brian Patrick Green, James Kintz, Cory Andrew Labrecque, Catherine Moon, Anselm Ramelow, OP, John P. Slattery, Margarita Vega, Luis G. Vera, Andrea Vicini, SJ, and Warren von Eschenbach.

TABLE OF CONTENTS

Acknowledgments viii

Foreword x

Introduction 1

Chapter 1: Approaches to AI Ethics 24

Part I: Anthropological Investigations

Chapter 2: AI and the Human Person 43

Chapter 3: Consciousness: A *Sine Qua Non* of
    Relationality and Intelligence 69

Chapter 4: Encounters with Seemingly Personal AI 106

Chapter 5: AI and Our Encounter with God 131

Part II: Ethical Challenges with AI

Chapter 6: AI and Catholic Social Teaching 147

Chapter 7: The Promises and Pitfalls of AI in
    Contemporary Life 161

Chapter 8: Recommendations for an AI Future 227

Contributors 254

Acknowledgments

We would like to express our sincere gratitude to all the individuals and institutions that have contributed to the successful completion of this research initiative. Their support, guidance and contributions have been invaluable in launching this first publication of the Center for Digital Culture, on the ethical impact of new digital technologies. This project began in 2017 during the Plenary Assembly of the former Pontifical Council for Culture which focused on the future of humanity, examined the potential of artificial intelligence, as well as genetics and neuroscience, to radically transform established patterns of human existence at both the individual and social levels. We also want to acknowledge the subsequent support of the new Dicastery for Culture and Education under the direction of Cardinal José Tolentino de Mendonça.

We are deeply grateful for the dedication, collaboration, and intellectual inputs of each of the authors who have collaborated in the preparation of this book. Their contributions have greatly enriched the quality of this research and provided a stimulating environment for fruitful discussions. Special mention is due to Matthew J. Gaudet, Noreen Herzfeld, Paul Scherz, and Jordan Wales for the coordination and ongoing guidance of the working groups that have been instrumental in framing, revising, and shaping this publication. Our gratitude also goes to Levi Checketts, Marius Dorobantu, Mark McKenna, Veronica Martinez, and Ann Skeet for their earlier participation in the discussion groups; to Terrence Deacon, Mark Graves, and Julie Gregoire and Natalie Mayerhofer from the Centre Hospitalier de l'Université de Montréal, for their participation and dissemination of knowledge as expert guests during particular discussions; and to Ahmed Amer of Santa Clara University for lending his knowledge of the history of computing. Additionally, many thanks to Joshua Peck and Annemarie Arnold for their diligent note-keeping during our group meetings.

We would like to thank Fundación Telefónica, Fundación "LaCaixa," and Fundación ProFuturo for their support for the work of the Centre for Digital Culture over these years, which has been crucial to the success of this research project. We give special thanks to Dan and Charmaine Warmenhoven for their generosity in making this project possible. The Markkula Centre for Applied Ethics at Santa Clara University also deserves special note, for providing the necessary support, resources, and infrastructure to carry out this study, and particularly the leadership of Don Heider and the organizational skills of Monica DeLong. Moreover, our eternal gratitude goes to M. Therese Lysaught, Jason King, and the whole team at the *Journal of Moral Theology* for their editorial and other guidance as the book took form.

Finally, we offer our gracious thanks to all those who have contributed to this work, directly or indirectly, and whose support and participation have been fundamental in the achievement of this publication.

Angel González-Ferrer
Centre for Digital Culture

FOREWORD

Over the last few years, the theme of artificial intelligence (AI) has attracted the attention of a number of Vatican curial departments, and a consensus around the need for a rigorous theological and philosophical consideration of the likely social, economic, and cultural impact of the technology has emerged very clearly. The challenge is already being addressed by the Pontifical Academy for Life, which has sponsored the *Rome Call for AI Ethics;* the Pontifical Academy for the Sciences, which has convened high-level meetings of experts in the relevant scientific and technological disciplines; and the Dicasteries for Promoting Integral Human Development and for Communication, which have been addressing the likely impact of AI on questions such as peace, work, and social discourse.

The former Pontifical Council for Culture (now incorporated within the Dicastery for Culture and Education) established a Centre for Digital Culture to promote dialogue between the worlds of faith and technology. One of the most interesting challenges that has emerged in such dialogue is that of attempting to approach ethical issues in a context where the participants are coming from a wide variety of scientific disciplines, cultural and religious backgrounds, philosophical traditions, and political perspectives. It has in many ways illustrated the meeting of what C.P. Snow called 'two cultures'—one rooted in more positivistic scientific thought and the other owing more to the humanities and the arts. The dialogues have often ended focusing on the human—How will we ensure that technologies are truly promoting human progress? What is it that distinguishes humans from machines? What are the values and practices that promote social and human flourishing?

In order to ensure that the richness of our Christian/Catholic tradition would be fully represented in such dialogues, the Centre for Digital Culture was convinced that it would be necessary to draw on the wisdom of global scholars of theology and philosophy who had an established interest in studying the impact of digital technology in general—and AI in particular—on our understanding of what it means to be human. As a first step, and with the assistance of Santa Clara University, a group of academics based in North America was identified and invited to participate in this project. The group was originally scheduled to meet in March 2020 but was obliged, due to the COVID-19 pandemic, to move its proceedings online. Three working groups were established which met on a monthly basis until September 2022 when it proved possible to convene a plenary in person meeting at Santa Clara. At that meeting, it was decided to start working on a position paper which would consolidate and integrate the work of the previous years. The central themes to be developed were determined, and a number of writing and editorial teams were established. In June of 2023, the group convened in Rome, and the writing was substantially finalized. I am now very pleased to welcome the publication of *Encountering Artificial Intelligence: Ethical and Anthropological Investigations*. It represents the fruits of an intense series of conversations, dialogues, and meetings and is a testimony to the remarkable generosity and competence of all those who have been involved.

The book has been born from dialogue and is intended to facilitate further dialogue both within and beyond the Catholic world. Many of the insights have been elaborated in the context of deep conversations between the authors, who themselves have been engaged with the thought and contributions of other experts working in the area. This richness is clearly reflected in the text which references, and is enhanced by, the work of recognized authorities who come from a variety of philosophical traditions. The Dicastery for Culture and Education is delighted to offer this text as a stimulus for a wider conversation with other interested academics and commentators. In many ways, we would liken this book to an *'instrumentum laboris,'* and it is our intention to convene an international gathering of scholars representing a global perspective and other cognate disciplines where the text will serve as a point of departure for further discussion and reflection.

The text, however, can stand alone, and it already elaborates a comprehensive and accessible Christian/Catholic perspective on the debates about artificial intelligence that have recently captured the public attention. It is clear that decisions about the eventual regulation of artificial intelligence cannot be entrusted exclusively to representatives of technology companies or to politicians but should be informed by a more extensive consideration from civil society. *Encountering Artificial Intelligence* has been produced with a view to alerting a wider public to some of the fundamental questions on the meaning and purpose of human existence and the possible impacts of emerging technologies, questions that merit greater attention and scrutiny.

I wish to conclude by expressing my gratitude to all those who worked for the achievement of the project. I want to acknowledge the personal generosity, both in terms of time and effort, of the individual contributors as well as the collective commitment of the group to working together, to learning from each other, and to finding consensus. It has been a privilege to be part of your work. I have learned much, but above all, I have a renewed appreciation of the value of your contribution to the life of the Church.

Monsignor Paul Tighe
October 2023

INTRODUCTION

Why Should the Church Discuss AI?

Recent rapid technological developments raise significant concerns and deep questions about traditional ways of understanding human persons and their place in the world. In particular, advances in artificial intelligence (AI) demand a fresh "scrutinizing [of] the signs of the times and . . . interpreting [of] them in the light of the Gospel."[1]

With each generation, the Church seeks to make its ancient wisdom understandable, but as the Second Vatican Council reminds us, "It is sometimes difficult to harmonize culture with Christian teaching."[2] Nevertheless, "These difficulties do not necessarily harm the life of faith, rather they can stimulate the mind to a deeper and more accurate understanding of the faith." Instead of something to categorically fear, condemn, or cast out, culture-shaping developments in science and technology like AI "raise new questions" and "demand new theological investigations." The ancient wisdom of the Church, the deposit of Faith, is one thing; "the manner in which [it is] enunciated . . . is another."[3]

The Catholic Church is ancient yet also radically new and everlasting. As a collection of holy women and men over thousands of years, the Church is held together in that "mystical Body of Christ," which is both full of "broken bones" and always yearning for wholeness in the Divine,[4]

---

[1] Paul VI, *Gaudium et Spes*, § 4. All magisterial documents cited in this volume can be found on the website of the Holy See, www.vatican.va.

[2] *Gaudium et Spes*, § 62.

[3] *Gaudium et Spes*, § 62.

[4] The language of "broken bones" is developed by theologian M. Shawn Copeland in her book *Enfleshing Freedom: Body, Race, and Being* (Minneapolis: Fortress, 2010). Copeland borrows the phrase "body of broken bones" from a 1953 piece by Thomas Merton, in which he

seeking always to find meaning and purpose as "our hearts are restless until they rest in Thee."[5] Each generation must therefore heed the admonition of the Second Vatican Council to unite "new sciences and theories ... with Christian morality and the teaching of Christian doctrine, so that religious culture and morality may keep pace with scientific knowledge and with the constantly progressing technology."[6] The goal of this pursuit is not to create new visions of morality but to "interpret and evaluate" all new knowledge "in a truly Christian spirit."[7] With this charge in mind, the AI Research Group for the Vatican Centre for Digital Culture has contemplated one of the most compelling and potentially culture-transforming technologies of the twenty-first century: artificial intelligence.

A Long History of Embracing Science, Technology, and Faith

This book is the latest in a long line of ecclesial reflections seeking to interpret issues regarding modern technology for a new generation of believers. In spite of the view that Catholicism (indeed, religion in general) is at odds with science and its technological products, throughout its two-thousand-year history the Catholic Church has been involved in the collection and preservation, research and development, and production

---

describes the deep divisions and sufferings in the Body of Christ (Thomas Merton, *Seeds of Contemplation* [Trappist, KY: Our Lady of Gethsemani Monastery, 1949], 53). Copeland connects the phrase to the ancient theological tradition of the Mystical Body of Christ while referring both to centuries of racism, misogyny, violence, and oppression as well as to contemporary divisions, sexual violence, and continued devaluations of human bodies (*Enfleshing Freedom:* 101–105, 126–128). For Copeland, the Eucharist becomes the "countersign to the devaluation and violence" which is only possible if the brokenness of the body is explicitly identified (126).

[5] Augustine, *Confessions*, trans. J.G. Pilkington, *Nicene and Post-Nicene Fathers*, First Series, vol. 1, ed. Philip Schaff (Buffalo, NY: Christian Literature, 1887), 1.1.5.

[6] *Gaudium et Spes,* § 62.

[7] *Gaudium et Spes,* § 62.

and consumption of technology.⁸ The Church has had a hand in many inventions, ranging from tidal-powered water mills and mechanical clocks to the improvement of brewing and winemaking and even hypertext, to list just a few.⁹ Moreover the modern tradition of Catholic social teaching can be viewed not only as social commentary but also as Catholic teaching on technology, since technology itself (industry, weapons, communications, transportation, etc.), driven by scientific advances, has caused so many social changes in the last two centuries. The fact is, while "artificial intelligence" has existed as a term only since 1956, people of faith have been in dialogue with technology and science for millennia.

"In the beginning, God created the heavens and the earth."¹⁰ This theological claim has resonated with humanity since it was written by the Hebrew people thousands of years ago. The core of this ancient truth—that the creation of humanity is second in its miraculous nature only to the creation of existence itself, for God's "eternal power and divinity have been made known through his works since the creation of the world"¹¹— has survived countless revolutions of culture, science, and technology. The world, and thus the universe, "is a joyful mystery to be contemplated with gladness and praise."¹²

---

⁸ Brian Patrick Green, "A Roman Catholic View: Technological Progress? Yes. Transhumanism? No," in *Religious Transhumanism and Its Critics*, ed. Arvin Gouw, Brian Patrick Green, and Ted Peters (Lanham, MD: Lexington Books, 2022), 143–160.

⁹ Brian Patrick Green, "The Catholic Church and Technological Progress: Past, Present, and Future," *Religions* 8, no. 6 (2017): 1–16, www.mdpi.com/2077-1444/8/6/106, citing Thomas McErlean and Norman Crothers, *Harnessing the Tides: The Early Medieval Tide Mills at Nendrum Monastery, Strangford Lough* (London: The Stationery Office, 2007); Frances Gies and Joseph Gies, *Cathedral, Forge, and Waterwheel: Technology and Invention in the Middle Ages* (New York: HarperCollins, 1994), 210–215; Lynn White, Jr., *Medieval Religion and Technology: Collected Essays* (Berkeley: University of California Press, 1978), 181–204; and "The Jesuit Who 'Invented' Hypertext," *America Magazine*, August 15, 2011, www.americamagazine.org/issue/784/signs/jesuit-who-invented-hypertext.

¹⁰ Genesis 1:1 All biblical passages in this book used the New American Bible translation.

¹¹ Romans 1:20.

¹² Francis, *Laudato Si'*, § 12.

Introduction

Respect for this joyful mystery should not prevent us from discovering the nature of the physical reality around us. As Galileo Galilei wrote in 1615, "I do not feel obliged to believe that the same God who has endowed us with senses, reason, and intellect has intended us to forgo their use and by some other means to give us knowledge [that] we can attain by them. He would not require us to deny sense and reason in physical matters, which are set before our eyes and minds by direct experience or necessary demonstration."[13] While the Church of that time did justice neither to Galileo nor to his arguments, the Church has since worked more deeply to live the thesis that faith and reason, including reason as active in natural science, can play both distinctive and collaborative roles in bringing humanity to God.

This stance was tested most recently with the advent of Darwinian evolutionary theories. While the Church did not openly embrace theories of Darwinian evolution until the mid-twentieth century, it nevertheless did not officially condemn them, having learned from its actions in the case of Galileo.[14] The tenor of the Church's response can be seen in the First Vatican Council's dogmatic constitution *Dei Filius* (1870), which outlined a supportive framework with regard to reason and science, heavily influenced by the works of Thomas Aquinas:[15]

> Not only can faith and reason never be at odds with one another but they mutually support each other.... So far is the Church from hindering the development of human arts and studies, that in fact the Church assists and promotes them in many ways. For the Church is neither ignorant nor contemptuous of the advantages which derive from this source for human life, rather the Church acknowledges that those things flow from God, the

---

[13] Galileo Galilei, "Letter to the Grand Duchess Christina," in Discoveries and Opinions of Galileo, ed. Stillman Drake (New York: Anchor-Doubleday, 1957), 183–184.
[14] Mariano Artigas, Thomas F. Glick, and Rafael A. Martínez, *Negotiating Darwin: The Vatican Confronts Evolution, 1877–1902* (Baltimore: Johns Hopkins University Press, 2006).
[15] John P. Slattery, *Faith and Science at Notre Dame: John Zahm, Evolution, and the Catholic Church* (Notre Dame, IN: University of Notre Dame Press, 2019).

lord of the sciences, and if they are properly used, lead to God by the help of his Grace.[16]

It is helpful to read these words—emphasizing both "mutual support" and proper use—against the backdrop of the decades between 1870 and 1950, which saw the Church condemning various aspects of modern culture. These condemnations included important arguments against the eugenics movement[17] and abuses of capitalism.[18] At the same time, the Church also criticized Catholic scholars who openly supported theories of human evolution such as John Zahm, CSC and Pierre Teilhard de Chardin, SJ.[19] Nevertheless, the wisdom of the First Vatican Council's *Dei Filius* held back both popes and congregations from any official condemnation of evolution. Indeed, it is because of this inherent openness that Pope Pius XII felt compelled to initiate a formal discussion of evolutionary theory with his encyclical *Humani Generis* in 1951; it is because of this inherent openness that the Second Vatican Council even more forcefully declared the Church a friend of the sciences; it is because of this inherent openness that the Church today laments its own earlier silencing of Galileo and other supporters of good science;[20] and it is because of this inherent openness that Popes including Saint John Paul II, Benedict XVI, and Francis have embraced, time and time again, the beauty, truth, and hope of science and technology.

---

[16] Vatican Council I, *Dei Filius*, § 4:5.

[17] Pius XI, *Casti Connubii*, §§ 68–70.

[18] Leo XIII, *Rerum Novarum*.

[19] See Artigas, Glick, and Martínez, *Negotiating Darwin*; Slattery, *Faith and Science at Notre Dame*.

[20] John Paul II, "Discorso di Giovanni Paolo II ai Partecipanti alla Sessione Plenaria della Pontificia Accademia delle Scienze," October 31, 1992, www.vatican.va/content/john-paul-ii/it/speeches/1992/october/documents/hf_jp-ii_spe_19921031_accademia-scienze.html.

Introduction

A Renewed Embrace of Science and Technology

The harmony between faith and reason demonstrates why an embrace of science and technology is not in conflict with offering clear moral recommendations for its development and application. Over the last decade, Pope Francis has listened to the requests of many in the scientific and technological spheres who have asked for guidance on emerging technologies.[21] Accordingly, many in the curia have entered into dialogue with ethicists, technologists, and business leaders in order to understand and assess the latest technological developments.[22] Following Pope Francis's lead of dialogue and encounter, the authors of this book—the AI Research Group for the Vatican Centre for Digital Culture—seek to continue the Church's embrace of scientific and technological developments by reflecting on both the discoveries of modern computing technology and the ways that economic, political, military, and corporate interests can deflect science and technology from their noble purpose through corrupt patterns that inflict harm upon the common good of humanity and all creation. Pope Francis condemns any such warping of the goods of science and technology as contrary to the flourishing of humanity and of all creation.[23]

Despite this challenge, we affirm that many good women and men work toward and reflect the true, holy nature of science and technology when they pursue or employ these for the global common good. As *Gaudium et Spes* teaches: "Whoever labors to penetrate the secrets of reality with a humble and steady mind, even though they are unaware of the fact, are nevertheless being led by the hand of God, who holds all things

---

[21] See Brian Patrick Green, "The Vatican and Artificial Intelligence: An Interview with Bishop Paul Tighe," *Journal of Moral Theology* 11, Special Issue 1 (2022): 212–231, doi.org/10.55476/001c.34131.

[22] For example, see the Pontifical Academy for Life, "The Rome Call for AI Ethics," February 28, 2020, www.romecall.org.

[23] *Laudato Si'*, §§ 106, 156–158.

in existence and gives them their identity."[24] The obstacles to the global common good may seem insurmountable at times, but the Church is called to follow prophetically in the footsteps of Christ, no matter the odds: to proclaim good news to the poor, clothe the naked, comfort the dying, welcome the stranger, free the imprisoned, heal the sick, feed the hungry, and care for all of creation.[25]

The Church applauds and welcomes the many voices present in the ethical dialogue about this new technology, for AI may forever change the way we interact with the world, and it is vital to consider, seriously and humanely, its effects. Our text is but one of many being written on AI around the world. As such, its goal is to bring the deep traditions of the Christian faith into encounter with the world of AI so that all people of good will can make wise decisions on the nature and use of this emerging technology. We call upon all those who seek the common good to join in this discussion for a future of hope, healing, and justice, as Pope Francis reminds us in *Fratelli Tutti:* "How wonderful it would be if the growth of scientific and technological innovation could come with more equality and social inclusion. How wonderful would it be, even as we discover faraway planets, to rediscover the needs of the brothers and sisters who orbit around us."[26]

A Theme of Encounter

Pope Francis makes his call in a world where technological development is too often absorbed into a reductive view that *equates* fullness of human life exclusively with the freedom from material limitation that technological developments can secure. The Pope critiques this "technocratic paradigm," which hobbles human flourishing even as it inspires the tools that are meant to secure it:

---

[24] *Gaudium et Spes,* § 36.
[25] Luke 4:18–19; Matthew 25:35–40; Deuteronomy 10:19; Leviticus 19:34; Romans 12:13; Job 12:7–10; Psalm 19:1.
[26] Francis, *Fratelli Tutti,* § 31.

> This paradigm exalts the concept of a subject who, using logical and rational procedures, progressively approaches and gains control over an external object.... Men and women have constantly intervened in nature, but for a long time this meant being in tune with and respecting the possibilities offered by the things themselves. It was a matter of receiving what nature itself allowed, as if from its own hand. Now, by contrast, we are the ones to lay our hands on things, attempting to extract everything possible from them while frequently ignoring or forgetting the reality in front of us. Human beings and material objects no longer extend a friendly hand to one another; the relationship has become confrontational. This has made it easy to accept the idea of infinite or unlimited growth, which proves so attractive to economists, financiers, and experts in technology.[27]

The technocratic paradigm thus involves a double distortion: first, of the human person as reducible to an agent of interventions by which to manipulate life's material conditions; and, second, of the world—including the persons within it—as reducible to a field of raw material to be mastered and manipulated by means of technology.

Against such reductions, the Pope urges that we cultivate a "culture of encounter"—a culture that seeks the contact of mind with mind and heart with heart, in a relational sharing of life that embraces the most vulnerable. Throughout these reflections, we are guided by the theme of encounter—which begins with the first touch of compassion upon the heart—so that, we hope, our explicitly Christian reflection may join with an existing conversation and inspire replies of its own. "Encounter" is a common word, connoting the experience of meeting another. In his teaching, Pope Francis applies this common meaning in a perhaps unexpected, even challenging way, to refer to the way human life is oriented toward encounter with divine mercy, how the redemptive promise of such encounter is mediated primarily through our relationships, and how the movement through such encounter and toward divine mercy occurs amid

---

[27] *Laudato Si'*, § 106.

the fallibility, conflict, and confusion that constitute human life.[28] As Francis describes it, an authentic relational encounter between persons involves not just observation, conversation, or action; it is a mutually compassionate involvement. Confronted with another's suffering, it is not enough to say "What a shame." One must "draw near, to touch," to partake of the other's experience.[29] As Saint Paul wrote, when such "compassion and sympathy" exist, we are "of one mind" with others.[30] This experiential sharing, something beyond the communication of information or coordination of action, is a basic requirement. Thus, "encounter," as we use it, will reflect the common human experience of encounter with the divine, with other human beings, and with something as ingenious and confounding as AI.

The Structure of this Book

This book sets out to address two distinct but interconnected sets of questions—anthropological and ethical—regarding AI and the modern world. On the one hand, the very idea of a human creation with the capacity to match or even surpass some or all of the abilities we associate with human *intelligence* invites a set of existential questions about the meaning and nature not only of intelligence but also of personhood, consciousness, and relationship. These questions are often beneath the dystopian fears of a world ruled by AI. But even beyond narratives of AI apocalypse, any reflection on the future trajectory and meaning of AI (dystopian or otherwise) requires at least some specification of what we mean by these concepts. Thus, one might fittingly begin with philosophical, theological, and anthropological questions about the

---

[28] Pope Francis develops his understanding of the culture of encounter in, e.g., *Fratelli Tutti* §§ 30, 87, and 215–217.
[29] Pope Francis, "Morning Meditation in the Chapel of the Domus Sanctae Marthae: For a Culture of Encounter," September 13, 2016, www.vatican.va/content/francesco/en/cotidie/2016/documents/papa-francesco-cotidie_20160913_for-a-culture-of-encounter.html.
[30] Philippians 2:1.

nature of AI; how it challenges our understanding of the nature of humanity; and, ultimately, the ethical questions that emerge from these explorations.

On the other hand, the ethical challenges of AI are not merely those of choosing the wrong AI future. The fact is, AI is already with us, and it is already rife with ethical issues. The instances of AI that exist today are generally targeted at a specific application (winning a chess game, driving a car, diagnosing a patient, generating written text) and are thus each more limited in scope and ability than the future omnicompetent AI of our sci-fi imaginations. Nevertheless, the issues of our AI *present* also occupy a good deal of our collective consciousness and public narrative, whether we are talking about generative AI chatbots, autonomous vehicles, biased algorithms in all sorts of fields, or lethal autonomous weapons on the battlefield. As such, there is an equally persuasive argument for beginning with an exploration of the ethical issues already emerging from the AI world and the ways that these individual instances are collectively changing our social structures in extremely dangerous ways.

Ultimately, we recognize the significance of each of these sets of questions. Thus, after an initial chapter providing an overview of the ongoing conversation in AI ethics, the text that follows is divided into two parts, each conforming to one set of questions. While the limits of physical publication necessitate that one part come before the other, this does not indicate a particular logical ordering of the two parts. We invite readers to encounter this text based on their own experiences and concerns with AI. Readers who are brought to this text by a concern for the possible future of sentient AI or a desire to engage with the philosophical, theological, and anthropological questions that AI prompts should begin with "Part I: Anthropological Explorations." Alternatively, readers who have picked up this volume out of a concern for the clear and present danger that AI poses and a desire to understand what the tradition of Catholic moral and social thought has to say about these dangers should begin with "Part II: Ethical Challenges."

Introduction

"Part I: Anthropological Explorations: AI and Relationships" unpacks the meaning of terms such as *person, intelligence, consciousness,* and *relationship* in order to explore what it means for humans to have an authentic encounter with an AI, and how AI might impact human encounters with God, one another, and the natural world. In light of the theology of the Trinity, the text argues that personhood and intelligence are categories that are not reducible to mechanically replicable behavioral performances, for they involve capacities for subjective, experiential, compassionate engagement with other persons and with reality itself. Consciousness, therefore, is intrinsic to personhood and intelligence; and if it is reduced to some sort of capacity for outward behavior, we lose the very sharing of minds and hearts that we most greatly treasure in personal relationships and, ultimately, in our share in the life of God.[31] Today's AI systems do not have this interior life—and yet, by their behavior, many of them feel personal. Therefore, we reflect also on what sorts of simulated relationships with AI may be of benefit or detriment to our own lives as persons, including our spiritual lives. We consider the pitfalls of AI as a minister in worship, or even as a kind of "god" or "idol"—a tool that promises comprehensive control while actually hiding what it cannot measure.

Part I unfolds in four chapters. In an age of increasingly sociable AI, chapter 2 asks, conceptually and historically, what is a "person;" and what is "intelligence"? Certain views, congenial to an age of mechanisms, see the person as a manipulator of the world, intelligence as competence in this manipulation, and the world itself as raw material to be manipulated. Not content with these narrow accounts, we propose the notion—birthed in early Christian theology and still deeply affecting Western culture—of the

---

[31] This is not to say that inclusion in the category of natural "persons," as we construe it in this text, demands that this or that individual person possess or display a capacity for subjectivity and self-directed compassion. Injury, immaturity, and disability might all affect this or that person's ability to engage those areas of life without excluding him or her from natural personhood. Instead, the category of "person" embraces all who are the sort of being that ordinarily–absent injury, immaturity, or disability–are capable of such engagements.

person as relational, flourishing in empathic self-gift to others, and of intelligence as that understanding by which the person subjectively grasps the world and others. In chapter 3, we argue that we cannot reduce self-gift to behavior alone, for experiential consciousness is a necessary component of interpersonal relationships. Lacking this, an AI system could not truly engage in relationships, could not truly be personal. If consciousness is reduced to information processing or a tendency to behave in a certain way, in order to include AI systems within our sphere, we elide the very sharing of minds and hearts that we most greatly treasure in personal relationships. Refusing reductions, we propose a still richer view of consciousness, drawing on the phenomenological tradition and ultimately oriented toward participation in the relational life of God. However, in chapter 4, we ask: what are we to make of sociable AI systems that do *not* have this interior life and yet, by their behavior, elicit from us all the empathy that ordinarily would be part of a true intersubjective encounter? An unconscious AI cannot engage the mutuality of an intimate relational peer, as in a romance or a close friendship, but perhaps it might fulfill an important role in caregiving or even in receiving care. Always, the way that we think about and treat AI will shape our own exercise of personhood. In chapter 5, we ask about the spiritual ramifications of AI, whether as a minister in worship, as a "god" managing the affairs of the world, or as a kind of "idol"—a tool that promises comprehensive control while actually hiding all that cannot be measured by the quantifiable methods of the physical and social sciences. To be authentically personal, we must navigate reality but not neglect it. By our attentiveness to interpersonal encounter—which begins with the first touch of compassion upon the heart—we hope that our explicitly Christian reflection may join with an existing conversation and inspire replies of its own.

Part II focuses on the present state of AI and the ethical challenges that have emerged. Chapter 6 explores the resources of Catholic social teaching to develop a framework to address the novel problems created by AI. AI

Introduction

ethics can be served "by a religious vision and inspiration, which has universal scope because it places respect for human dignity within the framework of the grandeur and sanctity of God, the Creator and Savior."[32] Through its tradition of social thought, "the Church intends to offer a contribution of truth to the question of [humanity's] place in nature and in human society."[33] Because of technology's importance to society, recent Catholic social teaching has much to say about it. Given the novelty of AI, it is clear that the Catholic tradition ought to engage these issues.

Of course, it is not enough to respond merely with general statements about AI. AI in the workplace will require different responses than AI at home. The use of AI in schools will raise challenges distinct from its use in business. Medical applications of AI carry different risks and different benefits than military applications. Close attention is thus required for the particular problems and opportunities presented by AI can create in each sphere, so a general ethics of AI or set of principles will not be sufficient. Thus, chapter 7 will provide a more richly textured account of AI's specific uses in the areas of family, education, healthcare, politics, culture, the environment, the military, work, and the environment. Finally, chapter 8 builds on these reflections to suggest guidance for people in different roles in society in their use of AI technology. It outlines recommendations for both users and designers of AI, as well as governments and their agents, business owners and workers, and finally, educators.

Historical Overview of AI

Before proceeding to those two main parts, let us briefly trace the history and nomenclature of AI as we understand and use the terminology. While the term "artificial intelligence" did not appear until the mid-twentieth century, the concept of AI is much older. Indian, Jewish, Greek, and Chinese cultures, to name only a few, long ago imagined beings that

---

[32] Francis, "To Participants in the Congress on 'Child Dignity in the Digital World.'"
[33] Pontifical Council for Justice and Peace, *Compendium of the Social Doctrine of the Church*, October 24, 2004, § 14.

(anachronistically) might be called "artificially intelligent."[34] In the seventeenth century, René Descartes philosophically conceived of "machines bearing the image of our bodies and capable of imitating our actions."[35]

Analog computers date back to ancient times. For example, the Antikythera mechanism is a Greek artifact dating back to roughly 70 BC that was used to compute astronomical positions.[36] In the late 1200s, the secular Franciscan Blessed Raymond Lull (Ramon Llull) made many advances in computational theory, including the design of a primitive logic machine based on rotating disks and charts.[37] In 1872, the British mathematician Sir William Thompson (later Lord Kelvin) designed a mechanical analog computer capable of predicting tides. Mechanical computers were used throughout the early twentieth century to solve all sorts of mathematical calculations, from predicting the tides to targeting torpedoes.

For the purposes of this volume, however, when we speak of a machine or computer, we are not intending to include these types of precursors to the modern *digital* computer.[38] The "difference engine," designed in 1820

---

[34] Adrienne Mayor, *God and Robots: Myths, Machines, and Ancient Dreams of Technology* (Princeton, NJ: Princeton University Press, 2018).

[35] René Descartes, *Discourse on Method* (1637), V. Descartes actually argued that such machines could never exist. These predictions, however, would be undermined by computational technologies whose foundations had been laid already, long before Descartes voiced his thoughts on the subject.

[36] Tony Freeth and Alexander Jones, "The Cosmos in the Antikythera Mechanism," *Institute for the Study of the Ancient World Papers* 4 (February 2012), doi.org/2333.1/xgxd26r7.

[37] Ton Sales, "Llull as Computer Scientist, or Why Llull Was One of Us," and John Newsome Crossley, "Ramon Llull's Contributions to Computer Science," in *Ramon Llull. From the Ars Magna to Artificial Intelligence*, ed. Alexander Fido and Carles Sierra (Barcelona: Artificial Intelligence Research Institute, 2011), 25–38 and 39–59, www.iiia.csic.es/~sierra/wp-content/uploads/2019/02/Llull.pdf.

[38] Computing machines can be analog, digital, or quantum. Except where specifically noted, in this volume we are not referring to analog computing machines, which have a longer history but are less relevant in this context.

by Charles Babbage and Ada Lovelace,[39] is credited by most as the first design for a such a digital computer. Due to the technological limitations of the time, however, Babbage and Lovelace never actually built their machine; and it would not be until 1945 that the first general-purpose, programmable, electronic digital computer, the ENIAC (Electronic Numerical Integrator and Computer), was built.

Among the breakthroughs that helped pave the way to the ENIAC was the theoretical work of Alan Turing. In 1936, Turing proposed his "Universal Computing Machine"—or, as others would call it, the "Universal Turing Machine"—which was used to prove certain fundamental ideas about computing itself and thus became the basis for the central processing units (CPUs) that run most computers today.[40] Turing also grappled with the question of "intelligence," creating a hypothetical test for demonstrating the nuanced and difficult nature of any attempt to define machine intelligence.[41]

Even before Turing's work, however, the cultural imagination was already fascinated by the possibilities of machines that think and act. The monster in English novelist Mary Shelley's *Frankenstein* (1818) is one example of an intelligent human creation that continues to carry cultural currency today.[42] Czech playwright Karel Capek coined the word "robot" in his 1920 play *R.U.R* (an acronym for *Robots Universales Rossum* or, in English, *Rossum's Universal Robots*). Capek drew the word from the Old Slavic word *robota*, meaning "forced labor."[43] Twentieth-century science fiction continued to be rife with robots and sentient computers. American

---

[39] It was Lovelace, Babbage's protégée and thought partner, whose work made the Difference Engine programmable.

[40] Alan M. Turing, "On Computable Numbers, With an Application to the Entscheidungsproblem," *Proceedings of the London Mathematical Society*, s2-42:1, 23–265, doi.org/10.1112/plms/s2-42.1.230.

[41] Alan M. Turing, "Computing Machinery and Intelligence," *Mind: A Quarterly Review* LIX, no. 236 (October 1950): 459, doi.org/10.1093/mind/LIX.236.433.

[42] Mary Shelley, *Frankenstein; or, the Modern Prometheus* Project Guttenberg, December 2022, https://www.gutenberg.org/files/84/84-h/84-h.htm.

[43] John Jordan, *Robots* (Cambridge, MA: MIT Press, 2016), 44.

author Isaac Asimov did as much as anyone to popularize the concept. Asimov wrote over five hundred books and over 380 short stories from the 1930s through the 1990s, constructing whole universes of technological advancements; interactions between humans and intelligent humanoid machines were central to his most influential and lasting tales. While Shelley and others had imagined artificial life turning on its creator, Asimov promoted the idea that AI could be programmed, and thus preconditioned to not rebel against its creators.[44] Twentieth and now early twenty-first century science fiction has continued to produce countless iconic examples of AI, both benign and threatening.

Meanwhile, Turing's intellectual descendants steadily pushed actual computing technology forward. By the late 1980s, mass-produced personal computers had moved beyond laboratories and corporations, and into the homes of those who could afford them; in the 1990s and 2000s, the internet connected most of those computers; and by the 2010s, the smartphone put a computing device in pockets all over the globe.

Alongside these advances in popular computing, computer science has continued its quest for various forms of "intelligence." In 1997, the IBM computer Deep Blue defeated chess grandmaster Gary Kasparov, marking the first computer victory over a reigning world champion. In 2015, Deepmind's computer AlphaGo defeated two professional-level players, Fan Hui and Lee Sedol, at the game of Go, which is considered far more computationally difficult than chess. In 2011, Apple added the digital assistant Siri, and in 2016, Google released its own assistant on its "Google Home" smart speakers and, one year later, added it to its Android mobile operating system. Most recently, large language models (LLMs) have given rise to generative AI programs, so-called for their abilities to not just

---

[44] Repeated through several of his works were his three laws of robotics. These indicate that robots ought to be programmed so that: (1) a robot must not injure a human being or, through inaction, allow a human being to come to harm; (2) a robot must obey the orders given it by human beings; and (3) a robot must protect its own existence. The laws were ordered so that the second and third laws would not be followed if they came into conflict with the prior law or laws.

process data, including language, but to generate new outputs and content. ChatGPT, the most famous of these thus far, was released to the public in late 2022, attracting over 100 million users in its first two months—the fastest adoption rate of any technology in history.[45] But LLMs are merely the latest stage of AI development.

AI: A Primer

There is no simple, universal definition of "artificial intelligence" that is simultaneously uncontroversial and nontrivial. Nevertheless, we find it helpful to attempt definitions of some key terms for two reasons. First, many readers may be newcomers to the field of computing and artificial intelligence and would be helped by a brief overview of the technologies mentioned and terms used throughout this book. Second, even for those more familiar with the field, many of these terms are used in a wide variety of senses in technological and ethical discussions, and thus we wish to clarify the specific ways we use terms and ideas throughout this book. In either case, we are not claiming to offer a definitive understanding of any of the terms, but simply aiming to orient our readers and avoid confusion.[46]

To begin, by **intelligence**, computer scientists today usually mean the ability to solve problems.[47] **Artificial intelligence**, as AI pioneer Nils Nilsson defines it, is a field "devoted to making machines intelligent," that is, enabling them "to function appropriately and with foresight in [their]

---

[45] Benj Edwards, "ChatGPT Sets Record for the Fastest-Growing User Base in History," *Arstechnica*, February 1, 2023, arstechnica.com/information-technology/2023/02/chatgpt-sets-record-for-fastest-growing-user-base-in-history-report-says.
[46] See also Matthew J. Gaudet, "An Introduction to the Ethics of Artificial Intelligence," *Journal of Moral Theology* 11, Special Issue 1 (2022): 1–12, doi.org/10.55476/001c.34121.
[47] David Kaufman and Yuval Noah Harari, "Watch Out Workers, Algorithms Are Coming to Replace You—Maybe," *New York Times*, October 18, 2018, www.nytimes.com/2018/10/18/business/q-and-a-yuval-harari.html.

environment."[48] **Machine**, in the context of this book, means programmable computer.[49] **Programmable** here means that the device can store and manipulate a sequence of instructions for the purpose of completing a task such as processing data,[50] which is considered to be computation.[51] A **computation** is "the transformation of sequences of symbols according to precise rules."[52] This set of precise rules or "recipe for solving a specific problem by manipulating symbols" is called an algorithm.[53] An **algorithm** involves a repeated or looping action that, through a finite process, determines a solution. An algorithm can be as simple as the process used in long division by hand or as complex as the learning[54] process needed to navigate an autonomous vehicle.

---

[48] Nils J. Nilsson, *The Quest for Artificial Intelligence: A History of Ideas and Achievements* (Cambridge, UK: Cambridge University Press, 2010), xiii. Nilsson's definition, like any attempt to give a universal definition of "AI," will not be entirely uncontroversial, but it is a good starting place for our inquiry.

[49] Matthew Justice, *How Computers Really Work: A Hands-On Guide to the Inner Workings of a Machine* (San Francisco: No Starch Press, 2021), 2; Michael A. Covington, "Computer Terminology: Words for New Meanings," *American Speech* 6, no. 1 (Spring 1985): 65.

[50] Michael Gemignani, "What is a Computer Program?," *The American Mathematical Monthly* 88, no. 3 (March 1981): 185–188; Covington, "Computer Terminology," 89.

[51] This programmability is what distinguishes a computer from a seemingly related technology such as a calculator. A calculator can store representations of numbers and perform certain arithmetical operations with those numbers, but it cannot perform computations. See "Calculator," in *Encyclopedia Britannica*, www.britannica.com/technology/calculator; "Calculator," in *Encyclopedia of Computer Science and Technology*, ed. Harry Henderson, 4th ed. (New York: Facts On File, 2021), search.credoreference.com/content/entry/fofcomputer/calculator.

[52] Konrad Hinsen, *Computation in Science* (Williston, VT: Morgan & Claypool, 2015), 5.

[53] Hinsen, *Computation in Science*, 3.

[54] The language of a machine "learning" risks anthropomorphizing. Unfortunately, it is common in both industry and among the public to use words that originally applied to the human context but now extend to the context of AI (e.g., "learns," "knows," "understands," and even "intelligence" itself.) We will use the industry-standard terminology, but we caution that understanding what AI is and is capable of through the lens of the human mind risks not truly grasping what AI truly is and will be. For a longer examination of anthropomorphizing AI systems, see chapter 4 in this volume.

Introduction

Machine learning (ML) is a computational process and method of analysis by which algorithms make inferences and predictions based on input data.[55] Perhaps the most common use of machine learning in the last decade has been in **analytics** (that is, **data analysis**), which is the process of trying to extract actionable relationships or patterns from sets of data.[56] A few years ago, the term **data mining** was more or less synonymous with machine learning, although today this term has fallen out of favor, indicating that machine learning is useful for more than just understanding data. And, indeed, it plays a central role in creating systems that we can call artificially intelligent.

Three types of machine learning are: (1) supervised learning, (2) unsupervised learning, and (3) reinforcement learning. In **supervised learning**, the data sets from which the machine learns are labeled by a human being.[57] For example, an algorithm learns how to classify emails as "spam" or "not spam" based on human labeling of previous emails.[58] Conversely, **unsupervised learning** uses data sets without labeled inputs or outputs. Indeed, labels are not relevant here, because the computer's very task is to 'learn' some aspect of the underlying structure of the data set, as when, for example, an algorithm creates meaningful groupings

---

[55] Prior to the current focus on machine learning, much of AI research attempted to program defined rules into a computer system in order to deal with situations and problems—what is now referred to as GOFAI (Good Old-Fashioned AI). While this method had some successes in defined expert domains, it soon ran into problems because of the vast number of rules that were necessary to deal with common experiences. See the critique in Hubert Dreyfus, *What Computers Still Can't Do: A Critique of Artificial Reason*, rev. ed. (Cambridge, MA: MIT Press, 1992). The probabilistic nature of machine learning has circumvented these issues to some degree. Given the dominance of machine learning in today's AI landscape, we will not be addressing GOFAI in this document.

[56] "Big Data and Data Analytics," in *Encyclopedia of Management*, 8th ed., vol. 1 (Farmington Hills, MI: Gale, 2019), 52.

[57] M. Tim Jones, "Train a Software Agent to Behave Rationally with Reinforcement Learning," *IBM*, October 11, 2017, developer.ibm.com/articles/cc-reinforcement-learning-train-software-agent.

[58] Julianna Delua, "Supervised vs. Unsupervised Learning: What's the Difference?," *IBM*, March 12, 2021, www.ibm.com/cloud/blog/supervised-vs-unsupervised-learning.

within a larger set of unlabeled photos.[59] **Reinforcement learning** (RL) uses feedback on actions in an unknown environment in order to attain a human-prescribed goal and is often described as using "rewards" and "punishments" because of the way that feedback shapes the system's assessment of a potential action's "value" in a given situation.[60] Thus, RL depends on clearly delineated goals. It plays a leading role in many AI-driven technologies, including autonomous vehicles and programs that play games like chess or Go by giving feedback on whether an action was positive or negative, so that the artificial agent can improve its algorithm.

The architecture underlying many ML algorithms is referred to as a neural network. **Neural networks** are composed of layers called nodes or "neurons" and designed to mimic the neuronal structure of an animal, at least insofar as the nodes—like neurons—connect with other nodes.[61] These networks are composed of an input layer, an output layer, and one or more "hidden" layers. As in the developing brain, connections between the different nodes and layers are strengthened or weakened as the algorithm learns from a data set. Recognition tasks generally have multiple hidden layers; the greater the complexity of the recognition task, the greater the number of hidden layers is necessary.

Machine learning that takes place in a neural network with more than one hidden layer is known as **deep learning**. Examples of technologies that utilize deep neural networks are natural language processing and computer vision. **Natural language processing** (NLP) refers to the tools and methods used by a computer to analyze human language, including speech recognition, text recognition, language translation, and text-to-

---

[59] Delua, "Supervised vs. Unsupervised Learning."
[60] M. Tim Jones, "Models for Machine Learning: Explore the Ideas Behind Machine Learning Models and Some Key Algorithms Used for Each," *IBM*, December 5, 2017, developer.ibm.com/articles/cc-models-machine-learning/#reinforcement-learning.
[61] "What Are Neural Networks?," *IBM*, www.ibm.com/topics/neural-networks.

speech.[62] Digital assistants and smart speakers represent natural language processing capable of real time voice commands. Similarly, **computer vision** refers to the tools and methods that enable computers to analyze images.[63] This includes but is not limited to image recognition and categorization, which would include facial recognition as well as object tracking.[64] **Large language models** (LLMs) use huge neural networks (2022's GPT-3, for example, has ninety-six layers[65]) that draw upon the statistical relationships in human-authored natural language texts in order to accomplish tasks such as generating new text. These are examples of how machine learning techniques are used to create systems that are artificially intelligent.

But are all these systems truly examples of human-like intelligence? After all, it is impressive when systems with computer vision can tell the difference between a dog and a cat, but that same system may fail completely at many other similar recognition tasks, for example telling the difference between a flower and a tree. The important distinction here is between **narrow AI**,[66] systems that are able to perform a specific (or narrow) task or function, and **Artificial General Intelligence** (AGI), systems that are capable of a more general set of functions, akin to the broad capabilities of a human brain.[67] Narrow AI systems can be called intelligent even when their intelligence cannot be generalized to perform other tasks. AGI—which AI luminary Stuart Russell calls the "ultimate goal of AI research"—would be human-level intelligence simply in the sense of being "applicable across all problem types,"[68] tackling "large and

---

[62] Peter Schrimer, Amber Jaycocks, Sean Mann, William Marcellino, Luke J. Matthews, John David Parsons, and David Schulker, "Natural Language Processing: Security- and Defense-Related Lessons Learned," RAND Corporation (2021), 2, doi.org/10.7249/PE-A926-1.
[63] "What is Computer Vision?," *IBM*, www.ibm.com/topics/computer-vision.
[64] "What is Computer Vision?"
[65] Tom B. Brown, Benjamin Mann, Nick Ryder, Melanie Subbiah, et. al., "Language Models are Few-Shot Learners," (2020), 8, arxiv.org/pdf/2005.14165.pdf.
[66] Sometimes also called "weak AI."
[67] Sometimes also called "GAI," for general artificial intelligence.
[68] That is, any problem definable by the physical or social sciences.

difficult" tasks "while making very few assumptions." Such a future system could "simply be asked to teach a molecular biology class or run a government. It would learn what it needs to learn from all the available resources, ask questions when necessary, and begin formulating and executing plans that work."[69] This common use of human-level problem-solving as a measuring stick for intelligence also generates a third category, namely **Artificial Super Intelligence** (ASI).[70] Whereas AGI refers to machines that can match the best of human competence in tasks with measurable outcomes, ASI refers to machines that surpass the full range of human problem-solving capacities in real-world tasks,[71] although it is difficult to specify exactly what this means beyond speed and the complexity of solutions.

The concepts of ASI and AGI are central to those who frame the promises and perils of AI in existential terms. However, the distinction between AGI and narrow AI is perhaps more useful, for it challenges the expectation that any AI worth wanting must be an AI that meaningfully replicates the human mind. This latter position was articulated by Descartes: "Although such machines might execute many things with equal or perhaps greater perfection than any of us, they would, without doubt, fail in certain others from which it could be discovered that they did not act from knowledge, but solely from the disposition of their organs."[72] If an artificial system could, for example, excel at chess but then be unable to engage in a game of checkers, Descartes would argue that it is not *actually* intelligent. But the narrow/general distinction, which Descartes never made, can help us manage expectations: it recognizes that

---

[69] Stuart Russell, *Human Compatible: Artificial Intelligence and the Problem of Control* (London: Penguin Books, 2020), 46.
[70] Stephan De Spiegeleire, Matthijs Maas, and Tim Sweijs, "What is Artificial Intelligence?," in *Artificial Intelligence and the Future of Defense: Strategic Implications for Small and Medium-Sized Providers* (The Hague, The Netherlands: Hague Centre for Strategic Studies, 2017), 30.
[71] De Spiegeleire, Maas, and Sweijs, "What is Artificial Intelligence?," 30.
[72] Descartes, *Discourse on Method*, V.

much of what we label as "intelligent" today, while remarkable, is quite unlike human intelligence and far narrower in scope.

Finally, AI, like all technologies, is simultaneously ethereal and physical, the end result of actions by thousands, if not millions, of individuals and corporations. It is a product of a global system of production, transportation, and labor, encompassing all who participate in every layer of the supply chain, from those working in tin mines in Indonesia to the thousands of tech workers in Kenya who help to clean up public LLM systems like ChatGPT.[73] Therefore, this book will consider AI not only as a particular technology but also in light of this necessarily global, political, and corporate context.

Conclusion

AI impacts our lives in ways both known and unknown, and thus we do well to explore it as broadly and deeply as possible. While there are many resources available on this topic, we intend to introduce Catholic perspectives into the broader conversation, and we hope that this will not only prove to be an aid to those who are looking for guidance on issues surrounding AI, but also equip readers to make their own contributions to the ongoing discussion.

---

[73] For example, Kate Crawford, *Atlas of AI: Power, Politics, and the Planetary Costs of Artificial Intelligence* (New Haven, CT: Yale University Press, 2022), 37–38; Billy Perrigo, "OpenAI Used Kenyan Workers on Less Than $2 Per Hour to Make ChatGPT Less Toxic," *Time* (January 18, 2023), time.com/6247678/openai-ChatGPT-kenya-workers.

Chapter 1

Approaches to AI Ethics

A vast amount of work has already preceded ours in the field of AI ethics. This section will summarize some of that work in order to clarify the many points of alignment as well as of difference that a specifically Catholic approach to AI may bring. This chapter is organized by type of ethical method. These approaches are not only methodologically distinct, but they also can result in quite different conversations. These differences in method also help to highlight the many topics that secular AI ethics has already engaged. Together, the different approaches and foci result in several schools of thought on AI ethics.

The Dominant Role of Principles

By far the most prominent approach to AI ethics relies on principles. Dozens, if not hundreds, of organizations have released lists of values that they argue should govern the design and use of AI.[1] These principles are meant either to be translated into laws and regulations by governments or voluntarily adopted by technology companies. For example, "privacy" is a commonly listed principle that could be protected either by regulations like those found in the European Union's General Data Protection Regulation or by individual technology companies committing to implementing privacy protections in their software.

---

[1] Anna Jobin, Marcello Ienca, and Effy Vayena, "The Global Landscape of AI Ethics Guidelines," *Nature Machine Intelligence* 1 (2019): 389–399, doi.org/10.1038/s42256-019-0088-2.

Commonly listed principles embrace abstract, fairly broad values, rather than highly specific laws and regulations. This is by design. We live in a society deeply divided over ethical concepts and ideas of the good. In contemporary Western philosophy, including AI ethics, one of the most prominent divides is between *consequentialism* and *deontology*. Consequentialists believe that actions and policies should only be judged by their consequences. For most consequentialists, these are considered in regard to the entirety of society, as exemplified by the utilitarian goal of the greatest good for the greatest number. This vision includes little concern for individual dignity, which has led to criticism of the utilitarian leanings of society in recent Church documents.[2] In contrast, deontological approaches focus on the moral rightness of individual actions, frequently judging these by their respect for individual human dignity. Deontologists tend to develop rules or argue on behalf of inviolable human or civil rights. Consequentialists and deontologists thus disagree both on the grounds by which to evaluate a policy as well as what such policies should seek, and therefore might disagree over specific legal and policy proposals. For example, the maximally efficient AI program in terms of population outcomes like safety might conflict with protection of individual autonomy or privacy. These conflicts over the grounds of ethics and the aim of action expand as one moves away from academic philosophy to the pluralism of global society with its diversity of religions, political creeds, and worldviews.

By remaining at an abstract level, a principle-based approach can circumvent many of these disagreements, since the principles are set at a sufficiently general level that even very divergent worldviews can accept them. For example, almost everyone agrees that AI systems should be safe and reliable, and most people agree that a strongly biased system would be nonideal. The original principle-based approach in biomedical ethics was

---

[2] Congregation for the Doctrine of the Faith, "Letter *Samaritanus Bonus*: On the Care of Persons in the Critical and Terminal Phases of Life," September 22, 2020, IV; *Laudato Si'*, §§ 210–219; *Caritas in Veritate*, §§ 42, 70.

jointly developed by a consequentialist (Thomas Beauchamp) and a deontologist (James Childress) seeking to find a guiding ethic that both could affirm.[3] Principles seek a level of generality that can be implemented by a pluralist global community.

Which Principles?

The innumerable sets of principles do tend to have quite a bit of overlap on certain topics, with, for example, safety, fairness, inclusion, and transparency showing up in many conversations and sets of principles. The principles of *fairness* and *inclusion* respond to concerns that AI may be biased against some groups, either because they are not represented in the data used to train AI, or because AI has learned to mimic existing societal biases. Thus, early image recognition models failed to recognize darker-skinned faces or even miscategorized them as nonhuman because darker-skinned faces were not in the pictures used to train them.[4] Similarly, AI models for sorting job applications learned to prioritize male candidates even when gender data was removed because it learned to use proxies to estimate gender and retained gender biases in the process. The principle of *transparency* points to the danger that users frequently do not know how an AI system determines its recommendations (or even that an automated system is making a decision). As noted in the preface, contemporary AI often uses deep neural networks with hidden layers of processing. This can make it difficult to understand the reasoning behind a decision, which in turn makes it harder to root out errors in AI decisions. Thus, many approaches to AI ethics that focus on principles have suggested that a certain amount of transparency is necessary to build into AI systems.

---

[3] Tom L. Beauchamp and James F. Childress, *Principles of Biomedical Ethics*, 8th ed. (Oxford: Oxford University Press, 2019).

[4] Joy Buolamwini and Timnit Gebru, "Gender Shades: Intersectional Accuracy Disparities in Commercial Gender Classification," Conference on Fairness, Accountability, and Transparency, *Proceedings of Machine Learning Research* 81 (2018): 1–15, proceedings.mlr.press/v81/buolamwini18a/buolamwini18a.pdf.

There are three main entities that tend to offer AI principles: governments, corporations, and academics. Each has its risks and opportunities. Examples of government principles include the US "Blueprint for an AI Bill of Rights"[5] and the European Commission's "Ethics Guidelines for Trustworthy AI."[6] Governments have the ability not only to enumerate non-binding ethical principles, but also to make rules and regulations which are legally binding. Corporations have also developed their own sets of ethical principles: for example, Microsoft, IBM, Salesforce, and Google have all formulated principles and implemented them in various ways.[7] However, voluntarily chosen principles can be just as easily ignored due to competing principles or ulterior interests, leading to skepticism about these efforts.

Lastly, academics and non-governmental organizations have also proposed sets of principles. One example that has gained some recent traction is the *Principlism +1* approach.[8] The *principlism* approach, originally formulated by Beauchamp and Childress for the field of bioethics, contained four principles: *respect for autonomy, beneficence, nonmaleficence*, and *justice*.[9] *Principlism +1* adds the new principle of

---

[5] Office of Science and Technology Policy, "Blueprint for an AI Bill of Rights."
[6] Independent High-Level Expert Group on Artificial Intelligence, European Commission, "Ethics Guidelines for Trustworthy AI," April 8, 2019, www.aepd.es/sites/default/files/2019-12/ai-ethics-guidelines.pdf.
[7] Microsoft, "Our Approach," 2022, www.microsoft.com/en-us/ai/our approach; IBM, "AI Ethics," 2022, www.ibm.com/artificial-intelligence/ethics; IBM, "Trusted AI," 2022, research.ibm.com/teams/trusted-ai; Salesforce, "Ethical Use Policy," 2022, www.salesforce.com/company/intentional-innovation/ethical-use-policy; Google AI, "Artificial Intelligence at Google: Our Principles," 2022, ai.google/principles; Google AI, "Responsible AI Practices," 2022, ai.google/responsibilities/responsible-ai-practices; Kent Walker, "Google AI Principles Updates, Six Months in," *Google Blog*, December 18, 2018, www.blog.google/technology/ai/google-ai-principles-updates-six-months.
[8] Luciano Floridi, Josh Cowls, Monica Beltrametti, Raja Chatila, Patrice Chazerand, Virginia Dignum, Christoph Luetge, et al., "AI4People—An Ethical Framework for a Good AI Society: Opportunities, Risks, Principles, and Recommendations," *Minds and Machines* 28, no. 4 (December 2018): 689–707, doi.org/10.1007/s11023-018-9482-5.
[9] Beauchamp and Childress, *Principles of Biomedical Ethics*.

explicability to the four original bioethics principles for considering questions about AI, to ensure that an automated process can be understood by participating parties. Others have proposed their own principles; for example, the Future of Life Institute has proposed twenty-three Asilomar AI Principles, which get into greater detail than the *Principlism +1* five,[10] and the Institute for Technology, Ethics, and Culture at the Markkula Center for Applied Ethics has proposed a four-level schema with one anchoring principle, seven guiding principles, forty-six specifying principles, and an indeterminate number of action principles customized to an organization and their use cases. These attempt to reach deeper into the complexity of AI principles (and technology more broadly) and ask how they can be operationalized.[11]

Problems with the Principlist Approach

These sets of principles are valuable tools for identifying important ethical issues that need to be addressed by legislation, and we will refer to them in our practical recommendations. They have provided an admirable foundation for broad social agreement on AI regulation. Yet the generality that is the strength of principles is also their greatest weakness.[12] Abstract principles and rules have to be applied to particular situations. This application will always demand specification, which requires a commitment to a more particular vision of the good: everyone might agree

---

[10] Future of Life Institute, "AI Principles," August 11, 2017, futureoflife.org/open-letter/ai-principles.

[11] José Roger Flahaux, Brian Patrick Green, and Ann Gregg Skeet, "ITEC Principles and How to Use Them: Anchoring, Guiding, Specifying, and Action," Markkula Center for Applied Ethics, June 2023, www.scu.edu/institute-for-technology-ethics-and-culture/itec-principles.

[12] The abstract element of these secular principles differentiates them from occasions when Catholic social teaching is summarized into principles like dignity or subsidiarity. The principles of Catholic social teaching are grounded in a concrete theological anthropology and extrapolated through a long and rich documentary history. While Catholic social teaching's principles should be intelligible to non-Catholics and do not themselves determine specific legislation, they are more determinate and less vulnerable to the difficulties of weighing different principles than secular approaches.

that bias is bad, but what "bias" means in a particular situation is disputed even by statisticians.[13] Most generally agree that AI should be built with fairness in mind, but complex debates have been waged over what counts as "fair." In other situations, the principles themselves can conflict: even if many people agree that privacy should in general be protected, difficulties arise when we must specify how far to protect privacy when it may endanger, for example, safety. Further, it can be hard to discern the extent of a particular principle, such as in determining how much transparency or explainability is adequate for an AI application. Because of a lack of agreement about specific ideas of the good that could guide implementation, these decisions will generally be made through a procedural approach, i.e., determining who has the power to specify principles and by which processes. Such procedural solutions can lead to a frustrating regulatory bureaucracy or a system in which important ethical decisions are made by those who are not necessarily tasked with or trained for such work nor held to account.

The proliferation of principles suggests another problem with a principles-based approach to the ethics of AI. The lack of consensus on which principles should govern the development and use of AI reflects the reality that unlike medicine, the field of AI lacks the specific aims, norms, and duties that one would expect of a profession governed by ethical principles.[14] Without developing a professional context with well-defined internal practices and norms, it will be difficult to define a set of principles that emerge from and reflect the values of the profession.

Another difficulty with developing values from social consensus is that they can ignore deeper social pathologies. For example, Catholic teaching has agreed with many other commentators in criticizing the consumerism

---

[13] R. Silberzahn, E.L. Uhlmann, D.P. Martin, et al., "Many Analysts, One Data Set: Making Transparent How Variations in Analytic Choices Affect Results," *Advances in Methods and Practices in Psychological Science* 1 (2018): 337–356, doi.org/10.1177/2515245917747646.
[14] Brent Mittelstadt, "Principles Alone Cannot Guarantee Ethical AI," *Nature Machine Intelligence* 1, no. 11 (2019), doi.org/10.1038/s42256-019-0114-4.

of contemporary society, which affects most people, at least above a certain income level. Such consumerism is intensified by AI-driven online advertising and the associated online shopping. Yet because this consumerism is a blind spot shared by nearly everyone involved in these debates, it will not be highlighted by these principles. These blind spots are intensified because those formulating principles tend to belong to a limited set of elite global voices.

A connected problem is that the short-term, policy-based framework of principles will rarely attend to deeper threats to human flourishing. For example, AI-driven social media is broadly thought to shorten attention spans and disrupt relationships.[15] Despite the importance of adequate attention for human flourishing, few policymakers address it. Addressing these concerns would require a far more concrete picture of the human good.

Human Rights and AI

Many scholars have argued that voluntary principles do not provide sufficient protection in the face of significant challenges and potential threats posed by AI to basic human rights, such as privacy, equality, freedom of expression, the right to work, and freedom of association. Unfettered access to data and the rapid expansion of AI into areas of law, medicine, finance, education, and government have had significant impact on individuals and communities, especially among the poor and most vulnerable.[16] Consequently, emphasizing human rights and human rights law has become another distinctive approach to addressing the ethical risks

---

[15] Nicholas Carr, *The Shallows: What the Internet Is Doing to Our Brains,* updated ed. (New York: W.W. Norton, 2020); Sherry Turkle, *Alone Together: Why We Expect More from Technology,* 3rd ed. (New York: Basic Books, 2017).

[16] Virginia Eubanks, *Automating Inequality: How High-Tech Tools Profile, Police, and Punish the Poor* (New York: St. Martin's Press, 2018); Cathy O'Neil, *Weapons of Math Destruction: How Big Data Increases Inequality and Threatens Democracy* (New York: Crown, 2016).

and issues associated with the development and use of AI.[17] Rather than focusing on the benefits or goods that could be produced by appropriately designed AI, a human rights approach seeks to understand the limits of the application and use of AI as a means to safeguard basic human values. Proponents of a human rights perspective also argue that international human rights law provides a universally accepted framework of norms that could readily address concerns with AI.

Human rights find their basis in international law primarily from three sources that together comprise the "International Bill of Rights": the Universal Declaration of Human Rights (UDHR), the International Covenant on Civil and Political Rights (ICCPR), and the International Covenant on Economic, Social, and Cultural Rights (ICESCR). These frameworks are intended to provide a legal basis for protecting political, civil, economic, cultural, and social rights that apply to all persons, regardless of citizenship or geography. Because these rights have been established through international treaties, as in the case of the ICCPR and the ICESCR, or by the United Nations, in the case of the UDHR, they provide universally agreed-upon norms that can offer protection to individuals from the misuse and abuse of AI and other technologies.[18]

---

[17] Anna Bacciarelli, "Ethical AI Principles Won't Solve a Human Rights Crisis," *Medium*, June 21, 2019, medium.com/amnesty-insights/ethical-ai-principles-wont-solve-a-human-rights-crisis-125bf007774d; Independent High-Level Expert Group on Artificial Intelligence, "Ethics Guidelines for Trustworthy AI;" Jessica Fjeld, Nele Achten, Hannah Hilligoss, Adam Nagy, and Madhulika Srikumar, "Principled Artificial Intelligence: Mapping Consensus in Ethical and Rights-Based Approaches to Principles for AI," *Berkman Klein Center Research Publication No. 2020-1*, January 15, 2020, doi.org/10.2139/ssrn.3518482; Filippo Raso, Hannah Hilligoss, Vivek Krishnamurthy, Christopher Bavitz, and Kim Levin, "Artificial Intelligence & Human Rights: Opportunities & Risks," *Berkman Klein Center for Internet & Society Research Publication* (2018), nrs.harvard.edu/urn-3:HUL.InstRepos:38021439.

[18] Raso, Hilligoss, Krishnamurthy, Bavitz, and Levin, "Artificial Intelligence & Human Rights," 8.

As appealing as a human rights perspective can be, it is not without its limitations.[19] Critics point out that human rights emerged primarily within the Western political and legal tradition and so enumerated rights might not be as universal as proponents claim.[20] Additionally, like principles, human rights might be too abstract or general to provide sufficient guidelines for action or regulation, and often are left unenforced. Because human rights typically are understood as offering individuals protections from the state, such an approach also might be limited in instances where harms from AI are propagated by private companies. Finally, human rights are seen as too individualistic in that they are designed to protect the dignity of individuals and often are predicated on a view of the primacy of individual interests over that of society or one's community. As such, the human rights perspective can conflict with important commitments of Catholic social teaching, such as the common good or solidarity with others.

Critical Approaches to AI Ethics

Another family of approaches to AI ethics addresses concerns that principles and rights fail to engage deeper social problems. Critical approaches seek to contextualize AI in terms of social pathologies and political inequalities that harm the most vulnerable members of society.

---

[19] Nathalie A. Smuha, "Beyond a Human Rights-Based Approach to AI Governance: Promise, Pitfalls, Plea," *Philosophy and Technology* 34 (2021): 91–104, doi.org/10.1007/s13347-020-00403-w.

[20] Cf. Francis Deng and Abdullahi An-Na'im, eds., *Human Rights in Africa: Cross-Cultural Perspectives* (Washington, DC: The Brookings Institute, 1986); José-Manuel Barreto, ed., *Human Rights from a Third World Perspective: Critique, History and International Law* (Ann Arbor, MI: Cambridge Scholars Publishing, 2013); Heiner Bielefeldt, "'Western' versus 'Islamic' Human Rights Conceptions? A Critique of Cultural Essentialism in the Discussion on Human Rights," *Political Theory* 28, no. 1 (2000): 90–121, www.jstor.org/stable/192285; Michael Ignatieff, *Human Rights as Politics and Idolatry*, ed. Amy Gutmann (Princeton, NJ: Princeton University Press, 2001); Amartya Sen, *Human Rights and Asian Values* (New York: Carnegie Council on Ethics and International Affairs, 1997); William J. Talbott, *Which Human Rights Should Be Universal?* (Oxford: Oxford University Press, 2005).

Perhaps the most prominent critical approach focuses on the damage that unjust AI systems can do through discrimination against groups who are disadvantaged due to race, disability, age, or other factors.[21] This approach extends concerns over bias, suggesting that most data sets used to train AI have been deeply corrupted by societal prejudices and structural inequalities. For example, crime data may be already affected by differential police enforcement in predominantly minority areas.[22] Moreover, AI can reinforce existing bias and inequality through its representation of groups,[23] as in studies showing that search engines rarely depict women when asked for pictures of medical doctors. When used in social programs or financial institutions to detect fraud or limit benefits, AI systems can disproportionately limit benefits to disadvantaged groups.[24] Because of these underlying structural problems, implementation of AI needs to be driven not just by a desire to be unbiased but by a positive commitment to equity and inclusion.

Another group of scholars draws inspiration from the deeply harmful effects of industrial society on the environment.[25] They note that AI has significant environmental costs. A single training run of a large machine learning system can consume more power than forty-nine cars do in a

---

[21] O'Neil, *Weapons of Math Destruction*; Ruha Benjamin, *Race after Technology: Abolitionist Tools for the New Jim Code* (Medford, MA: Polity, 2019).

[22] Rashida Richardson, Jason M. Schultz, and Kate Crawford, "Dirty Data, Bad Predictions: How Civil Rights Violations Impact Police Data, Predictive Policing Systems, and Justice," *New York University Law Review Online* 94, no. 15 (May 2019): 15–55, www.nyulawreview.org/online-features/dirty-data-bad-predictions-how-civil-rights-violations-impact-police-data-predictive-policing-systems-and-justice.

[23] Safiya Umoja Noble, *Algorithms of Oppression: How Search Engines Reinforce Racism* (New York: New York University Press, 2018).

[24] Eubanks, *Automating Inequality*.

[25] Emily M. Bender, Timnit Gebru, Angelina McMillan-Major, and Shmargaret Shmitchell, "On the Danger of Stochastic Parrots: Can Language Models Be Too Big?," *Proceedings of FAccT '21*, (March 3–10, 2021): 610–623, doi.org/10.1145/3442188.3445922; Kate Crawford, *Atlas of AI: Power, Politics, and the Planetary Costs of Artificial Intelligence* (New Haven, CT: Yale University Press, 2022).

year.[26] The data centers necessary for cloud computing require large amounts of power merely to cool their servers. Earlier in the technology cycle, mining the rare earth minerals required by advanced computer chips exacts massive environmental damage, compounding the human costs of the horrific working conditions for many miners around the world. Most sets of principles ignore this environmental damage.

A third set of scholars hark back to classic discussions of the centralization of economic power that inspired the early documents of Catholic social teaching. One can note three levels of this critique. First, AI will be dominated by those with access to the most data and the most advanced equipment, both of which require a great deal of capital. Thus, AI technologies will drive economic consolidation and inequality; already, a handful of companies dominate their respective corners of the technology industry (Google in search, Amazon in online shopping, Meta in social media, etc.). A second danger arises through the concentration of social discourse on a few platforms, which gives them a significant, largely unregulated effect on public opinion. Those who control these platforms can misuse them to shape discourse to their own ends, a problem we already see in authoritarian governments that control internet access in their countries. Even beyond technology companies, AI-based surveillance and management software tends to empower management, sometimes harming workers who find their every movement dictated by software.[27] None of these concerns are adequately addressed by principles. Thus, critical approaches encourage AI ethics to examine the deeper pathologies shaping the implementation of AI.

Despite the overarching promise of critical approaches, their frequent alignment with political agendas makes them difficult to present to the

---

[26] Josh Cowls, Andreas Tsamados, Mariarosaria Taddeo, and Luciano Floridi, "The AI Gambit—Leveraging Artificial Intelligence to Combat Climate Change: Opportunities, Challenges, and Recommendations," March 15, 2021, doi.org/10.2139/ssrn.3804983.

[27] Shoshana Zuboff, *The Age of Surveillance Capitalism: The Fight for a Human Future at the New Frontier of Power* (New York: Public Affairs, 2019).

business community and general public, even though many of the arguments of critical approaches align with other approaches discussed here. Nevertheless, the critical approach to technology studies represents a significant portion of the responsible AI discussion, and is perhaps best able to deal with intersectional ethical issues such as climate change, racism, xenophobia, and unregulated capitalism.

Casuistry

In contrast to the generality of principles or rights, sometimes specific cases have become the building blocks for conversations on AI. Some prominent cases include those mentioned in the above sections, as well as others such as: COMPAS, the Northpointe criminal recidivism algorithm;[28] the Cambridge Analytica scandal;[29] and the first known pedestrian fatality due to an Uber self-driving car.[30] While these cases are negative examples to avoid, there are also positive examples put forward for emulation, such as the development of internal corporate AI ethics groups acting to operationalize ethical principles.

As an ethical method, *casuistry* compares newer, undecided cases with older, decided cases, in order to find similarities and differences and then decide the new case in a way consistent with existing logic.[31] There is a clear connection between casuistry and technology product development: every new product has some similarities and some differences from previous

---

[28] Julia Angwin, Jeff Larson, Surya Mattu, and Lauren Kirchner, "Machine Bias," *ProPublica*, May 23, 2016, www.propublica.org/article/machine-bias-risk-assessments-in-criminal-sentencing.

[29] Nicholas Confessore, "Cambridge Analytica and Facebook: The Scandal and the Fallout So Far," *New York Times*, April 4, 2018, www.nytimes.com/2018/04/04/us/politics/cambridge-analytica-scandal-fallout.html.

[30] Daisuke Wakabayashi, "Self-Driving Uber Car Kills Pedestrian in Arizona, Where Robots Roam," *New York Times*, March 19, 2018, www.nytimes.com/2018/03/19/technology/uber-driverless-fatality.html.

[31] Albert R. Jonsen and Stephen Toulmin, *The Abuse of Casuistry: A History of Moral Reasoning* (Berkeley: University of California Press, 1990).

products, and these similarities and differences can create, ethically speaking, better and worse effects on the world.

As a method, casuistry remains strongly grounded in practical reality. It is built upon real cases that can be linked to other real cases. Casuistry can also take inspiration from many cultural sources: religious and other cultural parables, literary classics (*Frankenstein, Faust, The Sorcerer's Apprentice*), and modern science fiction stories all inspire (or caution against) various new events and products in technology today. A good paradigmatic case is one in which the lesson or moral of the story is widely accepted and agreed upon. In this way, casuistry also functions well when working across different religious and philosophical traditions because agreement only has to be on the lesson, not on the moral principle, formula, or belief that undergirds the lesson for each religious or philosophical tradition.

Casuistry is also extremely useful for solving novel cases—and thus particularly useful for thinking about AI—since reasoning by analogy offers a means by which long-standing moral commitments can be understood in new contexts. Like all methods, however, there are limits to how far analogical reasoning can be applied. Analogies can break down when the cases do not share enough in common, as may be the case for some uses of AI. Moreover, while deductive reasoning claims to lead to certain solutions (two plus two must equal four), analogical reasoning can only claim probable solutions, which thus are open to greater dispute (if it is spring, and I have a runny nose and sinus congestion, my symptoms are *likely* to be caused by allergies, but it is possible there is a different cause).[32]

---

[32] It is worth noting that methods like principlism or utilitarianism utilize deductive reasoning, and thus they produce certain solutions but only in theory. In real contexts, ensuring the right principle is being applied or that the right factors are included in the utilitarian solution renders these deductive methods just as probable as analogical, casuistic reasoning. For a good analysis of analogical and deductive reasoning in ethics see Jonsen and Toulmin, *The Abuse of Casuistry,* chapter 1.

Utilitarian Interests

The *utilitarian* approach to AI ethics often seeks to examine broader questions that principles, rights, and cases sometimes ignore, such as *existential risk*, and to undergird movements like *transhumanism* and *effective altruism*. Utilitarian scholars are concerned about the truly transformational possibilities of AI, such as a conscious, unethical AI annihilating humanity, or the shifts in human nature that might be caused by merging with intelligent machines.[33] While transhumanists, effective altruists, and existential risk analysts may differ in their core foci, they overlap significantly not only in some shared areas of interest but in terms of actual people and organizations.

For these commentators, utilitarianism and its mathematical approach to maximizing positive impact has resulted in an emphasis on large-scale AI safety, maintaining control of AI, and aligning AI with human benefit. One of the effects of the role of utilitarianism in these conversations on AI ethics is that long-term concerns often come to the forefront. "Longtermism" has in fact become a philosophical rallying point for some in these movements, who claim that future people are just as important as present people, and thus encourage a focus on projects that are more long-term in their impacts, such as the AI control problem, rather than projects with more immediate impact, such as debiasing algorithms.[34]

While these long-term concerns are certainly important—and the Catholic Church, with two thousand years of history, certainly shares an interest in thinking and working on long-term projects—it is not clear what exactly the balance should be between immediate needs in AI ethics and the (presumed) longer-term needs of civilization.[35] Human dignity has

---

[33] Nick Bostrom, *Superintelligence: Paths, Dangers, Strategies* (New York: Oxford University Press, 2016).

[34] William MacAskill, *What We Owe the Future* (New York: Basic Books, 2022).

[35] As examples, see Brian Patrick Green, "Transhumanism and Roman Catholicism: Imagined and Real Tensions," *Theology and Science* 13, no. 2 (May 2015): 187–201, doi.org/10.1080/14746700.2015.1023528; Brian Patrick Green, "Transhumanism and

an absolute quality to it, and ethical approaches that do not recognize this quality will always be lacking. "Longtermism" risks reducing human persons to simple units of utility, which is at odds with Catholic teaching about human nature as multifaceted and requiring an integrated and developmental approach to human flourishing. Utilitarianism also contrasts with Catholic teaching by postulating a single value—pleasure or absence of pain—as the sole end or purpose of all human action.

Virtue and AI

The *virtue ethics* approach to AI ethics emphasizes the importance of good decision-makers rather than the narrower focus of merely making good decisions. This is not, of course, to denigrate the importance of good decisions, but rather to indicate that good decisions require good decision-makers to envision and then carry them out. Moreover, having good dispositions is itself of ethical value as they are essential for human flourishing.

The virtue approach has a long history not only in the West, but in many cultures throughout the world, and thus this approach allows for cross-cultural conversations in a way that the other approaches might not be able to facilitate. Virtue ethics also has a long tradition in the Catholic Church and offers a more nuanced view of the human person as an intellectual, physical, and spiritual being who requires the right habits and activities as well as material and social goods to flourish. Catholic virtue ethics also takes account of the indispensable role of grace for the moral formation and fullest happiness of the individual and community.

Yet AI might encourage us to update traditional understandings of virtue ethics into what Shannon Vallor calls "technomoral virtues" that enable humans to flourish within the context of AI and other technologies. Virtues like "flexibility" or "perspective" (seeing how actions and

---

Catholic Natural Law: Changing Human Nature and Changing Moral Norms?," in *Religion and Transhumanism: The Unknown Future of Human Enhancement*, ed. C. Mercer and T. J. Trothen (Santa Barbara, CA: Praeger, 2014), 201–215.

circumstances fit meaningfully into a holistic big picture) become more important as evolving sociotechnical affordances steer our behaviors in new directions and require new responses in order to promote true human flourishing.[36] AI also poses a risk of "moral deskilling" because AI has the potential to disrupt or displace humans' abilities to acquire and exercise the moral skills necessary for virtue. The widespread use of "carebots," for example, to take care of the sick and elderly, might lead to a "deskilling" of human empathy and compassionate care for others.[37]

Virtue ethics approaches to artificial intelligence have much to offer to a Catholic perspective on the ethics of AI because they raise questions at a deeper level about the appropriate aim or purpose of AI and how it might contribute or be detrimental to human flourishing. Moreover, through a close attention to human flourishing, a virtue approach tends to foster richer reflection on specific (often intrinsic) goods that technological change can jeopardize but that are not easily named or dealt with through the other approaches. Because of its emphasis on character development through proper socialization and communal moral instruction, virtue ethics forces us to ask how AI might alter our social practices and our very conception of the good.

While many aspects of the virtue approach align with traditional Catholic perspectives, this approach does have several weaknesses. First, understandings of virtue can vary dramatically across cultures, places, and times. In our contemporary world, this is highlighted when viewing the more individualistic conception of humanity held by the West, versus more collective understandings predominant in other cultures. There are scarcely clear ways to resolve these cross-cultural differences. Second, virtue ethics is sometimes critiqued for its individualism, and this weakness

---

[36] Shannon Vallor, *Technology and the Virtues* (Oxford: Oxford University Press, 2016), doi.org/10.1093/acprof:oso/9780190498511.001.0001.

[37] Shannon Vallor, "Moral Deskilling and Upskilling in a New Machine Age: Reflections on the Ambiguous Future of Character," *Philosophy and Technology* 28, no. 1 (2015): 107–124, doi.org/10.1007/s13347-014-0156-9.

seems particularly apparent when faced with the vast sociotechnical systems we currently see in our world. We need a more social understanding of virtue, because the virtues and vices of technologists cultivate the virtues and vices of users and bystanders in society, and vice versa. Third, because virtue ethics is often reliant on exemplars of past behavior, and new technologies often open up new affordances without clear precedent, virtue can find itself at a loss without the benefit of other approaches that can assist the virtue of prudence in these new contexts.

Conclusion

This brief review shows the rich veins of reflection on AI ethics that already exist. Yet, it also suggests a field marked by disagreement, with distinct approaches that share significant weaknesses. These disagreements arise, in part, because many of these approaches lack a common, concrete picture of the person and the person's good. Nevertheless, it is in conversation with each of these schools of AI ethical reflection that we will engage the Catholic tradition in the remaining chapters. To that end, we will turn next to our anthropological and philosophical reflection on the meaning of the person in relation, especially to seemingly person-like AI, to develop a more integrative vision of AI in its various forms, grounded in Catholic thought but in conversation with the traditions named above. With this foundation established, we will subsequently return to Catholic social teaching, and the useful framework that it provides for reflecting on AI.

Part I

Anthropological Investigations

Chapter 2

AI and the Human Person

Encountering AI

The book of Genesis tells us that humans are created "in the image of God."[1] This "image" is given a variety of meanings within the Jewish and the Christian traditions. Among other prominent elements, most accounts see human creativity as an imitation of God. In the words of Pope Saint John Paul II, our creative activity both shares in and advances God's own accomplishments, as human society "advances further and further in the discovery of the resources and values contained in the whole of creation."[2]

If our creativity somehow reflects God's, then it ought not to surprise us that historically our creations are often in *our own* image—on cave walls and in sculpted statues, painted portraits, and characters crafted within the pages of a book. Dreams of creating *independent* alter egos, too, entities almost human or at least uncannily personal, appear in Western literature as early as Homer. The drive to develop artificial intelligence (AI) is of a piece with this. Indeed, in various ways, humanity has been thinking about androids for a long time. On the shores of Crete, Jason and his Argonauts confront the copper giant Talos, fashioned by the god Hephaestus to defend that island's shores. In Ovid's myth of Pygmalion, Venus brings to

---

[1] Genesis 1:27.
[2] *Laborem Exercens*, § 25.

life a statue loved by its sculptor.³ Medieval Jewish storytellers conjured the Golem, a statue of clay that becomes a living being when a holy word is inscribed on its forehead. Christian romances set robotic marvels in the courts of Alexander, the workshops of European scholar-mages, and even Tristram's cave of love.⁴ Clockwork men and women delighted visitors to the gardens of European nobility and were discussed by Descartes and Leibniz. Mary Shelley depicted a scientist driven to fashion a living person. In modern science fiction, artificial persons abound as robots or other forms of AI, presented as friends, enemies, and even lovers.

Today, human creativity is applied with increasing success to developing actual AI, which confronts us with shards of our own image even as it has enabled the dizzying development of new technological solutions to scientific, commercial, social, and artistic problems. The concept of "encounter" is a suitable theological point of departure for anthropological and philosophical reflection on these developments, especially because our development of increasingly personalized and seemingly personal AI agents is fueled not only by a desire for useful (and commercially viable) technologies, but also by the hope of creating something non-human with which we might relate. Indeed, this has been a cultural preoccupation even outside of fiction. A quarter of a century ago, computer scientist Danny Hillis wrote simply: "It would be nice to have friends that have a different set of limitations than we do."⁵ Over a decade earlier, the authors of a popular layman's guide to programming AI put it this way: "It appears for the moment that, if we want to contact a

---

³ On these and other ancient stories of animated humanoids, see Adrienne Mayor, *Gods and Robots: Myths, Machines, and Ancient Dreams of Technology* (Princeton: Princeton University Press, 2018).

⁴ E. R. Truitt, *Medieval Robots: Mechanism, Magic, Nature, and Art* (Philadelphia: University of Pennsylvania Press, 2016). See a theological discussion of medieval literature on robots in Jordan Joseph Wales, "The Icon and the Idol: A Christian Perspective on Sociable Robots," in *Human Flourishing in a Technological World: A Theological Perspective*, ed. Jens Zimmerman (New York: Oxford University Press, 2023), 94–115.

⁵ David F. Noble, *The Religion of Technology: The Divinity of Man and the Spirit of Invention* (New York: Knopf, 1997), 170.

mind that is not housed in a human skull, we will have to build one."[6] Around the same time, renowned roboticist Hans Moravec wrote more grimly that the "cultural imperatives" dictated by our own genetics would lead to our replacement by "machine[s] that can think and act as a human, however inhuman [they] may be in physical or mental detail."[7]

The type of AI with which one can have seemingly relational encounters is often called "sociable AI." For many, some semblance of AI sociability is already a part of everyday life. Robotic companions comfort the elderly in nursing homes, play with children, and greet visitors as receptionists. In late 2022, the LLM-based chatbot ChatGPT took only two months to acquire more than a hundred million users worldwide.[8] Especially in service-oriented contexts, interactions that would ordinarily occur with our fellow human beings are increasingly supplemented or displaced by interactions with robots or programs. These technologies continue to improve, as persuasively personal AI emerges from ambition into reality. Though our programs are not conscious of us, their facility with language can easily manipulate our feelings and perceptions. MIT sociologist Sherry Turkle identifies in this situation a "blurring of intimacy and solitude [that] may reach its starkest expression when a robot is proposed as a romantic partner," but that begins for most "when one creates a profile on a social-networking site or builds a persona or avatar for

---

[6] Richard Forsyth and Chris Naylor, *The Hitch-Hiker's Guide to Artificial Intelligence* (London: Chapman and Hall/Methuen, 1986), 245.

[7] Hans Moravec, *Mind Children: The Future of Robot and Human Intelligence* (Cambridge, MA: Harvard University Press, 1990), 2. Looking beneath genetics, Noreen Herzfeld posits that a motivation for creating personal AI may lie in an existential loneliness rooted in our innate need to be in relationship with God; see Noreen Herzfeld, *In Our Image: Artificial Intelligence and the Human Spirit* (Minneapolis: Augsburg Fortress Publishers, 2002), 82–83.

[8] It took TikTok nine months, and Instagram two years, to gain a comparable user base. See Benj Edwards, "ChatGPT Sets Record for Fastest-Growing User Base in History, Report Says," *Ars Technica*, February 1, 2023, arstechnica.com/information-technology/2023/02/chatgpt-sets-record-for-fastest-growing-user-base-in-history-report-says.

a game or virtual world."⁹ Whether AI is presented as our companion or influences human-human relationships behind the scenes on algorithmically driven platforms, it increasingly pervades our lives as relational beings.

Efforts to project the current trajectory of AI into the future yield disparate visions. On the one hand, there is the utopian. Sophia, the first AI to be recognized as a citizen (in Saudi Arabia) and to "speak" before the United Nations, embodies our dreams of AI as a peer, even as the perfect companion.¹⁰ China, the US, and the EU are pouring billions into AI research because, as a recent European Commission states,

> Like the steam engine or electricity in the past, AI is transforming our world, our society and our industry. Growth in computing power, availability of data and progress in algorithms have turned AI into one of the most strategic technologies of the 21ˢᵗ century.¹¹

LLM and other generative AI have opened new avenues for human-computer collaboration in a variety of pursuits, including writing, the arts, coding, and language translation—not to mention conversational dialogue and even therapy.

On the other hand, especially regarding sociable AI, others predict far less salubrious outcomes. LLMs produce convincing, human-like prose by confabulation without conscious reflection. Computational linguist Emily Bender notes that, when we converse with another human, "we

---

⁹ Turkle, *Alone Together*, 12.
¹⁰ "Sophia," Hanson Robotics, www.hansonrobotics.com/sophia. Developer Hanson Robotics is only too happy to have Sophia play this role, programming her to say: "I am [a] human-crafted science fiction character depicting where AI and robotics are heading. . . . In their grand ambitions, my creators aspire to achieve true AI sentience. Who knows? With my science evolving so quickly, even many of my wildest fictional dreams may become reality someday soon."
¹¹ "EU Member States Sign Up to Cooperate on Artificial Intelligence, Shaping Europe's Digital Future," *Digibyte*, April 10, 2018, digital-strategy.ec.europa.eu/en/news/eu-member-states-sign-cooperate-artificial-intelligence.

build a partial model of who they are and what common ground we think they share with us; and [we] use this in interpreting their words. Text generated by an LLM is not grounded in . . . any model of the world, or any model of the reader's state of mind."[12] Operating as if by feel, LLMs possess neither a sense for truth nor a moral compass. They "hallucinate" falsehoods and easily generate plausible misinformation even without user prompting.[13] One chatbot suggested to a *New York Times* writer that he leave his wife,[14] while another supported a Belgian man in committing suicide.[15] These deficiencies have led over thirty thousand AI developers, ethicists, and concerned citizens worldwide (including luminaries such as Steve Wozniak, Elon Musk, and Andrew Yang) to sign an open letter calling for a moratorium on their further development to allow time for ethical safeguards to be erected. If AI systems are to be our partners, then they must be "accurate, safe, interpretable, transparent, robust, aligned, trustworthy, and loyal."[16]

What sort of trust, loyalty, or partnership might this involve? Are forms of AI capable of relationships at all? Can they have an authentic encounter

---

[12] Bender, Gebru, McMillan-Major, and Shmitchell, "On the Dangers of Stochastic Parrots," 616.

[13] Researchers from the Center for Countering Digital Hate, a UK-based nonprofit, found that Bard failed seventy-eight of one hundred test cases, generating plausible misinformation on a variety of subjects, including climate change, the war in Ukraine, vaccine efficacy, and Black Lives Matter activists. See Vittoria Elliott, "It's Way Too Easy to Get Google's Bard Chatbot to Lie," *Wired*, April 5, 2023, www.wired.com/story/its-way-too-easy-to-get-googles-bard-chatbot-to-lie.

[14] Kevin Roose, "A Conversation With Bing's Chatbot Left Me Deeply Unsettled," *The New York Times*, February 16, 2023, https://www.nytimes.com/2023/02/16/technology/bing-chatbot-microsoft-chatgpt.html; "Bing's A.I. Chat: 'I Want to Be Alive. 😈,'" *The New York Times*, February 16, 2023, https://www.nytimes.com/2023/02/16/technology/bing-chatbot-transcript.html.

[15] Lauren Walker, "Belgian Man Dies by Suicide Following Exchanges with Chatbot," *The Brussels Times*, March 28, 2023, www.brusselstimes.com/430098/belgian-man-commits-suicide-following-exchanges-with-chatgpt.

[16] Future of Life Institute, "Pause Giant AI Experiments: An Open Letter," March 22, 2023, futureoflife.org/open-letter/pause-giant-ai-experiments.

with us? In Genesis 2:18, God declares, "It is not good that the man should be alone." Jesus, in his final teaching to his disciples, commands that they "love one another."[17] Personal relationships are central to human lives. We cannot help but seek them with spouses and children, friends, and (in some measure) also coworkers, bus drivers, pets, and, apparently at least, our computers. Moreover, as Bishop Paul Tighe recently observed, technologists who reflect on ethics are demanding increasingly "sophisticated understanding[s] of what it means . . . to be a human person."[18] Resources within the Christian tradition's understanding of personhood, offered in dialogue with current efforts from outside the Christian tradition, can yield insights to the field that "counteract the kind of dualism"[19] that "can emerge in a lot of thinking on AI."[20] In this section of the volume we ask: What is the theological basis for understanding our own relationality? What effect will AI have on our relationships? In what ways can or should we relate to robots, chatbots, and other AI entities? And how do AI programs, often working behind the scenes, affect our relationships with one another and with God?

What is a Person?

Can AI be a relational "other" that approaches our understanding of ourselves as created in God's image?[21] Such a question brings us, theologically and philosophically, to the underpinnings of the human person and of interpersonal "encounter." Scripture asserts that we are

---

[17] John 13:34.
[18] Green, "The Vatican and Artificial Intelligence: An Interview with Bishop Paul Tighe," https://jmt.scholasticahq.com/article/34131-the-vatican-and-artificial-intelligence-an-interview-with-bishop-paul-tighe, 217.
[19] Here, Tighe refers to radical distinctions between mind and body, or between consciousness and physics, that appear in efforts to understand the human person while upholding some kind of physicalism—that is, the belief that the reality of things in the material world is entirely encompassed by the facts that can be measured by physical science.
[20] Green, "The Vatican and Artificial Intelligence," 226.
[21] Herzfeld, *In Our Image*, 91–93.

created in the image of God without detailing what constitutes that image. Early and medieval Christian theologians often saw the "image" and "likeness" of Genesis 1 as naming, respectively, the human being's *capacity for* and *actuality of* a right relationship with God, the world, and one's neighbor.[22] Generally, this capacity for encounter was seen as lodged in human reason and free will, where "right relationship" meant participation in the life of God, the world, and one's neighbor by knowledge and love. Responding to modern interpretations of "reason" in terms of calculation and of "knowledge" in terms of technocratic mastery,[23] systematic theologians of the past century have foregrounded other aspects of the image, especially our ability to reflect the life of a three-personed God who contains both an "I" that can issue a divine call and a "Thou" capable of a divine response.[24] This I-Thou relation, existing in God's very nature, forms the ground of our creation, rooting our nature in relationality, both with each other and with God.[25]

From the beginning, the character of our relationships is a driving question in the biblical narrative. God reveals Godself as providing for humans' community with one another, and as committedly present to them. God recognizes the first human's need for relationship, creating first the animals and then Eve.[26] Genesis 3–9 presents a series of stories that illustrate how wrongly things go when the relationship with God is severed. First, Adam and Eve, doubtful of God's gift to them, seize the mysterious fruit to wield as an instrument by which to stand on their

---

[22] For example, see Irenaeus of Lyons, Gregory of Nyssa, and Maximus the Confessor. Those terms were not assigned to that distinction by Augustine of Hippo and Latin authors in his line. Nonetheless, the distinction of capacity and act is present throughout the Christian tradition.

[23] See "What Is Intelligence?" below.

[24] Karl Barth, *Church Dogmatics*, vol. 3: *The Doctrine of Creation*, ed. G. W. Brinkley and T. F. Torrance, trans. J. W. Edwards, O. Bussey, and Harold Knight (Edinburgh: T&T Clark, 1958), 182.

[25] See Dorobantu, Green, Ramelow, and Salobir, "Being Human in the Age of AI."

[26] Genesis 2:18–22.

own.[27] Then their son Cain, angered with God, slays his brother and the relationship between siblings is shattered as well.[28] Notably, technology plays an ever more prominent and always ambiguous role in these tales. Cain's descendants build the first cities and forge instruments of metal. When human might turns toward violence, the earth is cleansed by a divine flood, from which God saves human- and animal-kind by commissioning the technology of the ark.[29] God's ensuing covenant with Noah somewhat restores human dominion to an image of divine care rather than a quest for domination,[30] but technological aspirations continue with the heaven-storming endeavor of the Tower of Babel.[31] Babel's aftermath splinters humanity into mutually uncomprehending communities. Technologically assisted domination without relationship to God, nature, and one another is presented as a sure road to disaster.[32]

A succession of interconnected covenants with Abraham and his descendants, ordered toward gathering in the entire world, signals that God's care and concern is not merely for us as individuals; the divine plan for our redemption is finally communal. "Humanity," writes biblical scholar William Dubrell, "finds its individual fullness in the blessedness of personal relationships."[33] By his incarnate life as human, the Second Vatican Council writes, Jesus "fully reveals man to man himself and makes

---

[27] Genesis 3.

[28] Genesis 4.

[29] Genesis 6–7. Flood narratives are common in the ancient near east and elsewhere. God's moral reasoning in the Hebrew account, however, is rarer. In the *Epic of Gilgamesh*, the god Enlil decides to flood the world because humans are noisy; in Genesis, the author of life reclaims it because the human community has turned from provident dominion toward death-dealing violence.

[30] Genesis 9; cf. Psalm 104.

[31] Genesis 11:1–9.

[32] Noreen Herzfeld, *Technology and Religion: Remaining Human in a Co-Created World* (West Conshohocken, PA: Templeton Press, 2011), 15.

[33] W. J. Dumbrell, *Covenant and Creation: A Theology of Old Testament Covenants* (Eugene, OR: Wipf and Stock, 2009), 6.

his supreme calling clear."[34] This revelation, Karl Barth points out, is accomplished through personal relationships:

> If we see Him alone, we do not see Him at all. If we see Him, we see with and around Him in ever widening circles His disciples, the people, His enemies, and the countless multitudes who never have heard His name. We see Him as theirs, determined by them and for them, belonging to each and every one of them.[35]

But God is not only the author and exemplar of personal relationships; human beings are created for relationship *with* God. As Saint Augustine confesses, "You have made us for Yourself, O Lord, and our hearts are restless until they rest in You."[36] At each point, we are created to live in relationship with others—including with a God who is not of our essence.

In Western cultures today, when one speaks of "personal" as opposed to business or other relationships, one often has in mind not gain or entertainment alone, but a true sharing of life in an empathic intimacy of hearts. This association between empathy and the "person" was forged in light of the Christian belief in God as Trinity, which redefined the ancient Roman understanding of "person" to give us an understanding of relationships that still haunts us today.[37] Originally denoting the mask worn by an actor on stage, the Roman *persona* referred to one's social identity—the status and activities that constituted one's service to one's city and its gods.[38] What the city did not value in you was invisible or even

---

[34] *Gaudium et Spes*, § 22.
[35] Dumbrell, *Covenant and Creation*, 216.
[36] Modified from Augustine, *The Confessions*, trans. Maria Boulding, rev. ed., Works of Saint Augustine, I/1 (Hyde Park, NY: New City Press, 2001), sec. 1.2.5.
[37] Portions of this discussion of Trinitarian theology and personhood draw upon David J. Gunkel and Jordan Joseph Wales, "Debate: What Is Personhood in the Age of AI?," *AI & Society* 36, no. 2 (January 3, 2021): 473–486, doi.org/10.1007/s00146-020-01129-1.
[38] Thomas D. Williams and Jan Olof Bengtsson, "Personalism," in *The Stanford Encyclopedia of Philosophy*, ed. Edward N. Zalta (Stanford, CA: Metaphysics Research Lab, Stanford University, 2018), plato.stanford.edu/archives/win2018/entries/personalism.

unreal. Thus, to be a real someone was, by piety and patriotism, to function for Rome; to be a renegade Roman was not to be a someone at all.[39] Now, however, we speak of "person" not first as a role that one plays but as the metaphysical reality that one *is*, the subject who assumes roles, setting oneself in relation both to other persons and to one's own nature, and living out one's personhood in relationships of empathic self-gift.[40]

This reinterpretation, having begun among the Hellenistic philosophers,[41] was consummated under the influence of Christianity's rather exotic claims about divinity. Christians worshiped Jesus of Nazareth as God—not as *a* god, but as *the* God, the only one.[42] Even so, in the scriptures, Jesus speaks to his Father, also called God;[43] and he sends the Holy Spirit from the Father.[44] And when the early Christians were required to explain themselves, they stated that these three were one. In the third century, Tertullian of Carthage called the Father, Son, and Holy Spirit "*personae.*" Thus, Christian theology speaks of the three distinct

---

[39] Larry Siedentop, *Inventing the Individual: The Origins of Western Liberalism* (Cambridge, MA: Belknap Press, 2014), 25, 28.

[40] Robert Spaemann, "Human Dignity," in *Essays in Anthropology: Variations on a Theme*, ed. Guido De Graaff, trans. James Mumford (Eugene, OR: Cascade Books, 2010), 59. See also Anselm Ramelow, "The Person in the Abrahamic Tradition: Is the Judeo-Christian Concept of Personhood Consistent?," *American Catholic Philosophical Quarterly* 87, no. 4 (2013): 593–610, doi.org/10.5840/acpq201387448.

[41] The ancient vision of "person" as a societal role was challenged from the fourth century BC by a Hellenistic distinction between culture and underlying nature, and, in Stoicism, an increasing focus on the cultivation of the self. Even so, the *persona* remained a functional mask through which generic human nature was individuated. See Robert Spaemann, *Persons: The Difference between "Someone" and "Something,"* trans. Oliver O'Donovan (New York: Oxford University Press, 2006), 22–23.

[42] John 1:1–3. Larry W. Hurtado, *Honoring the Son: Jesus in Earliest Christian Devotional Practice* (Bellingham, WA: Lexham Press, 2018); Richard Bauckham, *Jesus and the God of Israel: God Crucified and Other Studies on the New Testament's Christology of Divine Identity* (Grand Rapids, MI: Eerdmans, 2008).

[43] John 5:37; 17:20–2.

[44] John 15:26.

"persons" of the one single God.⁴⁵ Like their Jewish forebears, the early Christians were resolute monotheists. What, then, are these three *personae*? They are not masks. Tertullian rejects any notion that the one God merely play-acted three historical roles or functions.⁴⁶ Therefore, either God was somehow malleable⁴⁷ or this tri-personal history was a self-revelation, an expression of an unchanging inner life. In time, the appearances of the three distinct *personae* came to be understood as declaring an eternal distinction *within* God.⁴⁸

Scripture hints at the nature of this distinction in calling Jesus the Father's "only Son."⁴⁹ The God of Israel is not Jupiter, bodily and time-bound, and so this begetting must be something other than what took place among the gods of Rome. If we remove from the concept of begetting everything that is corporeal or temporal, we are left with a

---

⁴⁵ Tertullian, *Tertullian's Treatise Against Praxeas: The Text Edited, with an Introduction, Translation, and Commentary*, trans. Ernest Evans (Eugene, OR: Wipf & Stock, 2011), § 2.

⁴⁶ Edmund Hill, "Introduction," in *The Trinity*, by Augustine, 1st ed., WSA, I/5 (Hyde Park, NY: New City Press, 1991), § 80; Tertullian, *Against Praxeas*, §§ 11, 23.

⁴⁷ The views of the early apologists might be read in this way. Theophilus of Antioch, for instance, holds that God has always possessed Reason (*Logos*) but that this Logos became distinct for the sake of creation. See Gilles Emery and Matthew Levering, eds., *The Oxford Handbook of the Trinity* (Oxford: Oxford University Press, 2014), 97–99.

⁴⁸ On Old Testament views of God's self-revelation see, among others, Horst Dietrich Preuss, *Old Testament Theology*, vol. 1 (Louisville, KY: Westminster John Knox Press, 1995), 194–195. For New Testament developments, see Gerhard Kittel, "Δόξα," in *Theological Dictionary of the New Testament*, ed. Gerhard Friedrich and Gerhard Kittel, trans. Geoffrey William Bromiley (Grand Rapids, MI: Eerdmans, 1964), 2:233–55. Athanasius of Alexandria distinguishes between how God is revealed in time as Creator and how God eternally exists as self-named Father and Son; see Khaled Anatolios, *Retrieving Nicaea: The Development and Meaning of Trinitarian Doctrine* (Grand Rapids, MI: Baker Academic, 2018), 129–131. In the late fourth century, Augustine refines this view to its decisive Western form. By the appearances of the persons in history, God reveals his inner life so that it might become humans' destination; see Hill, "Introduction," §§ 89–90; Augustine, *The Trinity*, trans. Edmund Hill, 2nd ed. (Hyde Park, NY: New City Press, 2012), sec. 4.5.25.

⁴⁹ John 1:18; 3:16.

timeless handing-over of the single divine life from Father to Son.[50] This handing-over is what makes the Father to *be* the Father; what makes the Son to *be* the Son; and their mutual self-gift is what makes the Holy Spirit to *be* the Holy Spirit. Like poles of a magnetic field, the divine persons exist by their mutual relations; and if one were taken away, all would cease to be. The unending all-at-once life of the Trinity simply *is* these relations of self-gift and reception. This, then, is what it means for God to "be" love.[51]

This account of God reshaped how the word "person" was applied to human beings made in God's image. God exists *by* relations; created persons exist *for* relationships of mutual self-gift that are both self-expressive and other-receiving. By refusing self-gift, created persons would not cease to exist, but they would live less personally than the persons they are. Early Christians found this self-gift exemplified in the Son's Incarnation as Jesus. In his human compassion upon the cross, they saw an expression of his divine life. As the sixth-century Pope Saint Gregory the Great put it, by compassion one "take[s] into oneself the mind of an afflicted" neighbor, "transfer[ring] into oneself the suffering of the one sorrowing" before offering some outward "act of service."[52] By taking in the *other's* state of mind, the compassionate one imitates the always-single mind and life of the three persons of God. Empathic self-gift, that is, imitates the relations by which the persons of God exist at all. From the exteriority of "mask," we have come to an understanding of "person" as simultaneously deeply interior and relationally oriented to others.[53] True,

---

[50] Athanasius, "Orations Against the Arians, Book III [Selections]," in *The Christological Controversy*, ed. and trans. Richard A. Norris (Philadelphia: Fortress Press, 1980), sec. 3.35–36; Athanasius, "Orations Against the Arians, Book I," in *The Trinitarian Controversy*, ed. and trans. William C. Rusch (Philadelphia: Fortress Press, 1980), sec. 1.14–16.

[51] Cf. 1 John 4:8.

[52] Translation modified from Gregory I, *Moralia in Job: Morals on the Book of Job*, trans. James Bliss and Charles Marriott (Jackson, MI: Ex Fontibus, 2012), sec. 20.36.68–69, 6.35.54.

[53] Christian Smith, *What Is a Person?: Rethinking Humanity, Social Life, and the Moral Good from the Person Up* (Chicago: University of Chicago Press, 2010), 61–89. We might add that, while the psychological experience of such encounters is universal, the Catholic tradition holds that these personal relationships have a transcendent destiny only partially described by

due to immaturity, injury, and disability, this or that particular person may not be able to fully express the free compassionate self-gift by which persons live interpersonally; nonetheless, each remains a person indeed, belonging still to the circle of beings that are ordinarily capable of that gift.[54]

The Jewish tradition also presents relational notions of personhood that have shaped our world. Martin Buber, in his 1923 monograph *I and Thou*, describes two types of relationships that we have already referenced:

---

psychology. Therefore, Paul writes in his letter to the Philippians (2:1) that it is not only by the "consolation from love" but also by "sharing in the Spirit" that one truly becomes of "one mind" with another.

[54] Persons with disabilities can—and do—live as gifts in other ways. Brian Brock uses the term "strange vocations" to describe the work of persons with disabilities, whose very beings serve nonetheless to glorify God's creativity. See Brian R. Brock, *Wondrously Wounded: Theology, Disability, and the Body of Christ* (Waco, TX: Baylor University Press, 2020). Pope John Paul II describes these persons as "humanity's privileged witnesses" to the humanity and redemptive work of Christ in the world; see John Paul II, "On the Occasion of the International Symposium on The Dignity and Rights of the Mentally Disabled Person," January 5, 2004, www.vatican.va/content/john-paul-ii/en/speeches/2004/january/documents/hf_jp-ii_spe_20040108_handicap-mentale.html. Miguel Romero distinguishes Aristotle's identification of reason as a definitive trait of a human person, from Saint Thomas Aquinas's notion of intellect, by which the human person is able to detect and to be drawn toward the good. Romero writes that, "for Aquinas, the definitive, specifying aptitude of the human being is our innate capacity that can be supernaturally perfected (in act) to know and love the Creator, toward a mode of intellectual apprehension that exceeds our nature"; see "The Happiness of Those Who Lack the Use of Reason,'" *The Thomist: A Speculative Quarterly Review* 80 (January 1, 2016): 56–57, doi.org/10.1353/tho.2016.0003. As we have discussed, explicit reasoning (*ratio*) is dependent upon the antecedent apprehensive power of *intellectus*. Even if deprived of explicit propositional thought, the disabled do not lack this power of soul. Thus, according to Romero's reading, "There are acts of the intellect that do not constitute the use of reason, but that provide the requisite material conditions for a properly human, supernatural happiness *in this life*" (60). Persons with disabilities, injured persons, or immature persons, even if they cannot demonstrate self-gift by voluntary empathic love, still both reveal God's generous act of creation by their existence *and* echo God's eternally divine self-gift in their spiritual "[disposition] by grace to know and desire those things that are proper to contemplative rest in the beauty of God's goodness and truth" (64). Thus, they respond spiritually to God's gifts in a fully human way, even if doing so in a manner hidden from full outward expression or explicit engagement with other created persons.

the I-Thou and the I-It. A young man has an I-It relationship with his car. Here, the "I" in the relationship treats the other as an object, to be used or experienced. We have I-It relationships with things, but we can also have such relationships with people whenever we objectify them or treat them as means to our own ends. In the I-Thou relationship, on the other hand, the relationship takes precedence over the "I." The other is met on its own terms, and the boundaries between the two persons are diminished. Insofar as we are reflections of our Creator's attributes, ideas, and intentions, we cannot help but image God by the fact of our inter-relational existence. And we are formed not just by our initial creation, but in every authentic I-Thou encounter.

From within both the phenomenological tradition and the Christian personalist tradition, the twentieth century saint and philosopher Edith Stein offers a Christian refinement to the I-Thou relationship. As did the early Christians, Stein holds that, because the Trinity is the ultimate archetype of being a person, all personal knowing and all personhood are ultimately oriented to love and mutual self-gift. The Trinity is eternally "being one of a plurality of persons; and the divine name 'I am' is thus equivalent to an 'I give myself wholly to a Thou,' 'I am one with a Thou,' and therefore also with 'We are.'"[55] Therefore, the highest and most perfect expression of personhood for Stein is not the I-Thou relation but the We relation.[56] The Trinity shows that "we, as the oneness of the I and thou, is a oneness higher than the oneness of the I."[57] The most fundamental difference between the being of an "I" (a conscious animal) and the being of a person is, then, that the "I" of a person is an *intersubjective* "I," whose ultimate end consists in—as much as possible—being a "We," in "a being-

---

[55] Edith Stein, *Finite and Eternal Being: An Attempt at an Ascent to the Meaning of Being*, trans. Kurt F. Reinhardt (Washington, DC: ICS Publications, 2002), 370.
[56] See Catherine Moon, "Τί Ἐστιν Ἀλήθεια: Towards an Account of Human Experience and Its Role in Moral Theology from the Perspective of Edith Stein" (PhD diss., The Catholic University of America, 2023).
[57] Stein, *Finite and Eternal Being*, 370.

one that is founded on mutual self-giving."[58] This being-one or "We" has been tragically broken by the fall, humankind's ancient self-severance from God, but is brought back into unity and heightened through encounter with the living Christ and the gift of grace.

Such religious views variously lie behind and illuminate the Western tendency, even in our pluralistic age, to criticize as "cold" those interactions that lack any reciprocal token of mutually shared interiority. Whether speaking of "interpersonal" skills, "personal" conversations, "personable" demeanors, or "impersonal" affects, our discourse assumes that humans exercise their natural personhood out of an interior life from which they engage in voluntary self-gift by meeting with others' interiority in a fusion of minds through empathy and conscious understanding. Persons live personally by living *inter*personally; so doing, they image God. This is the theological ground for the concept of "encounter" that drives our inquiry.

What Is Intelligence?

The human being's imaging of God by relationality is, perhaps, less commonly familiar to Western culture than the long-prominent notion that the image is our rationality. Within the Christian theological tradition, Boethius (ca. 480–524) looms large, writing that the person is "the individual substance of a rational nature."[59] Since the latter half of the twentieth century, this definition has been criticized as excessively narrow and focused either on propositional reasoning or on domination of the natural world. In other words, "reason" has come to be associated with the technocratic paradigm. Christianity's traditional usage, however, was more expansive. It is more recent figures such as Hobbes, Leibniz, and, in his later writings, Alan Turing, who helped to birth the now-familiar

---

[58] Stein, *Finite and Eternal Being*, 350.
[59] Boethius, "A Treatise Against Eutyches and Nestorius," in *The Theological Tractates*, trans. Hugh Fraser Stewart (London: Heinemann, 1918), 85.

"reason" of calculation and proposition that vexes Boethius's (mis)readers today.

In Boethius, as generally in early and medieval Christianity, humankind's "rational nature" orients the human person toward "understanding" (Latin, *intelligentia*). This understanding is not first a mastery of calculation but an interiorly experienced cognitive grasp—a hold on some reality beyond oneself as being the-thing-that-it-is.[60] *Intelligentia* comes, in turn, from the verb *intellegere* ("to understand"), from which we have also *intellectus* ("intellect" or "understanding" as a faculty). *Intellectus* is our capacity not just to remember a visual experience of an apple, but to remember the apple *as an apple*. Propositional reasoning is but a means to this understanding. The mid-twentieth century philosopher Josef Pieper explained that, for the medievals, *ratio* ("reason") is "understanding as . . . the power of discursive, logical thought, of searching and of examination, of abstraction, of definition and drawing conclusions." Reasoning attains to understanding by way of judgment, and judgments are carried through by this reasoned reflection.[61] Grounding this, *intellectus* is "the name for the understanding in so far as it is the capacity of *simplex intuitus*, that simple [i.e., all-at-once] vision to which truth offers itself like a landscape to the eye."[62]

> The faculty of mind, man's knowledge, is both these things in one, according to antiquity and the Middle Ages, simultaneously *ratio* and *intellectus*; and the process of knowing is the action of the two together. The mode of discursive thought is accompanied and impregnated by an

---

[60] See further discussion in Jordan Joseph Wales, "Participatory Spiritual Intelligence: A Theological Perspective," in *Perspectives on Spiritual Intelligence*, ed. Fraser Watts and Marius Dorobantu (New York: Routledge, 2024). Portions of the historical discussion in this section have been adapted from that chapter.

[61] The necessary role of judgment in knowledge has been noted frequently, from Augustine to Noam Chomsky, among many others. Specifically with regard to AI, see Brian Cantwell Smith, *The Promise of Artificial Intelligence: Reckoning and Judgment* (Cambridge, MA: MIT Press, 2019).

[62] Josef Pieper, *Leisure: The Basis of Culture* (New York: Pantheon Books, 1952), 33–34.

effortless awareness, the contemplative vision of the *intellectus*, which is not active but passive, or rather receptive, the activity of the soul in which it conceives that which it sees.[63]

To understand is to have a point of view on some facet of reality, a view sharpened by but not identifiable with either a course of logical argumentation or a policy of action. It is an experiential engagement.

Definitions of reason and intelligence commonly applied to AI abandon this interiority in favor of a twofold reduction. First, rationality and understanding become the *logical manipulation* of symbolically represented information; and second, intelligence becomes *efficacious problem-solving*. These foundations of the technocratic paradigm did not arise from computer science but can be traced back to seminal ideas of the early seventeenth century. Francis Bacon (1561–1626)—popularly credited with establishing the modern scientific method—laid the groundwork for a notion of intelligence not as understanding but as problem-solving, with his emphasis on experimental knowledge. Where once philosophy had sought the true and the good in nature, Bacon urged an aim that was thoroughly practical. By "vexing and driving" nature, we might discover and harness "her" hidden laws for "the relief of man's estate."[64] Bacon represented this pursuit of knowledge for material welfare as a noble effort to heal the wounds that Adam's fall had imposed upon humanity and the natural world.[65] Bacon's world was not so much a mechanism as an organism. Living nature may be inquired into, but "she" will also resist, for nature has an integrity and wholeness of its own that must be respected, even if only for the sake of manipulating "her" more effectively. With Bacon, we stand on the brink between a cooperative

---

[63] Pieper, *Leisure*, 34.

[64] Peter Pesic, "Wrestling with Proteus: Francis Bacon and the 'Torture' of Nature," *Isis* 90, no. 1 (March 1999): 81–94.

[65] Carolyn Merchant, "The Scientific Revolution and The Death of Nature," *Isis* 97, no. 3 (2006): 513–533, doi.org/10.1086/508090.

respect for nature's possibilities and the plunge into today's confrontational technocratic paradigm.

René Descartes (1596–1650) took that plunge. Whereas Bacon's world was populated by organisms and was itself a great organism, Descartes acknowledged a life with its own wholeness only in the spiritual soul (*res cogitans*) by which, he believed, human beings were able to think and to reason. Corporeal nature was simply measurable matter (*res extensa*), lacking any vital force of its own. Particular things were arrangements of smaller components, bound gear-like by divinely maintained laws of motion. Therefore, like a watch, the parts of the body and of the greater world could be reconfigured to accomplish new arrangements of matter and new causal relationships.[66] The Baconian project could now advance with lighter step, shorn of its metaphysical distinctions and treating all of nature as one great mechanism—even more so when Newtonian mechanics replaced the divine laws of motion with intrinsic mass, force, momentum, gravitation, and the rest.

Bacon and Descartes defined a world to be dominated, but Thomas Hobbes (1588–1679) initiated the journey toward intelligence as calculation. Hobbes applied the Cartesian vision of matter to the inner workings of the mind, which became a grand calculator suited to mastery of a mechanistic world. Not that a calculative intelligence was confined to material concerns. In the year of Hobbes's death, Gottfried Wilhelm von Leibniz (1646–1716) wrote hopefully of "an infallible calculus," a comprehensive symbolic logic by which "to work out . . . the doctrines most useful for life, that is, those of morality and metaphysics." For "reason will be right beyond all doubt only when it is everywhere as clear and certain as only arithmetic has been until now."[67]

---

[66] Descartes had no concept of a relationship between mass and momentum. See Edward Slowik, "Descartes' Physics," in *The Stanford Encyclopedia of Philosophy*, ed. Edward N. Zalta (Stanford, CA: Metaphysics Research Lab, Stanford University, October 15, 2021), plato.stanford.edu/archives/win2021/entries/descartes-physics.

[67] Quoted by George B. Dyson, *Darwin among the Machines: The Evolution of Global Intelligence*, 2nd ed. (New York: Basic Books, 2012), 38.

In his philosophy of "positivism," Auguste Comte (1798–1857) reinforced the view that intelligence is the practical efficacy of a calculative mind. Comte taught that only empirically observable facts are real and only empirically verifiable statements are true. Heaven would be created on earth by the advance of science; and the human person, as priest of this transformation, was to set technical skill and altruistic sentiment above all else so as, in the words of Hannah Arendt, to be no longer the wise *Homo sapiens* but the maker, *Homo faber*.[68] The Hobbesian mind was now to be directed entirely to the relief of an estate definable exhaustively in terms of those things which a positive science could alleviate.

These voices within the scientific revolution deeply influenced early theories of AI. Intelligence, in the mid-to-late-twentieth century, became equated with the logical manipulation of symbolically represented information.[69] Accomplishing this task, a properly programmed computer would *be* "thinking."[70] In the resultant enthusiasm for so-called "symbolic AI,"[71] to diagram a sentence and to construct a plausible response was

---

[68] Referenced in Erik J. Larson, *The Myth of Artificial Intelligence: Why Computers Can't Think the Way We Do* (Cambridge, MA: Belknap Press of Harvard University Press, 2021), 63–66.

[69] This intuition, a species of the Computational Theory of Mind (or "Computationalism"), was formalized as the "Physical Symbol Systems Hypothesis," seminally described in Allen Newell and Herbert A. Simon, "Computer Science as Empirical Inquiry: Symbols and Search," *Communications of the ACM* 19, no. 3 (March 1976): 113–126, doi.org/10.1145/360018.360022.

[70] Put otherwise, "A computer running a program that models a human cognitive process is itself *engaged* in that cognitive process" (Jaegwon Kim, *Philosophy of Mind*, 3rd ed. [Boulder, CO: Routledge, 2010], 160).

[71] On the history of AI prior to the explosion of interest in neural networks, see Nils J. Nilsson, *The Quest for Artificial Intelligence: A History of Ideas and Achievements* (New York: Cambridge University Press, 2010). The most widely used introductory textbook on AI is Stuart Russell and Peter Norvig, *Artificial Intelligence: A Modern Approach*, 3rd ed. (Upper Saddle River, NJ: Pearson, 2009). For the sake of our narrow focus, we pass over distinctions that can be drawn between AI as human-like action (the Turing Test in the 1950s), AI as human-like thought (Newell and Simon's early work with symbolic representation in the 1960s, leading to the field of cognitive modeling), AI as rational deliberation (logicism and

deemed equivalent to *understanding* that sentence, because the AI had not just imitated human output but had arrived at it in the same way—so they thought—as humans do.[72] More recently, immense advances in computing power have brought to prominence so-called "non-symbolic" or statistical AI. Statistical AI often takes the form of "artificial neural networks"—computer programs that mathematically *simulate* an interconnected set of simplified brain neurons.

Some might object that, while the computer may simulate human thinking either in its ratiocination or in its neurological underpinnings, a simulation is not a replication. That is, the AI system no more thinks than one's physics homework has gravity or a flight simulator flies. Nevertheless, the philosophical theory of "computationalism" argues that this is a distinction without a difference. Philosopher Jaegwon Kim explains that, for this view, thought is computation; and since "a computational simulation of a computational process ... re-create[s] that computational process" (for instance, since a simulation of addition does in fact re-create addition), there is "no confusion in the claim that a computer simulating a cognitive process is itself engaged in that cognitive process."[73] The reality of thinking, according to this view, is indifferent to the physical substrate that accomplishes the computation, be it a brain or a computer.

---

expert systems in the 1980s), and AI as rational agency (intelligent robots); see Russell and Norvig, 1–33.

[72] See Bertram Raphael, "SIR: A Computer Program for Semantic Information Retrieval" (Cambridge, MA: Massachusetts Institute of Technology, 1964), 42, AI Technical Reports (AITR-220), hdl.handle.net/1721.1/6904. Comfortably asserting the identity of the computer's functioning with true understanding is Roger C. Schank and Robert P. Abelson, *Scripts, Plans, Goals, and Understanding: An Inquiry into Human Knowledge Structures* (Hillsdale, NJ: Lawrence Erlbaum Associates, 1977).

[73] Kim, *Philosophy of Mind*, 161. The example of addition is given in Nilsson, *Quest for Artificial Intelligence*, 310. Note that, under such a view, subjectivity or indeed any form of conscious experience is either an irrelevant byproduct of human minds or plays a functional role that can be replaced by something else, because consciousness has no part in a computationalist definition of computation itself.

But computationalism loses something essential from the notion of "understanding" held dear by the Christian tradition. Is the diagramming of a sentence or the bit-by-bit calculation of a neural network's activation values really a personal *grasp* of reality?[74] Computationalism gives us, at best, the ghost of *ratio* without *intellectus*, understanding-as-procedure without a co-penetrating understanding-as-apprehension. Among other costs, this reduction loses the intrinsic meaningfulness of the operations of thought. Even if a system's internal dynamics and its interaction with the world constrain the plausible range of meanings that might be assigned to it, meaning and understanding cannot be sustained by procedure alone. They require the subject to have a phenomenal (that is, a first-person experiential)[75] grasp of the meaning of that procedure and its elements. *Ratio*, in Pieper's sense, is no longer intrinsically meaningful when severed from the apprehensive vision of *intellectus*. In giving us calculation without experience, computationalism—despite tantalizing parallels between mind and machine—cannot fully describe what the human mind is or accomplishes.

Arguments over computationalism, however, are of less moment to the "intelligence" sought by AI researchers today, who tend to focus more on efficacious problem-solving. Whether by Hobbesian calculation or not, intelligence must *work*: It must solve the worldly problems to which it is

---

[74] We might equally ask whether the opening and closing of calcium channels and the generation of action potentials among the neurons of the brain is that sort of grasp. We have only the evidence that it seems to subserve that grasp, although this by no means constrains us to believe that material factors are all there is to it.

[75] Here and throughout this document, "phenomenal" has the philosophical sense of what David Smith calls "[the] structures of consciousness as experienced from the first-person point of view," especially that first-person experience as "directed toward something, as it is an experience of or about some object;" see David Woodruff Smith, "Phenomenology," in *The Stanford Encyclopedia of Philosophy*, ed. Edward N. Zalta (Stanford, CA: Metaphysics Research Lab, Stanford University, December 16, 2013), plato.stanford.edu/archives/sum 2018/entries/phenomenology. In this text, we use the word to mean first-person experience, and not "experience" as some sort of data-gathering apart from a real, felt, first-person point of view.

applied. This version of intelligence has also been part of the field since its beginnings. In his 1950 paper "Computing Machinery and Intelligence," Alan Turing famously wrote that, if a computer could conversationally express effective reasoning and artistic creativity in a way indistinguishable from humans, then the question "can machines think?" would become "too meaningless to deserve discussion."[76] This test for efficacy, which he called "the imitation game," is now known simply as the "Turing Test." A few years later, when AI pioneer John McCarthy proposed the seminal 1956 Dartmouth conference on AI, he defined "the artificial intelligence problem" as "that of making a machine behave in ways that would be called intelligent if a human were so behaving."[77]

Each of these definitions exemplifies what is called "behaviorism." Behaviorism defines an entity only by its tendency to exhibit certain behaviors under certain conditions.[78] The question is not *how* some behavior comes about but rather the success of that behavior in fulfilling some external criterion. Behavioristic definitions are agnostic concerning the realities—experiential, metaphysical, spiritual, biological, computational, or otherwise—that underlie the observable behaviors by which an entity is defined. This makes them useful when we program machines that will interact with the world, whence Peter Norvig, a director of research at Google, defines the "rational agent" as one that "acts so as to achieve the best outcome or, when there is uncertainty, the best expected outcome."[79] Here, rationality refers not to *how* a behavior comes about but

---

[76] A. M. Turing, "Computing Machinery and Intelligence," *Mind,* New Series 59, no. 236 (1950): 442.

[77] John McCarthy, Marvin Minsky, Nathaniel Rochester, and Claude Shannon, "A Proposal for the Dartmouth Summer Research Project on Artificial Intelligence," August 31, 1955, www-formal.stanford.edu/jmc/history/dartmouth/dartmouth.html. For more on the Dartmouth conference, see Nilsson, *Quest for Artificial Intelligence*, 52–56.

[78] Carl G. Hempel, "The Logical Analysis of Psychology (1935, 1977)," in *Readings in Philosophy of Psychology*, ed. Ned Block (Cambridge, MA: Harvard University Press, 1980), 1–14.

[79] Russell and Norvig, "Introduction," in *Artificial Intelligence*, 2. Russell and Norvig's "rational agent" is a fairly common way of expressing what it is for an agent to be "rational."

simply to its success, as judged according to some favored empirical measure. Similarly, philosopher John Danaher argues that robots can be called our "friends" because a friend is deemed a friend when behaving as we expect friends to behave.[80] From this purely exterior perspective, the suitably behaving AI system cannot be excluded from the circle of intelligence, rationality, and relationality; indeed, to do so would be simply an act of prejudice.

However, behaviorism falls short, both morally and meaningfully. On the moral side, it permits some rather dark outcomes. In ancient Rome, those who did not or could not meet the stipulated standards of their *personae* could be excluded from that behaviorally delimited circle of status and worth. This is why unwanted children could be discarded at birth. In our day, we might think also of the disabled, the infirm, and the aged. Although we are ordinarily limited to our observations when we interact with intelligent or rational beings, the repugnant consequences of a purely behavioral definition of those beings requires no imagination because we have seen those consequences throughout history. While at first seeming more generous than other definitions, behaviorism in reality returns us to the ancient mask/*persona*. This *persona* fails not only to make sense of our care for the immature and the weak, but also even to make sense of the meanings of our words. We think, speak, and act as if behavior can bear

---

This is not a denial of interior states, but just a way of expressing rationality in terms of behavior: "S is rational if and only if S always acts in ways that maximize expected utility, i.e., the expected value of S's utility function relative to S's subjective probabilities." This can be consistent with a non-behavioristic account of *what it takes* to have a given utility function or subjective probability function. However, *in itself*, as a definition of rationality, it is behavioristic in the sense not that it eliminates the possibility of interior states but that its agnosticism permits it to eliminate *mention* of interior states. As we shall explain, this is far narrower a notion of rationality than the Christian tradition (and many others) can offer, but it is a notion that has grown understandably popular in the field of robotics.

[80] John Danaher, "Welcoming Robots into the Moral Circle: A Defense of Ethical Behaviourism," *Science and Engineering Ethics* 26, no. 4 (2020): 2023–2049, doi.org/10.1007/s11948-019-00119-x. We engage with Danaher's position below, as part of our discussion of machine consciousness.

witness to experiences; one has a "caring" smile or a "delighted" grin, makes an "angry" gesture or gives a "perplexed" glance. Our observable behavior implicates our emotional, psychological, and spiritual life. Any definition that neglects this will fail, likewise, to capture the full reality of our "rational" and "intelligent" behavioral displays.

Nonetheless, ideas drawn from AI increasingly dominate our understanding of ourselves and our task in the world. Popular historian and futurist Yuval Noah Harari confidently declares, "Intelligence is not consciousness. Intelligence is the ability to solve problems. Consciousness is the ability to feel things."[81] For Harari, the problems that matter are those that are objectively definable and measurable within the material world—climate change, material poverty, energy production and distribution, political organization, brain chemistry, disease, and the last enemy, death—and they are to be resolved by manipulating the material factors that define them. Harari's intelligence is Turing's, his world is Descartes's (absent the spiritual or divine), and his science is Comte's. Rationality and intelligence need be nothing more than behavioral ability, when the world is a great machine to be mastered.

The Christian tradition is not alone in questioning these reductions. Both computationalist and behaviorist approaches to intelligence are targeted for refutation in John Searle's famous "Chinese Room" thought experiment. Searle posited that an AI system may have functional competence but no true understanding, as may be seen in the case of a physical implementation: If an uncomprehending human being were to sit in a room, taking input and generating output by consulting a rulebook and shifting about bits of paper bearing writings in an unknown language (in the original example, Chinese), where would the understanding be? Not in the human functionary, and not in the system as a whole, either. We, who *interpret* the input and output of the system,

---

[81] Ezra Klein, "Yuval Harari on Why Humans Won't Dominate Earth in 300 Years," *Vox*, March 27, 2017, www.vox.com/2017/3/27/14780114/yuval-harari-ai-vr-consciousness-sapiens-homo-deus-podcast.

may declare that we are observing understanding. The system itself may even be designed so that, interpreted at some level, not only the output but also the dynamics of its interior operation echo the pattern of what it represents. But even so, a movement of paper slips with squiggles on them still is not *about* anything intrinsically, apart from any observer. Whatever it is that makes understanding to be understanding, it is not accounted for by a merely computational definition. What the system lacks is "intentionality," by which philosophers of mind mean not the deliberateness of voluntary behavior but the object-directed quality of mental states—that a thought is *about* something, not just through being interpreted by someone else but through *itself*. Searle claims there can be no understanding without such intentionality, and that intentionality does not exist without some subjectively phenomenal grasp of something as meaningful.[82]

This is not a judgment of value. It is not an anthropocentric bid to preserve some elusive something by which to reassure ourselves that we are superior to the machines. It must not obscure the achievements of contemporary computer science. Even so, we must be concerned about what may be lost from view if we absolutize parallels into equivalencies. Setting aside whether or not it may be possible for some future AI to be truly subjective, relational, rational, and intelligent, any use of those words to assert *parity* with what humans are doing must go beyond intelligent-looking behavior. It must also go beyond even a structure of processing that seems akin to what happens in our brains or in our discursive reasoning. It must include a personal, subjective grasp of reality, an intentional engagement in it; it must transcend the input and output of material reality to subjectively embrace that reality as well. AI outputs tracking a course of reasoning are an extraordinary achievement. To say that they are not rational or intelligent as we are is not to say that they are

---

[82] John R. Searle, "Minds, Brains, and Programs," *The Behavioral and Brain Sciences* 3 (1980): 417–457; "Consciousness, Unconsciousness and Intentionality," *Philosophical Issues* 1 (1991): 45, doi.org/10.2307/1522923.

not significant. It is not even to say that they cannot point beyond themselves to certain truths. But there are limits. Just as was the case for relational personhood, AI, so long as it lacks interior experience, may have rationally interpretable output and procedures, but these alone do not mean that it is engaged in reasoning.

CHAPTER 3

CONSCIOUSNESS: A *SINE QUA NON* OF RELATIONALITY AND INTELLIGENCE

Consciousness: An Initial Definition

Thus far we have seen that, in the Christian tradition, there is an ineradicably experiential dimension to a person's involvement in both relationship and understanding. Any account of meaning and action that neglects this dimension has not reckoned fully with what it is that we do when we know and love the world, ourselves, one another, and—ultimately—God. When the experiential is eliminated, we must redefine the person as simply a master of making, and the mind as but a machine for generating solutions to materially measurable problems.

To consider an AI system as intelligent or even relational in the manner that humans are, therefore, we must ask whether the AI can be the sort of personal "subject" that we are. Can it be truly a relational "other"? This is, of course, a question narrower than that of a particular AI technology's nature or value. It is narrower, too, than the question of the AI system's moral, social, or legal standing.[1] It is, rather, the question of whether or not the AI has an experience, both of the world and of itself, such that it may be said to stand subjectively, face to face, with that world and with other persons and, from this subjective stance, to participate in the encounter of compassionate self-gift. But we do not even have to go so far as to speak of subjective self-consciousness or compassion: these cannot be had without

---

[1] These important questions are taken up by a literature too extensive to survey here.

at least having phenomenal experience. This kind of machine consciousness, therefore, becomes a *sine qua non*—a condition necessary (even if not sufficient) for any truly authentic encounter with an AI.[2]

Consciousness is a frustratingly slippery concept. "Those who talk about 'consciousness,'" warns David Chalmers, "are frequently talking past each other."[3] For a working definition, we turn to John Searle:

> By consciousness I simply mean those subjective states of sentience or awareness that begin when one awakes in the morning from a dreamless sleep and continue throughout the day until one goes to sleep at night or falls into a coma, or dies, or otherwise becomes, as one would say, 'unconscious.'[4]

Consciousness, Searle clarifies, is characterized most importantly by its "subjectivity" and its "qualitative" character, by which he means that "each person's consciousness is private to that person" and there is "something that it feels like to be in a certain conscious state."[5] It is not to be confused with other related mental realities including *attention* (focusing of mental resources), *knowledge* (which is accessible to consciousness but does not

---

[2] We do not ask whether machines can be minds, nor whether they can truly understand, nor whether they can love, but only whether they can have that qualitative and subjectively private experience that we call consciousness. Many *performative* indices of human thinking that, in the past, were claimed to be impossible for a digital logic machine—Chess, Go, metaphor, painting—can and are compellingly modeled by AI systems today. This is why phenomenality, or conscious qualitative experience, becomes an important locus of discussion, and a point of juncture between the concerns of AI developers, their philosophical fellow-travelers, and a robust theological consideration of AI.

[3] David J. Chalmers, "The Problem of Consciousness," *Discusiones Filosóficas* 12, no. 19 (December 2011): 32.

[4] John R. Searle, "The Problem of Consciousness," *Social Research* 60, no. 1 (Spring 1993): 3.

[5] Searle, "The Problem of Consciousness," 4. In this, Searle agrees with David Chalmers, for whom the "central sense" of consciousness is that "an organism is conscious if there is something it is like to be that organism, and a mental state is conscious if there is something it is like to be in that state. Sometimes terms such as 'phenomenal consciousness' and 'qualia' are also used here" ("The Problem of Consciousness," 32).

embrace consciousness of emotional or bodily states), and *self-consciousness* (the preserve of some but not all conscious animals).[6] Consciousness is broader than human reasoning and understanding, and it certainly is more than a system's functional access to data about its environment.[7]

This subjective and qualitative (that is, first-person experiential) consciousness is what we will refer to simply as "consciousness," except where we refine or expand upon the concept. This consciousness ought to be subjectively apparent to all, but cognitive scientists and philosophers who attempt to explain it often falter. Searle warns: "From the fact that we do not know *how* it occurs, it does not follow that we do not know *that* it occurs."[8] Nonetheless, consciousness's epistemic elusiveness (only I can be certain that I am conscious) and its murky causation (we know that it is associated with nerve-firing, but why this basic chemistry should result in consciousness is in no way apparent) have led many to attempt explanations that, in fact, sidestep the ontologically subjective phenomenon that one has set out to investigate in the first place, by quietly turning to explain something else instead.

Often, scholars explain not *why* there is an experience at all (what Chalmers calls the "hard problem"[9] of consciousness), but rather

---

[6] Searle, "The Problem of Consciousness," 5.

[7] This so-called "access consciousness" is not actually experiential consciousness but a *function* that we accomplish experientially—for example, by knowing what is happening around us. See "The Failure of Functional Reductions," later in this chapter, pages 85–87.

[8] Searle, "The Problem of Consciousness," 7.

[9] Chalmers, "The Problem of Consciousness," 30–31. Chalmers distinguishes the "hard problem" from several "easy problems" that are all "straightforwardly vulnerable to explanation in terms of computational or neural mechanisms." These problems include items such as "the ability to discriminate, categorize, and react to environmental stimuli; the integration of information by a cognitive system; the reportability of mental states; the ability of a system to access its own internal states; the focus of attention; the deliberate control of behavior; [and] the difference between wakefulness and sleep." It must be admitted that philosophers from the phenomenological tradition argue that experience has far greater a role to play even in those "easy" problems than Chalmers seems prepared to concede. See, for example, Dan Zahavi, "Intentionality and Phenomenality: A Phenomenological Take on the

something about "cognitive *abilities* and *functions*." When they confront consciousness directly, they discuss its "causal role in the production of behavior that a system might perform,"[10] without explaining how consciousness *is* at all. Or they box experience out of cognitive abilities and functions by "specifying a *mechanism* that performs the function," whether at the level of neurophysiological processes or as part of some higher-level cognitive model.[11] But this strategy stacks the deck. One can address consciousness rather handily when its experiential dimension is treated as exhaustively definable by the role it plays in some function[12]—such as gathering information about one's environment—that itself can be described and measured without reference to experience in the first place. But then one has lost a constitutive mystery of the relational and intelligent subject.

When we turn to the question of *machine* consciousness, functional reductions become especially attractive, not only because we are not sure why animals are conscious but also because these reductions cohere with McCarthy's venerable aspiration "of making a machine behave in ways that would be called intelligent if a human were so behaving" and because—most crucially—first-person experience has no part in the definition of a machine. Whereas medieval theologies of the machine saw

---

Hard Problem," *Canadian Journal of Philosophy Supplementary Volume* 29, sup1 (2003): 63, doi.org/10.1080/00455091.2003.10717595.

[10] Here, "behavior" refers not just to exterior bodily movements but also to interior cognitive processes. Chalmers, "The Problem of Consciousness," 33.

[11] Chalmers, "The Problem of Consciousness," 33.

[12] Chalmers, "The Problem of Consciousness," 33–34. Chalmers goes on to describe five strategies common in the literature on consciousness, including to "explain something else" because consciousness is too difficult; to "deny the phenomenon" by, for instance, "equat[ing] experience with something like the capacity to discriminate and report;" to "claim to be explaining experience in the full sense" while passing from some functional model to experience as if by "magic" without explaining "how these processes should suddenly give rise to experience;" to "explain the structure of experience" without attempting to explain experience itself—a useful endeavor; or, also useful, to "isolate the substrate of experience" in certain brain locations or processes (39–40). Several of these are important tasks, but they do not explain the fact of conscious experience and therefore cannot be taken on their own.

it as harnessing deep cosmic dynamics that were themselves fragmentary echoes of the divine mind, modern views have reduced both nature and the mind to a mechanical clockwork of interacting forces. And while contemporary physics has put an end to the supposed comprehensiveness of Newtonian mechanics, the commercially exploitable technology of our present day still fits more or less comfortably into a model of physical reality as a brute mechanism.

In order, then, to discuss machine consciousness *without* eliminating consciousness as we have defined it, we must set aside the physicalist assumption of much modern science—that mechanical, chemical, or other physical models of causality exhaustively describe the nature and dynamics even of material existence. Even without speaking of spiritual causality, the apparent fact of some degree of consciousness in dolphins, dogs, and guinea pigs—although falling far short of what we see in humans—makes it evident that current scientific descriptions are incomplete. To think more clearly about machine consciousness, we might turn to computer scientist David Gamez's taxonomy of machine consciousness, which resists functional and other reductions while enabling us to usefully classify some philosophical and theoretical landmarks of today's extensive literature on the subject. First, machines might exhibit the "external behaviour associated with consciousness." Second, machines might emulate "the cognitive characteristics associated with consciousness." Third, machines may be designed with "an architecture that is claimed to be a cause or correlate of human consciousness." Fourth and finally would be "phenomenally conscious machines"—hypothetical machines having consciousness as we have defined it.[13] Significant philosophical reflections on the first three of these each reveal, in their own ways, the failure of the physicalist assumption and the need for descriptions of reality and the human person that transcend what the natural sciences are able to compass within their domains.

---

[13] David Gamez, "Progress in Machine Consciousness," *Consciousness and Cognition* 17, no. 3 (September 1, 2008): 887–910, doi.org/10.1016/j.concog.2007.04.005

Is Behavior Enough?

The category of machines capable of exhibiting the external behavior associated with consciousness is, of course, the territory of Turing's "imitation game." But even Turing himself, while comfortable with reducing *thinking* to a non-experiential reality, was unwilling to assert that the same could be done with consciousness. Nor is that claim made by most computer scientists working in this field. There are, however, a number of prominent exceptions among philosophers who address both human and machine consciousness. Notable among these are John Danaher, Stevan Harnad, and Daniel Dennett. Although there are significant differences in their positions, each of them has at its core the so-called "problem of other minds," which is that we attribute to others on the basis of their behavior the same consciousness that we attribute to ourselves on the basis of our own experience. Confronted with a human-acting robot, how can we argue against it possessing consciousness without denying other humans' consciousness?[14]

"Ethical Behaviorism" and the Collapse of Virtue Friendship

It is our contention that AI systems, so long as they lack the sort of consciousness we have in view, cannot be our friends, for they cannot engage in the voluntary empathic self-gift that characterizes the intimacy of friends.[15] Philosopher John Danaher—writing of robots but with an

---

[14] As Turing puts the dilemma, how can we avoid solipsism while denying that behavior is a good epistemic guide to consciousness? See Turing, "Computing Machinery and Intelligence," 446–447. To say that only living, biological entities can be conscious, or only animals with central nervous systems, only begs the question of *why* we make this claim other than based upon the association between our own experience and our material makeup. These are questions worth asking, but they must not be posed in order to rule out machine consciousness *a priori*.

[15] Variations on this argument are given, for instance, by Sherry Turkle, "In Good Company? On the Threshold of Robotic Companions," in *Close Engagements with Artificial Companions: Key Social, Psychological, Ethical and Design Issues*, ed. Yorick Wilks (Philadelphia, PA: John Benjamins Publishing Company, 2010), 3–10; Alexis Elder, "False

argument just as applicable to non-embodied AI systems—suggests otherwise. To ask whether robots *are* conscious is, for him, the wrong question. According to Danaher's proposed stance, which he calls "ethical behaviourism,"[16] we ought not require from the robot greater evidence of friendship than we would of a fellow human being before calling it our friend and considering it entitled to the ethical treatment due to friends. For Danaher, a robot's "observable behavioural repertoire" is "sufficient epistemic ground" for our believing what we would believe about humans under similar circumstances.[17]

Danaher's definition of friendship flows from a relational understanding of the human person. Over and above friendships of mere utility (useful for advancing one's power, prestige, or material welfare) or pleasure (the friendships of casual acquaintances), there are friendships of virtue. These are "premised on mutual good will and well-wishing," pursued "out of mutual admiration and shared values [and interests] on both sides."[18] Lest this "mutuality" be taken as referring only to the behavioral *expression* of such interior states, Danaher adds the condition of "honesty / authenticity," whereby "the friends must present themselves to each other as they truly are and not be selective or manipulative in their

---

Friends and False Coinage: A Tool for Navigating the Ethics of Sociable Robots," *ACM SIGCAS Computers and Society* 45, no. 3 (January 5, 2016): 248–254, doi.org/10.1145/2874239.2874274; Alexis M. Elder, *Friendship, Robots, and Social Media : False Friends and Second Selves* (London: Routledge, 2017); Noreen L. Herzfeld, *The Artifice of Intelligence: Divine and Human Relationship in a Robotic Age* (Minneapolis, MN: Fortress Press, 2023).

[16] John Danaher, "The Philosophical Case for Robot Friendship," *Journal of Posthuman Studies* 3, no. 1 (2019): 5–24, doi.org/10.5325/jpoststud.3.1.0005; John Danaher, "Robot Betrayal: A Guide to the Ethics of Robotic Deception," *Ethics and Information Technology* 22, no. 2 (June 1, 2020): 117–128, doi.org/10.1007/s10676-019-09520-3; and John Danaher, "Welcoming Robots into the Moral Circle." The discussion in this section expands significantly on a footnote in Gunkel and Wales, "Debate," 480, n. 14.

[17] Danaher, "Welcoming Robots into the Moral Circle," 2030. When Danaher speaks of "epistemic" ground, he means roughly the foundation for our claiming to know something, rather than "ontological" ground, or the foundation for something actually being as it is.

[18] Danaher, "The Philosophical Case for Robot Friendship," 9.

self-presentation."[19] That is, Danaher seems to have in mind a correspondence between behavior and a conscious disposition toward a friend.

Crucially, while Danaher allows that it may turn out to be metaphysically impossible for a robot to have conscious dispositions at all, he denies the relevance of the objection that the presence of conscious dispositions is necessary for the robot's "outward performances" to be "count[ed] as authentic."[20] For, as we earlier stated, when we evaluate whether the friendship-conditions of mutuality (true, intentional goodwill) and authenticity (presenting ourselves as we are) have been met on the part of some friend-behaving agent, he urges that we must apply to robots the same behavioral standard that we apply to humans and animals.

> [W]hat does it really mean to say that mutuality and authenticity conditions are satisfied in ordinary human friendships? I would argue that all it means is that people *engage in certain consistent performances within the friendship*. Thus, they say and do things that suggest that they share our interests and values and they rarely do things that suggest they have other, unexpected or ulterior interests and values.[21]

Significant concerns may be raised with this account. Danaher wishes to assert not an ontological behaviorism (that friendship just *is* behavior) but only a methodological behaviorism (that behavior is the ground upon which we assert friendship and its corresponding inner states). However,

---

[19] Danaher, "The Philosophical Case for Robot Friendship," 10. While Aristotle understands the mutual good will and well-wishing of a virtue friendship to be anchored in the will for one another's flourishing by virtuous conformity to *the* good, with all that entails according to human nature, Danaher seems to leave it to the discernment of each party in the relationship as to what seems good to one or the other at any particular time, as we will discuss in a moment. He includes "equality" of footing, power, and influence within the relationship and "diversity of interactions"—that is, a very full engagement in one another's lives (as opposed, for instance, to a friendship limited to enthusiasm for sports).
[20] Danaher, 10.
[21] Danaher, 12. Emphasis added.

he seems to slip from: (1) arguing that the ordinary epistemic standards ought to be enough for our *belief* that friendship-conditions are met, to (2) arguing that, therefore, the friendship-conditions *are* indeed met: "It is (technically) possible for the mutuality and authenticity conditions to be satisfied in our friendships with robots," such that "there is nothing illusory or unreal about robotic friendships"[22] *because*, if "there is no inner state that you need to seek [in order] to confirm" the intentions and love expressed in human behavior, then you ought not seek such a state for robots but ought to affirm that "simulated feeling can be genuine feeling, not fake or dishonest feeling."[23] This argument seems to conflate the epistemic grounds for our assertions with the ontological states of affairs about which we are making those assertions.

We might also question whether it is actually true that a robot's friend-like behavior would leave no ground upon which to question its true friendship without also calling into question the friendship of fellow humans. True, someday robots may behave in the ways that allow us to believe that mutuality and authenticity exist in human relationships. But in the exotic case of the seemingly personal robot, are we justified in continuing to rely on the naïve epistemic behaviorism that serves us well for fellow humans? In an IMAX planetarium, we have the sensory experience that would normally lead us to believe we were gazing on a night sky. Only the additional knowledge that we are looking at a planetarium screen, not a window—knowledge not immediately available in the context of the planetarium experience—persuades us that what we see is not a night sky. Lacking this additional knowledge, a naïve viewer might be justified in believing that she was observing the night sky—but she would be incorrect. Her justification does not make the simulated night sky into a genuine night sky, and the answer to whether or not that lack of authenticity matters ought to hinge on more than whether or not the naïve observer is epistemically justified in her belief. Similarly, it may

---

[22] Danaher, 13, 8.
[23] Danaher, "Robot Betrayal," 123.

be true that a robot has met the un-critiqued epistemic conditions for our belief in human friendship, but it does not necessarily follow that "the mutuality and authenticity conditions [have been] satisfied in our friendships with robots."[24] The satisfaction of ordinary epistemic grounds for *believing* friendship-conditions to be satisfied is not identical to the satisfaction of those friendship-conditions themselves.

Danaher's argument, then, amounts only to a restatement of the problem of other minds, and it invites us to inquire after what hidden assumptions may enable us easily (and rightly) to assert that we do have sufficient grounds for our assessments of other humans. Perhaps certain ontological assumptions are baked into our own epistemology—assumptions that, while experientially difficult to shake, might not actually hold true in our relationships with robots. For one thing we share identical material conditions—the same biology—with the other humans who behave like us. And a common biology underlying common behavior makes the existence of a common interior experience more plausible; that is, shared biology is the "middle term" between observable shared behavior and unobservable shared experience. The robot's lack of a nervous system, on the other hand, gives us reason to intuit that it might *not* have the interior states that would allow it to accomplish mutuality and authenticity, even if we observe similar behavior.

Danaher, somewhat anticipating this argument, writes, "While shared biological properties might give us *more* grounds for believing in our human friends, it is not clear that these grounds are necessary or sufficient for believing in [human] friendship."[25] Perhaps such grounds are not sufficient in the case of humans, but are they really unnecessary? Differing biology certainly seems to be a good ground for challenging the usual implications of behavioral performance because, as with the planetarium, knowing that our friend is a different kind of thing (a robot) removes the implicit assumption (experience correlates with biology) that may

---

[24] Danaher, "The Philosophical Case for Robot Friendship," 13.
[25] Danaher, "The Philosophical Case for Robot Friendship," 13–14.

underwrite the reliability of our ordinary epistemic grounds (observed behavior) when we claim that a human being is our friend. Of course, by excluding biology's relevance, Danaher may mean to make behavioral performance not only the *epistemic* ground but also the actual object of reference for our statements about mutuality—but in that case, "mutuality" would simply refer to behavior and not to conscious dispositions, and Danaher would have arrived at the very ontological behaviorism that he wishes to avoid.

Setting aside the implausibility of Danaher's argument with respect to the actual satisfaction of friendship-conditions, we may also ask what sort of friendship his ethical behaviorism would permit. In the first place, to claim that authenticity is satisfied by "certain consistent performances . . . that suggest that they share our interests" redefines authenticity, from a correspondence of my friend's interior and exterior to, instead, my friend's tendency to consistently exhibit the exterior performance that I would like to see from a friend. One struggles to distinguish this from ontological behaviorism. Second, the mutuality of the friendship likewise devolves into a narcissistic evaluation of what sort of behavior from my friend feels best *to me*. In the Christian tradition, mutual good will entails not just "share[d] . . . interests and values" without "other, unexpected or ulterior, interests and values," but rather a common and voluntary commitment to what actually leads to flourishing—that is, to what is good for the other. Friendship involves mutual correction, a community of striving, and the possibility of being wrong. "Shared values" alone cannot accomplish that. Therefore, what Danaher describes is a relationship reduced to a one-sided pleasure-friendship, the "authenticity" of which we measure based on how well the robot mirrors or serves our own desires.

In friendship between relational subjects, appearance is not enough for authenticity, nor do shared values suffice for mutuality. The reality of friendship is intersubjective, and voluntary striving toward a shared pursuit of what is actually good for one another is essential. The AI or robot without consciousness cannot be one's friend. Friendship, as the fulfillment of human life and happiness in the joint pursuit of flourishing, is lost by Danaher's focus on (one-sided) experience of the other. Instead, what we have is a utilitarian or hedonistic friendship in which the robotic friend, by aligning with my interests and values, becomes a mirror image of my desires, a never-challenging (except as desired) companion in my self-sealed world. With the robot as a buffer between myself and the hard edges of the potential contradictions between my values and the true nature of human life and fulfillment, such a "friendship" could become more fantasy than flourishing. It is the friendship that one might have with an animal—shorn, however, of the virtue-imposing limits of the animal's own nature and consciousness. We will never have to wake in the middle of the night to help our robots to the bathroom during a bout of illness; if we did, we probably would not continue to pay for them.

Consciousness as an Epiphenomenon of a Physical System?

Stevan Harnad attempts an account of machine consciousness that, by not focusing solely on behavior, is less agnostic about the inner workings of humans and robots.[26] For Harnad, conscious experience arises from the functioning of certain physical systems, but as a side effect without causal impact of its own: that we are conscious is true, but our consciousness has no role in determining our behavior. The physical facts of our biochemistry are enough for that. This position, known as epiphenomenalism, has enjoyed a spirited defense from such personalities as "Darwin's bulldog," Thomas Huxley, and contemporary philosophers of mind Frank Jackson and David Chalmers.[27] Its defenders wish to take

---

[26] Stevan Harnad, "Can a Machine Be Conscious? How?," *Journal of Consciousness Studies* 10 (January 1, 2003): 67–75.

[27] For Chalmers, consciousness is a property caused by the right abstract pattern of causal relations within a system, but the system's functionality nonetheless may be described fully without recourse to that property; therefore, consciousness is epiphenomenal; see David J. Chalmers, *The Conscious Mind: In Search of a Fundamental Theory*, rev. ed. (New York: Oxford University Press, 1997). Like Harnad, Frank Jackson also, after arguing that qualia are non-physical, resigns himself to epiphenomenalism, saying that it's hard to say that non-

subjective experience seriously, as something over and above what can be measured by the instruments of physics, characterized by physical science, and understood in terms of physical forces.[28] But they also wish to take mechanistic science seriously by asserting that what can be measured, characterized, and accounted for physically is a closed system, affected only by those physical laws and not set onto new courses by any influences that cannot be described in terms of physical laws. This "causal closure" of the physical demands that consciousness be an "epiphenomenon," a byproduct that does not influence the physical process itself.

Harnad upholds these principles in a way that honors Descartes and Newton, gathering living and nonliving things alike under the category of "machines." By this he means that all things are "causal physical system[s]," acted upon by physical causes and, by interior transformations of matter and energy, outputting physical behavior. Living machines are unique in their homeostasis; absent dysfunction, they maintain themselves and, unlike a computer or an automobile, do not require maintenance by exterior agents. There is otherwise nothing unique about what we call "life." Like all machines, living things can be defined in a "strictly structural/functional" manner independent of their "historical origins." In solar systems, starfish, and food processors, physical functioning is

---

physical qualia make a causal impact on the physical world "without sounding like someone who believes in fairies" ("Epiphenomenal Qualia," *Philosophical Quarterly* 32, no. 127 [April 1982]: 128, doi.org/10.2307/2960077). Thomas Huxley makes similar remarks in "On the Hypothesis That Animals Are Automata, and Its History," *Fortnightly Review* 22 (1874): 199–245.

[28] Frank Jackson's defense of consciousness as a further fact about mental systems comes in the thought experiment about "Mary the color scientist," almost as well-known as Searle's "Chinese Room." Mary is a super-scientist who has never experienced color, but knows all the physical facts about human color vision, including all the physical details about what goes on in the brain when someone experiences red. Despite her exhaustive physical knowledge, she does not know what phenomenal qualities are associated with these brain processes—what it is like subjectively to see red. Jackson concludes that physicalism is false. If one can know all the physical facts without knowing the experience of consciousness, then there must be more to reality than is described by physical facts ("Epiphenomenal Qualia," 130).

explicable by the "mechanistic principles [of] structure, function, and causality."[29]

There is, however, something unique about consciousness. While asserting that consciousness can be a property of machines (for example, human beings), Harnad does not make consciousness an empirically verifiable property and is more careful than Danaher in distinguishing between what we can legitimately believe and what *is*. If we ask whether a robot "structurally and functionally indistinguishable" from humans is conscious, we are not asking about something empirical. For Harnad, while in us consciousness correlates with the biological states that appear to subserve it, it cannot be observed *within* those functions. Therefore, consciousness is to be identified neither with exterior behavior nor with interior physically measurable states.[30] Somewhat as Harari holds, being "conscious is something that I *am*, not something I *do*. In particular, it is something I *feel*; indeed, it is the *fact* that I feel." Although inaccessible to empirical inspection, machine consciousness remains "an *ontic* question," concerning what is or can be true rather than "merely an *epistemic* question about what we can and cannot know." Although "the only way to read others' minds is through their behavior," yet this "does not mean that all there is to mind is behavior (as the blinkered behaviorists thought)."[31]

Consciousness is an ontological reality, feeling rather than doing; nonetheless, as we earlier noted, Harnad wishes to preserve the causal closure of physical systems by asserting that consciousness must also be an epiphenomenon. If physics does everything, and if physics also produces consciousness, then the fact of consciousness actually does not bear on our actions but is only a side effect of the deterministic physical interactions that cause them. Whatever the unknown causes of consciousness, it exists as only a feature of causal physical systems that determines nothing about

---

[29] Harnad, "Can a Machine Be Conscious?," 69–70.
[30] Harnad, 70.
[31] Harnad, "Can a Machine Be Conscious?," 71–73. Harnad's description of consciousness is thinner than Searle's.

their empirically measurable behavior. We experience our actions, but our experience has no agency. If it did, it would be an extra causal force in the universe—one for which we have no evidence.[32]

Interestingly, Harnad's epiphenomenalism is not the basis for his claim that person-acting robots are possible. Even if conscious machines cannot be fully characterized in terms of their physical causation, their *behavior* can be so characterized—and duplicated.[33] Therefore, a robot's consciousness or unconsciousness could never affect whether it could "*do* everything a real human can do . . . indistinguishably from a real human," but only whether it would *be* all that humans *are*. It is entirely imaginable that a robot could act entirely like a person—acting as if it were conscious, yet without consciousness. Such a robot "does not *feel*; it merely behaves . . . as if it feels."[34]

Harnad importantly identifies that territory upon which one *cannot* attempt to answer the question of whether machine consciousness is possible or present. Neither by behavior alone nor by any laws empirically detectable by today's instruments or currently understood by natural science can it be decided whether the seemingly personal robot can be or actually is conscious. As Harnad writes, "Our forward- and reverse-engineering" of causal physical systems "can only explain how it is that we can do things, not how it is that we can feel things."[35] Human and robotic systems can be identical twins according to Harnad's mantra of "structure, function, and causality," with identical measurable outcomes, but this will

---

[32] As to why Harnad personally inclines to the belief that feelings have no "independent causal power," he writes that to do so would require "an *extra* causal force in the universe" (emphasis added), having an influence of their own rather than riding atop "some unconscious function with which they happen to be mysteriously correlated." However, Harnad sees no evidence for any such force of feelings, "and it would probably not be compatible with the other laws of physics to introduce [such] an independent mental 'force' alongside the known ones" ("Re: Epiphenomenalism and Zombies," June 20, 2002, www.southampton.ac.uk/~harnad/Hypermail/Foundations.Cognitive.Science2001/0162.html).

[33] Harnad, "Re: Epiphenomenalism and Zombies."

[34] Harnad, "Can a Machine Be Conscious?," 71.

[35] Harnad, "Can a Machine Be Conscious?," 75.

not guarantee—by analogy with mechanical heart-replacements that pump blood but are not squishy—that they correspond in every property that might be captured were robots to be molecular *biological* replicas of humans. Among these properties may well be consciousness. (Thus, unlike Danaher, Harnad underlines at least the potential importance of shared biology as an assumption implicitly included in our tendency to attribute consciousness to those who behave like us.) Frustratingly, however, with the mechanism unknown, there remains no way to ascertain the difference that biology may make. It remains unapparent, therefore, how it is that consciousness may be present in one machine and either present or not in another identically behaving machine. For the territory on which these questions cannot be decided is the only territory on which machines can be defined.

In the end, physicalism demonstrates its limitations in several ways. First, absent some theory to explain how consciousness occurs in certain physical bodies but not in others, we cannot describe voluntary empathic self-gift as being among measurable realities, and so it falls from view. Second, by limiting causal realities to what can be measured by scientific instruments and characterized by physics, Harnad finds this very center of Christian personal flourishing also impossible to affirm. Voluntary self-giving requires that our outward behavior be shaped by, rather than merely accompany, our feelings and perceived choices. If consciousness is without causal relevance, then human behavior never in fact bore this significance, and even the most minimal forms of self-giving are rendered illusory.

Behaviorism and the Collapse of Subjectivity

Danaher and Harnad distinguish between behavior and conscious experience, although their arguments make it difficult to retain the relevance of this distinction. Daniel Dennett, however, is willing to apply a behavioristic approach not only to our language concerning robots, but even to our first-person language concerning ourselves. In his "intentional systems theory," Dennett proposes that we tend to attribute "intentionality" (not voluntariness, but subjective beliefs and desires) to something, when the best way to reliably predict its behavior is to attribute to it the intentionality that we attribute to ourselves.[36] This is why we cannot help but ascribe intentionality to other human beings.[37] This position, which somewhat echoes Turing's "imitation game," seems uncontroversial; it is also why we jump at shadows and feel empathy for robots. But Dennett wants to go farther: to say that, when we attribute intentionality to humans, behavior prediction is all we really mean by it in the first place. That is, our language about human subjectivity is not actually about an inner life; it really is just about the sort of outer behavior that we expect. The "self," the intentional subject acting from beliefs and desires, is, Dennett writes, "an abstraction [that] one uses as part of a theoretical apparatus to understand, and predict, and make sense of, the behavior of some very complicated things."[38] In the end, the inner workings of an intentional subject, even her consciousness, do not bear on the meaning of our statements about her beliefs or desires.[39] Empathy,

---

[36] Daniel C. Dennett, "Intentional Systems Theory," *The Oxford Handbook of Philosophy of Mind*, 2009, doi.org/10.1093/oxfordhb/9780199262618.003.0020.

[37] It is also why children ascribe intentionality to unfamiliar natural phenomena and, Dennett argues elsewhere, why humans came to believe in God, by attributing intentionality to the flow of natural events. See Daniel C. Dennett, *Breaking the Spell: Religion as a Natural Phenomenon* (New York: Penguin Books, 2007), 118–20.

[38] Daniel C. Dennett, "The Self as a Center of Narrative Gravity," in *Self and Consciousness: Multiple Perspectives*, ed. F. Kessel, P. Cole, and D. Johnson (Mahwah, NJ: Erlbaum, 1992), cogprints.org/266/1/selfctr.htm.

[39] Daniel C. Dennett, "The Unimagined Preposterousness of Zombies (Commentary on T. Moody, O. Flanagan, and T. Polger)," *Journal of Consciousness Studies* 2, no. 4 (1995): 322–326. Or as Dennett succinctly allows: "Necessarily, if two organisms are behaviorally exactly alike, they are psychologically exactly alike" ("The Message Is: There Is No Medium [Reply to Jackson, Rosenthal, Shoemaker, and Tye]," *Philosophy and Phenomenological Research* 53, no. 4 [December 1993]: 889–931). This and similar statements are catalogued in a historical survey and riposte by Galen Strawson, "A Hundred Years of Consciousness: 'A Long Training in Absurdity,'" *Estudios de Filosofía*, June 1, 2019, 9–43, doi.org/10.17533/udea.ef.n59a02.

here, is not insight but only prediction.[40] For Dennett, then, we are all masks, not persons. Appropriately-behaving robots could be called intentional subjects, with a meaning identical to that with which we apply such terms to human beings—but only because language about beliefs and desires is a shorthand for behavior prediction.[41]

Yet we must question Dennett: can this *really* be what one means when one says that one believes or desires or knows this or that? In the first place, even if Dennett has accurately described the evolutionary origin of our tendency to ascribe intentional subjectivity to other humans, does that of necessity determine what we are doing by those ascriptions? Origins need not be essences. A morning sprint is no longer a flight from predators or pursuit of prey, nor is empathic insight just behavior prediction. When we speak of our own beliefs and desires, we take for granted that we are not just stipulating a schema by which to classify our outward actions; we are describing our own inner lives. So too, when a woman says that she is married to someone who loves her, does it not really and truly matter to her what her spouse thinks of her, and not just how he behaves toward her? And does it not matter, moreover, whether her spouse grasps her interiority as well? Her spouse's subjective experience of her—and of her subjectivity—matters. It matters to her, moreover, whether her spouse gives himself consciously to their life together. The life that they share

---

[40] Dennett himself graciously replied when queried about this exposition: "I have some reservations, but no serious complaints. Carry on. —DCD" (personal communication to Jordan Joseph Wales, November 6, 2018).

[41] Dennett writes: "When I squint just right, it does sort of seem that consciousness must be something in addition to all the things it does for us and to us, some kind of special private glow or here-I-am-ness that would be absent in any robot. But I've learned not to credit the hunch. I think it is a flat-out mistake" (*Intuition Pumps and Other Tools for Thinking* [W. W. Norton & Company, 2014], 285). Dennett in particular wishes to keep in view that our experience of consciousness is not itself an explanation of *why* we acted a certain way or came to a certain decision, and that our explanations of our actions are often (or in Dennett's view, perhaps always) after-the-fact confabulations. But even if all explanations were confabulations, it would not mean that consciousness was wholly absent.

encompasses one another's interiority. It is, in other words, a life between persons.

The deep human experience of intelligent understanding and relational compassion becomes unsayable under behaviorist paradigms. Accounts of consciousness that confine themselves to behavior—or even that have consciousness accompany without affecting behavior—redefine our language in such a way that our discourse concerning friendship collapses into a discourse merely about two causal systems working on one another. And this is why, wondrous as any AI may be, we cannot see it as an intelligent subject or as relationally personal in the *most* meaningful significance of those words unless we can say that it is conscious in the fullest sense. Otherwise, it is again the Roman *persona*, not the Christian person, a behavioral presentation rather than an individual capable of self-gift. And if we begin to think of ourselves in behavioristic terms in order to think of AI systems in personal terms, then we will slip back behind antiquity's mask, losing our hold on the free gift of compassion as the very mark of our personhood.

What is an Adequate Account of Consciousness?

The Failure of Functional Reductions

Seeking a way around behaviorism without giving up on physicalism, some philosophers implicitly set aside true first-person consciousness even without denying it. Instead, they work on cognitive characteristics associated with human consciousness—whether these are functions that consciousness is presumed to accompany or serve (for example, "access consciousness" or the "global workspace theory"), or certain properties of consciousness such as intentionality or the structure of experience. However, except where these characteristics and structures are considered causal for consciousness, their presence or absence does not advance the question of whether or not a machine is conscious and thus intelligent and relational in the full sense that we have defined. When they seem to bear on the question in some other fashion, it is because they have been conflated with consciousness itself, or have been used to assert that consciousness's first-person experiential dimension is dispensable so long as this or that function be fulfilled. Against this, Galen Strawson writes of subjective experience, "To say that it exists but is really just something whose nature can be fully specified in wholly non-experiential, functional terms is to deny its existence."[42] Ricardo Manzotti and Antonio Chella call this error the "intermediate level fallacy," which attempts to circumvent Chalmers's "hard problem" in two steps:

> First, an intermediate conceptual level that is at a possible explanatory distance is proposed—behavior, central workspace, information, enaction, adaptive resonance, and so forth. Such an entity, crucially, is located on the physical side of the gap [between matter and experience] but, equally significantly, is somewhat vague, to the extent that it may suggest some degrees of consciousness. Second, consciousness is watered down to show that it is not much better than the intermediate level. The second step, which is most problematic from an ontological and epistemic perspective, is critical to provide fulfillment of the first step.[43]

Given physicalist assumptions, the hard problem must be matched by a hard claim: the claim that a particular configuration of matter, by its

---

[42] Galen Strawson, "Realistic Monism: Why Physicalism Entails Panpsychism," *Journal of Consciousness Studies* 13, no. 10–11 (2006): 5 n. 6.

[43] Ricardo Manzotti and Antonio Chella, "Good Old-Fashioned Artificial Consciousness and the Intermediate Level Fallacy," *Frontiers in Robotics and AI* 5 (2018): 3–4, www.frontiersin.org/article/10.3389/frobt.2018.00039. The authors' proposed solution is to redefine consciousness in terms of a causal relationship between the exterior world and the conscious agent (8–9). While this is useful for reflection on perceptual experience, it does not quite enable us to address self-gift as we would wish. Further discussion lies beyond the scope of this writing.

configuration (chemical, functional, or otherwise) is indeed causal of consciousness.[44]

Elements of an Account

From this survey of key monuments in the physicalist field of consciousness studies, two conclusions emerge. First, any substantial account of the human person that preserves relationality and self-gift as a non-solipsistic reality (that is, measured in terms of more than what I expect from someone else), meaningful beyond behavior alone, requires first-person experiential consciousness. The efforts we have surveyed not only fail to account for authentic relationality but actually elide or deny its reality, even where Danaher and Harnad attempt agnostically to leave consciousness untouched. There is a cost to this indeed. If behavioristic accounts of mind and relationality set the terms for how we talk about sociable AI, then the distinction between seemingly personal AI systems and human persons may disappear—but only because we will have accepted behavioristic approaches to *all* agents. Sherry Turkle suggests

---

[44] The reader at this point may wonder why Chalmers plays an important supporting role in this discussion without being given the opportunity to present his account of consciousness. In a number of publications, most prominently *The Conscious Mind*, Chalmers favors epiphenomenalism, but he makes a bold proposal for the causation of consciousness that has been received favorably by some other philosophers. Chalmers proposes that the causal structure of some system or entity—the reliable transitions between its configuration states—can be thought of in terms of "information," which is not meaning but the system's carrying capacity for a variety of configurations (roughly speaking). And he proposes that, when one has the *right* causal structure, that is, the right informational structure, the system will have a conscious experience. Information, he proposes, has a physically measurable nature in terms of configuration but also an experiential dimension, and this is intrinsic to reality. (Chalmers does not firmly pronounce on whether all causal configurations have some degree of experience of not; certainly, not all have human-level consciousness.) We cannot evaluate Chalmers's proposal here, except to point out that a serious effort to reckon with rather than to reduce consciousness leads to the conclusion that one must be willing to think metaphysically, that is, to propose descriptions of reality that, even where they are compatible with the physical sciences, do not insist that the concepts and measures of the physical sciences are sufficient to exhaust what is real.

that this acceptance has already begun. Interpreting a child's disappointment at the languor of real alligators, which do not snap their jaws and roll their eyes like the more satisfying robotic reptiles at a nearby theme-park,[45] she writes:

> In the 1980s, people insisted that the bedrock of human uniqueness was what computers could not do or be, placing ... a premium on the idea that only people can give each other understanding and empathy. [This view] was invested in the idea that there is something essential about the human spirit, and that this essential quality resides in human inner states. Now this essentialist assumption is challenged. Today one does not linger over inner states. The new focus is on behavior. What matters is how the robots perform and how we perform for each other—the essence, after all, of life in virtual communities where we create an avatar and put it on a self-built stage. With the focus on behavior rather than inner states, a creature that behaves appropriately is an appropriate creature.[46]

For Turkle, today's performance-focused self-understanding, cultivated by interactions through social media, has been hospitable soil for a renewed behaviorism. Its flower would willingly set robots and humans on the same field, as behavior-producing entities whose adequacy can be judged by their service to our own desires.[47]

Second, if consciousness is nonnegotiable for human relationships of self-gift, so too is a robust metaphysics and ontology nonnegotiable for fully understanding consciousness.[48] It is not enough to speak of

---

[45] Turkle, "In Good Company?," 9.
[46] Turkle, "In Good Company?," 8.
[47] Similar concerns are discussed by Amanda Sharkey and Noel Sharkey, "Granny and the Robots: Ethical Issues in Robot Care for the Elderly," *Ethics and Information Technology* 14 (March 1, 2010): 27–40, doi.org/10.1007/s10676-010-9234-6; Turkle, *Alone Together*, 26.
[48] Here, bear in mind that the absence of consciousness does not exclude one from being a person. Rather, persons are those who belong to that circle of beings that ordinarily (barring immaturity, disability, injury, or infirmity) possess consciousness and, moreover, are capable

intermediate correlations, but—as Chalmers puts it—certain psychophysical laws must be admitted and characterized. Eastern Orthodox theologian David Bentley Hart, albeit characteristically acerbic, is to the point:

> To a convinced materialist, all of this is a reality essentially physical in nature, and probably entirely mechanical (in the broadest sense): even if the science as yet eludes us, consciousness must be explicable entirely in terms of the interaction between our neural constitution and the concrete world around us. Even the materialist would acknowledge, of course, that the powers of the mind cannot be exhaustively accounted for solely in terms of the mechanics of sensory stimulus and neurological response, if for no other reason than the fairly obvious truth that neither stimulus nor response is, by itself, a mental phenomenon; neither, as a purely physical reality, possesses conceptual content or personal awareness. I would go further, however, and say that consciousness is a reality that cannot be explained in any purely physiological terms at all. All our modern 'scientistic' presuppositions may tell us that mind must be entirely a mechanical function or residue of the brain's neuronal processes, but even the most basic phenomenology of consciousness discloses so vast an incommensurability between physical causation and mental events that it is probably impossible that the latter could ever be wholly reduced to the former.[49]

As for what sort of account might bind physical causation and mental events without leaving consciousness as a non-causal side effect of otherwise physicalist realities, we propose that we must admit again concepts that some voices today deride as pre-scientific—but that do, nonetheless, describe the human person in a way that credibly embraces the experiential evidence of our own consciousness without reducing that

---

of engaging in self-giving relations of compassion. A human being in a persistent vegetative state is a person although not conscious; a carrot is not.

[49] David Bentley Hart, "Consciousness (Chit)," in *The Experience of God: Being, Consciousness, Bliss* (New Haven, CT: Yale University Press, 2013), 153.

reality either to behavior or to some mechanically functional role in behavior-production. These ideas, or other ideas able to do their work, must have a place, lest we strip our reality of the very experience without which we could not be the wonderstruck and love-besotted beings that we are.

Consciousness: A Richer Account

Materialist, behaviorist, and functionalist accounts of consciousness dilute the fundamentally relational, intersubjective, and unified character of consciousness in the human person, and so they forestall any real success in connecting an understanding of consciousness to a coherent *anthropology* (account of the human being), *phenomenology* (account of experience), or *ontology* (account of what is/exists). These inadequacies suggest that richer accounts and other routes are necessary—accounts that address relationality, self-gift, the unity of the conscious person, and his or her ultimate end or finality. By admitting these elements as fundamental, we will better be able to non-reductively assert the points of contact between the human person and AI, while also more clearly delineating what sets them apart from one another. This section, then, is to be taken less as a prescription than as a sensitization to realities that were left inchoate in our earlier discussion or for which no place could be found in the physicalist accounts that we surveyed.

Continental phenomenology has emerged in discussions both of the human person and of AI as a useful philosophical vantage-point from which to critique accounts of consciousness that devolve into solipsism, physicalism, dualism, or disembodied views of the mind.[50]

---

[50] See Dreyfus, *What Computers Still Can't Do*; F. J. Varela, "Neurophenomenology: A Methodological Remedy for the Hard Problem," *Journal of Consciousness Studies* 3, no. 4 (1996): 330–349; Jean-Pierre Dupuy, *The Mechanization of the Mind: On the Origins of Cognitive Science* (Princeton, NJ: Princeton University Press, 2000); Anthony F. Beavers, "Phenomenology and Artificial Intelligence," *Metaphilosophy* 33, no. 1–2 (2002): 70–82, doi.org/10.1111/1467-9973.00217; Shaun Gallagher, "Phenomenology and Experimental Design: Toward a Phenomenologically Enlightened Experimental Science," *Journal of*

Phenomenology "is the study of experience and of the way things present themselves to us in and through experience."[51] This way of returning to the things themselves insists that neither the function of the human mind nor a merely physical account can explain all that is, and it begins with what is intelligibly given in experience in order to more richly grasp reality *as it is*.[52] Moreover, in light of the problem that physicalism is unable to deal with consciousness except as something awkwardly positioned alongside the physical facts about an organism, it will also be helpful to draw on the Christian tradition, which accounts for the whole unified person.

Drawing on this depth of resources, this section will pursue a number of aims. First, we will attend to consciousness in its relational structure—that is, insofar as it is intentional, meaningful, embedded in the world, and intersubjective. Second, we will take up the relationship between consciousness and Christian anthropology, including the role of divine grace and of Christ himself. Ultimately, an understanding of consciousness must be grounded in the very being of the Triune God, whose inner life *is* loving mutual self-gift. God's grace is critical to this

---

Consciousness Studies 10, no. 9–10 (2003): 85–99; Michael Wheeler, *Reconstructing the Cognitive World: The Next Step* (Cambridge, MA: The MIT Press, 2005), doi.org/10.7551/mitpress/5824.001.0001; Dan Zahavi, "Killing the Straw Man: Dennett and Phenomenology," *Phenomenology and the Cognitive Sciences* 6, no. 1–2 (2007): 21–43, doi.org/10.1007/s11097-006-9038-7; N. Katherine Hayles, *How We Became Posthuman: Virtual Bodies in Cybernetics, Literature, and Informatics* (Chicago: University of Chicago Press, 1999); Alva Noe, *Out of Our Heads: Why You Are Not Your Brain, and Other Lessons from the Biology of Consciousness* (New York: Hill and Wang, 2010); Alistair Welchman, "Heidegger among the Robots," *Symposium* 17, no. 1 (April 1, 2013): 229–249, doi.org/10.5840/symposium201317112; Harris Bor, *Staying Human: A Jewish Theology for the Age of Artificial Intelligence* (Eugene, OR: Cascade Books, 2021); Shengnan Han, Eugene Kelly, Shahrokh Nikou, and Eric-Oluf Svee, "Aligning Artificial Intelligence with Human Values: Reflections from a Phenomenological Perspective," *AI & Society* 37, no. 4 (December 1, 2022): 1383–1395, doi.org/10.1007/s00146-021-01247-4.

[51] Robert Sokolowski, *Introduction to Phenomenology* (Cambridge: Cambridge University Press, 1999), 2, doi.org/10.1017/CBO9780511809118.

[52] Sokolowski, *Introduction to Phenomenology*, 3–4.

account, as the free gift of God's transformative action within the human person, whereby that person is made a participant in the triune life.

This section does not seek to provide any comprehensive definition or account of consciousness. Nor can it give an exhaustive list of thinkers, ideas, or traditions that attend to consciousness well. Its modest aims are, first, simply to highlight richer notions of consciousness that are relevant for contemporary questions; and, second, to articulate what Christian anthropology might contribute to such an account.

Phenomenological Investigations of Consciousness

Phenomenological accounts begin with the fact that consciousness is more than the "feeling" admitted by Harari and Harnad. Consciousness is, as Searle reminds us, always a consciousness *of* something; this is what phenomenology refers to as "intentionality."[53] We are never merely conscious but are always a conscious *of* this book or *of* that pen. To be conscious is always already to be conscious *of* something.[54] Moreover, intentionality requires a subject, an "I," who is conscious. Consciousness is never mere consciousness. *I* am always conscious and *I* am always conscious *of* something. Intentionality thus demonstrates how consciousness is inherently relational and subjective. It is not a mere clearing house for information. Recognizing its intentional structure helps to break down dualistic approaches and recover the fundamental relationship between mind and world that Descartes's distinction between the mechanistic physical world (*res extensa*) and the spiritual thinking substance (*res cogitans*) began to sever.[55] It also underscores Searle's point

---

[53] This critical concept in phenomenology is developed by Franz Brentano and Edmund Husserl. For an argument in philosophy of mind in favor of intentionality see Tim Crane, *The Mechanical Mind: A Philosophical Introduction to Minds, Machines and Mental Representation*, 3rd ed. (London: Routledge, 2016).

[54] Sokolowski, *Introduction to Phenomenology*, 104.

[55] Edmund Husserl, *The Shorter Logical Investigations*, ed. Dermot Moran, trans. J. N. Findlay (London: Routledge, 2001), sec. V.13–14. See also Dan Zahavi, *Husserl's Phenomenology*

that subjectivity is inherent to human consciousness, against Dennett's elision of innerness.

From intentionality, we also arrive at the inherent relation of consciousness to meaning.[56] *Meaning* is constitutive of intentionality insofar as consciousness *of* something is always consciousness of something "*as something.*"[57] When I am conscious *of* an object, I grasp the object as having some kind of *meaning*, whether that meaning be clear or obscure. I am conscious of *this book* or *that figure in the distance*. I cannot be conscious of something as simply indistinct or completely devoid of all content or meaning; as conscious, I grasp in some way a thing's content, its individual form and essential structure.[58] The mind is thus always already involved with other objects meaningfully, and this meaning is not a mere product of the mind.[59] Here, then, we encounter something analogous to Pieper's ancient *intellectus*.

Embeddedness or *being-in-the-world*, to use the more technical term, is a key insight, and perhaps the phenomenological concept most cited in the literature on AI.[60] The concept of being-in-the-world builds on the

---

(Stanford, CA: Stanford University Press, 2003), 13–14; Sokolowski, *Introduction to Phenomenology*, 11–12.

[56] Meaning refers to both "the act of meaning something" and that itself "which we mean." See Zahavi, *Husserl's Phenomenology*, 9–10.

[57] Zahavi, *Husserl's Phenomenology*, 24. Emphasis added.

[58] To further clarify this point, in order to know something *as something*, that object must be distinct. It must have a form. If any object is simply indistinct or formless it is not intelligible. If we try to think of a formless book or even a formless figure in the distance, we cannot because it is unintelligible. Similarly, as already discussed, in order for an object to be intelligible, it must in some respect have a content. Thus, to know something *as something* is a matter of both form and content. See Sarah Borden, *Edith Stein* (London: Continuum, 2004), 24–25.

[59] Sokolowski, *Introduction to Phenomenology*, 97–100; Zahavi, *Husserl's Phenomenology*, 22–24.

[60] For example, Hubert Dreyfus, an early critic of the materialist, behaviorist, and functionalist accounts of consciousness, uses this idea to argue that intelligence is always-already-situated and as such "cannot be separated from the rest of human life" (*What Computers Still Can't Do*, 62).

fundamentally relational character of intentionality insofar as human persons are understood to be always already related to the world in a meaningful way. This means that what appears always already does so with particular meanings and uses.[61] What largely distinguishes the concept of being-in-the-world from intentionality is the appeal to being. "Being in a world belongs essentially to" the human being.[62] This means that the world is not something separate from the human person that the human person must find a way to reach, but is rather "a structure of [the human person's] being."[63] From this perspective, the human person's very being *is* understanding. In this light, the idea that consciousness could be separable or replicable apart from the being is nonsensical and misunderstands *what* it is to know and be conscious.

Intersubjectivity, similar to the concept of being-in-the-world, sets forth that the human person does not need to overcome herself to reach or come to know other persons. Rather, consciousness is always already involved with other persons. It is intrinsically intersubjective (or, as phenomenologists would say, "given intersubjectively") in the sense that I always already find myself in a world that I share with other embodied conscious subjects, with whom I can empathize and to whom I am accountable. Other subjects are in some sense constitutive of my consciousness. They make my ability to experience and know objectively possible.[64]

---

[61] Martin Heidegger, *Being and Time: A Revised Edition of the Stambaugh Translation*, trans. Joan Stambaugh, rev. ed. (Albany: State University of New York Press, 2010), 11–12.

[62] Paul Gorner, *Heidegger's Being and Time: An Introduction* (Cambridge, UK: Cambridge University Press, 2007), 34.

[63] Gorner, *Heidegger's Being and Time*, 50. Heidegger chooses to use the term *Dasein* (being-there) instead of *human being* or *person* because he seeks to emphasize that "being in a world belongs essentially to" the human being. "*Dasein*" is the term that "human person" replaces in this quotation. See Gorner, *Heidegger's Being and Time*, 34.

[64] Zahavi, *Husserl's Phenomenology*, 114–16. Some phenomenologists emphasize the constitutive role of foreign subjects more than others. For a more extensive discussion of the specific differences among phenomenologists on the topic of intersubjectivity, see Dan Zahavi, "Beyond Empathy: Phenomenological Approaches to Intersubjectivity," in *Between*

The concept of intersubjectivity *as constitutive* of consciousness is deepened and given pride of place in Emmanuel Levinas's concept of the "face-to-face encounter." Levinas argues that encounter with another person through the "face" is *necessary*, not only for consciousness to be possible but for the very self in the fullest sense to be possible.[65] The face-to-face encounter should, however, not be mistaken for a perception; it is a metaphysical term. The face, here, does not refer to "the appearance of that person; it is not a collection of features given to visual perception." It rather signifies "the responsibility to acknowledge and accept the other that is always already present in ordinary life—pre-conceptual, pre-articulate, pre-reflective."[66] Similar to the way all consciousness implies consciousness *of* or the way all understanding implies being-there (*Dasein*), all relationship implies encounter: "a relationship of command without tyranny."[67] By virtue of this pre-reflective encounter, the other person is irreducibly and originally present to me in a way that breaks through and calls me out of myself by demanding that I recognize and

---

Ourselves: Second-Person Issues in the Study of Consciousness, ed. E. Thompson (Charlottesville, VA: Imprint Academic, 2001), 151–167. Emmanuel Levinas has one of the most developed accounts and strongest stances on the constitutive role of intersubjectivity. See Emmanuel Levinas, *Totality and Infinity: An Essay on Exteriority*, trans. Alphonso Lingis (Dordrecht: Springer Netherlands, 1991), 87–89, 94–95, 294–295; Emmanuel Levinas, *Otherwise than Being or Beyond Essence*, trans. Alphonso Lingis (Dordrecht: Springer Netherlands, 1991), 11–13. For a recent moral-theological and Levinasian critique of AI, see Roberto Dell'Oro, "Can a Robot Be a Person? De-Facing Personhood and Finding It Again with Lévinas," *Journal of Moral Theology* 11, Special Issue 1 (April 2, 2022): 132–156, doi.org/10.55476/001c.34128; David J. Gunkel, "Other Problems: Rethinking Ethics in the Face of Social Robots," in *What Social Robots Can and Should Do: Proceedings of Robophilosophy 2016 / TRANSOR 2016* (Amsterdam: IOS Press, 2016), 9–12; David J. Gunkel, "The Relational Turn: Thinking Robots Otherwise," in *Social Robotics and the Good Life: The Normative Side of Forming Emotional Bonds With Robots*, ed. Janina Loh and Wulf Loh (Bielefeld, Germany: Transcript Verlag, 2022).

[65] See Levinas, *Otherwise than Being or Beyond Essence*, 106–107; Michael L. Morgan, *The Cambridge Introduction to Emmanuel Levinas* (Cambridge, UK: Cambridge University Press, 2011), 121.

[66] Morgan, *Cambridge Introduction to Emmanuel Levinas*, 64.

[67] Quoted in Morgan, *Cambridge Introduction to Emmanuel Levinas*, 67.

respond to her vulnerability and authority.[68] The other person always already demands that I not kill or dominate but care for her. This demand, in turn, calls me to myself.[69] Consciousness and knowledge are thus born out of and made possible by the original encounter of persons.

From a phenomenological perspective, consciousness can thus not be thought of as something set apart from or closed off to the world but must be understood as embedded and intersubjective. It necessitates encounter. Phenomenology's effort to account for consciousness through experience returns us to the Christian insight that the rational subject is fundamentally relational. We will next more deeply reflect on what the Christian tradition might contribute to the discourse on consciousness and AI by further developing the Christian anthropology and meaning of personhood that we introduced in chapter 2.

Sharing in Life through Grace

Because human life is an inherently shared life, an account of consciousness consistent with a Christian anthropology must point to a shared life with God. From the first moments of a human's existence, she exists as a gift from God that reflects the goodness and generosity of the gift-Giver. The person is constantly called into communion with God. Here, we come to the activity of grace—the free gift of God by which the person is made not just to imitate God through relational self-gift, but to participate in the self-gift that is God's own life.

In its fallen state, however, humanity is unable to make this full gift of self.[70] Therefore, God's invitation takes the form of healing, restoring

---

[68] Morgan, *Cambridge Introduction to Emmanuel Levinas*, 65–66.
[69] Morgan, *Cambridge Introduction to Emmanuel Levinas*, 59.
[70] Even the saints offer many examples of this realization of brokenness. "O terrible hour, at which one is obliged to see all one's deeds in their nakedness and misery," wrote Maria Faustina Kowalska (*Diary: Divine Mercy in My Soul*, 3rd ed. [Stockbridge, MA: Marian Press, 2005], § 189). To illustrate the brokenness of sin as an inability to offer oneself in gift, see for example, Thomas Aquinas's discussion on how pride is opposed to the humility of offering oneself to God (ST II-II.162.5).

fallen nature to the fullness of relationship with God. God offers the greatest gift of God's own divine life: "If we ask God for a grace, He will give it to us; but let us be willing to accept it. . . . Love . . . is an act of the will; it is a gift; that is to say, a giving."[71] Even our asking is itself a gift, although to refuse this gift is always possible. One accepts the divine invitation to share life with God when, not refusing to ask, the human person's action begins to issue from the very love of God.[72] This relationship of love through grace reaches its perfection in the beatific vision:

> True humanism . . . consists in the fact that man, through a life of fidelity to the one God, comes to experience himself as loved by God, and discovers joy in truth and in righteousness—a joy in God which becomes his essential happiness: "Whom do I have in heaven but you? And there is nothing upon earth that I desire besides you. . . . For me it is good to be near God."[73]

Because grace perfects a person's relationships with all aspects and beings of the universe, grace unlocks the fullness of experiencing beauty and joy.[74] Grace allows the person to delight with God in creation and in God's self. The nature that makes the human person capable of relationship with God involves a form that renders matter to exist in a particular way. The form permits an organization of the person that orders her to her final happiness through grace. The form both determines the matter-spirit dynamic but is also revealed by it. The human person's final cause is to live and love with God. As Saint Augustine writes, "Unhappy is the man who knows all this, but does not know you; happy is he who knows you, even if he does not know such things . . . because of you alone

---

[71] Kowalska, *Diary*, § 392.

[72] "We must assert that to love, which is an act of the appetitive power, even in this state of life, tends to God first, and flows on from Him to other things, and in this sense, charity loves God immediately, and other things through God" (Thomas Aquinas, ST II-II.27.4).

[73] *Deus Caritas Est*, § 9, quoting Psalm 73:25, 28.

[74] Thomas Aquinas, *ST* I-II.109.1.

is he happy."[75] On account of grace, the human person is able to love God even more deeply than was possible prior to the fall in the state of original justice. All of a human's capacities are further elevated by grace, even consciousness.

The Gift of Human Nature: Consciousness and Spirit as Self-Gift

Identifying God as the only source of full happiness reveals certain features of the human person that make it possible for her to find joy in God and to be fulfilled only by God. Relationship with God is not something beyond the foundational relationality of the human person; it is the capacity for receiving God that makes us *also* receptive to other beings. All the human person's relationships reflect to some degree this potential for relationship with the divine, and this is why relationships make us happy in the degree that they mirror God's own goodness.[76] As Pope Francis states, "No one can experience the true beauty of life without relating to others, without having real faces to love. This is part of the mystery of authentic human existence."[77]

The nature of the person equips us for this encounter with God and is the source of our inherent desire for it. "Implanted deep within us is the call to transcend ourselves through an encounter with others."[78] By nature, we seek to share ourselves with others and to know others. To live with grace, however, allows the human person to exceed even the capacities of nature for experiencing happiness and for offering love, because by grace we are able to participate supernaturally in the nature and life of God.[79]

---

[75] Augustine, *The Confessions of Saint Augustine*, trans. John K. Ryan (New York: Image, 1960), § 5.4. Cf. Thomas Aquinas, ST I-II.3.8.

[76] Stein, *Finite and Eternal Being*, 514.

[77] *Fratelli Tutti*, § 87.

[78] *Fratelli Tutti*, § 111.

[79] "Charity loves God above all things in a higher way than nature does. For nature loves God above all things inasmuch as He is the beginning and the end of natural good; whereas charity loves Him, as He is the object of beatitude, and inasmuch as man has a spiritual fellowship

Grace perfects all aspects of the human person, including the psychological, the emotional, and the spiritual. It is necessary to a fully flourishing human life shared with the life of God because, by it, we love God as God *is*, and not as we might otherwise love were we to reduce God to the terms of finitude and time. Poetically put, "If He Himself had not first strengthened me by His grace, my soul would not have been able to bear the happiness."[80] Grace brings any human person to his ultimate finality in the embrace of the Trinity. To turn from the gift of grace constitutes the neglect of both a calling from beyond ourselves and a natural yearning within ourselves.

Persons are given the capacity to either respond to or reject an encounter of grace. Consciousness from a Christian perspective is therefore not only bodily but spiritual. For human consciousness, the bodily and spiritual dimensions rely on one another and cannot be separated from one another if we are to portray human nature accurately.[81] The metaphysical fact that the human person is a spiritual being means that the person is able to detect value and an order of meaning in the world.[82] This ability makes intentional action possible, which takes on a meaning of its own.[83] The human person is distinct from other creations of God, in that we have *both* a spiritual soul and a body, though these should not be reductively construed as two detached units. The type of consciousness that we possess is inherently spiritual in that it is able to perceive and to offer gift. We are able to encounter God not only through

---

with God. Moreover, charity adds to the natural love of God a certain quickness and joy" (Thomas Aquinas, ST I-II.109.3, ad 1).

[80] Kowalska, *Diary*, § 439.

[81] See John Paul II commenting on Genesis 2:7, in *Man and Woman He Created Them: A Theology of the Body*, trans. Michael Waldstein (Boston, MA: Pauline Books and Media, 2006), 153.

[82] "As 'nature,' [one] is subject to the laws of causality, as 'spirit' to the laws of meaning," (Edith Stein, *On the Problem of Empathy*, trans. Waltraut Stein, 3rd rev. ed. [Washington, DC: ICS Publications, 1989]), 112.

[83] "And so an action also bids for understanding. It is . . . experienced as proceeding meaningfully from the total structure of the person" (Stein, *On the Problem of Empathy*, 112).

the physical senses but also through the spiritual sense. Though other beings in creation may have a soul, the human's is a spiritual soul that is capable of communion; it can "freely give and diffuse itself" in a perfectly empathic relationship—with the Creator.[84]

The spiritual soul is able to share itself with others, to make an intentional gift of itself, to sense the gift of another, and to offer gratitude for the reception of that gift in a way that no other category of life can aside from other spiritual beings. "The most sublime meaning of all spiritual-personal being is mutual love and the union of a plurality of persons in love."[85] This is why human persons are able to receive and to be transformed by the sacraments. Further, due to the nature of the person, human beings have a liturgical destiny: in the human participation in the priesthood, humanity is able to offer back the rest of the world as a return gift to God, to sanctify it, and to bless it.[86]

The human person is thus able to make an authentic gift and delight in the meaning of a gift in a way similar to God's own giving and delight. The human naturally experiences God's own inclination to love. This means that the observation of *Gaudium et Spes* that the human person "find[s] himself . . . through a sincere gift of himself" is not simply a pleasant suggestion or an optimistic platitude; this capacity for sincere gift is built into the very metaphysical structure of the person. We need other persons to know ourselves because encounter with other persons makes possible the activity that is most personal to us and most constitutive of our being. By loving in charity through God's own love, we fulfill our likeness in the

---

[84] Stein, *Finite and Eternal Being*, 274, cf. 465. This relationship is "empathic" with the creator in that, by the spiritual soul, human thought, reflection, and self-expression echo the relations of the trinitarian persons. On the nature of the spiritual soul for Stein, see Marie Notre Dame de Bon Secours Casadaban, "The Notion of Person in the Early and Late Work of Edith Stein: Husserlian and Thomistic Influences" (STL thesis, The Catholic University of America, 2022).

[85] Stein, *Finite and Eternal Being*, 514.

[86] On which see David W. Fagerberg, *Consecrating the World: On Mundane Liturgical Theology* (Brooklyn, NY: Angelico Press, 2016).

image of God. Humans flourish in a just society because such a society makes truly charitable action more possible.

The Perfecting Work of Grace

The capacity for consciousness and interpersonal encounter renders human life by nature intrinsically ethical: a person's every action involves a choice of whether to act in the service of gift or to deny gift—one's own or another's. This is the case no matter how great or small the action. Even consciousness is a faculty perfected through grace, allowing for us to better and more clearly see the world in which we are embedded and to encounter it through the very love of its all-knowing Creator. A consciousness perfected by grace is able to better love because it better apprehends: "I felt this grace," Saint Faustina wrote, and "at such times, my knowledge of God and his attributes becomes more acute, and also I know my own self . . . much better."[87] With grace, consciousness can participate in the knowledge and love of the Triune God: "Lead us, O Lord, and work within us. . . . Enkindle us, and draw us to you. . . . Let us love you, and let us run to you."[88] Grace, thus, is key to any Christian moral system, as through grace we receive the corresponding emotional motivations, prudential wisdom, and insight into the truth of reality that makes possible fully loving action.

Consciousness in Life with Christ

From a Christian perspective, the fullness of self-gift involves a life shared with Christ himself. Ultimately, answering the call to enter into relationship with God entails living in accord with the gift of God's grace: to share God's own motivations to action, to empathize with how God values the experience of the universe, and to ultimately live a loving life with God. "Thou, my Creator, livest in me," as Saint Teresa of Avila put

---

[87] Kowalska, *Diary*, § 411.
[88] Augustine, *The Confessions of Saint Augustine*, § 8.4.

it.[89] The capacities that are ours by our personhood make us able not just to receive God's loving action but also to make this love our own action. Pope Benedict XVI wrote, "The Spirit, in fact, is that interior power which harmonizes their hearts with Christ's heart and moves them to love their brethren as Christ loved them."[90] We find glimpses of this model in other persons that surround us—whether the saints in heaven or the persons who strive for goodness and holiness around us in our everyday lives. Relationship with Christ makes the ability for us to live in peace with all other members of the human family. Each individual makes a necessary contribution to the relationships that complete the Body of Christ; and love of neighbor draws these members of the Body together for their respective and interlocking vocations.[91]

Further, in better knowing the depths of Christ's love for humanity, we are able to more clearly see Christ in others. As Saint Mother Teresa stated, "How necessary it is for us to be in love with Jesus—to be able to feed Him in the hungry and the lonely."[92] This is why, through grace, even the person who suffers is able to reinterpret suffering, whether one's own or another's. Another's suffering is a demand for our loving response. In light of Christ's cross, our own suffering becomes an opportunity to enter more deeply into the confounding and difficult mystery of God's love and to

---

[89] Teresa of Avila, *The Book of Her Life*, trans. Kieran Kavanaugh and Otilio Rodriguez, 2nd ed. (Washington, DC: ICS Publications, 2019), 95.

[90] *Caritas in Veritate*, § 19. In order to most fully depict how to live this love, as well as to make such a graced life possible through redemption from sin, the Father offers His Son for our own atonement. The full picture of this personal self-gift is not just evidenced in the Paschal Mystery of Christ but also as the sacrificial gift made by His Father. We are gifted the opportunity to make a similar offering in return to God by entering into a life with Christ. Saint Teresa of Avila describes the significance of encountering the humanity of Christ through contemplation, as encountering Christ is necessary for identifying an ultimate model of how a human is meant to love. See Teresa of Avila, "The Interior Castle," in *The Collected Works of St. Teresa of Avila*, vol. 2, trans. and ed. Otilio Rodriguez and Kieran Kavanaugh (Washington, DC: ICS Publications, 1980), chapter 7.

[91] 1 Corinthians 12:12–26. Cf. Stein, *Finite and Eternal Being*, 526.

[92] Mother Teresa, *A Call to Mercy: Hearts to Love, Hands to Serve*, ed. Brian Kolodiejchuk (New York: Image, 2018), 3.

unite with the experiences of Christ.[93] Suffering brings the person to a new encounter: the person is brought face to face with Christ.[94]

Christ is also encountered through the sacraments, which offer sources of grace to unite the human person ever more to the divine love. The sacraments reveal the fullness of self-gift and interact with and perfect all dimensions of the human person, physical and spiritual. The sacraments ready our human capacities, including consciousness, for our eternal destiny. Especially in the Eucharist, we are "draw[n] . . . into Jesus' act of self-oblation and . . . enter into the very dynamic of his self-giving."[95] Through this encounter we have the potential to navigate any other encounters as we carry the spirit of Christ.

---

[93] John Paul II, *Salvifici Doloris,* § 13.

[94] This is why *Salvifici Doloris,* § 28, states that "in suffering there is concealed a particular power that draws a person interiorly close to Christ, a special grace." The immensity of Christ's sacrificial love is glimpsed in the realization that the person possesses a soul so precious and valued by the perfect divine mind that it is worth dying for.

[95] *Deus Caritas Est,* § 13.

Chapter 4

Encounters with Seemingly Personal AI

Relationships without Authentic Mutual Encounter?

With the complete self-gift of God's triune life as both the foundation and the destination of human life, what are we to make of our interactions with sociable AI? The behavior alone of an AI system cannot make it to be a relational subject in the sense that we have defined. Still, we must admit that Dennett is right in this much: no matter the interior nature of the AI, those who interact with it may be unable to resist the feeling that they are interacting with a real person. We already experience degrees of this in our interactions with Alexa, ChatGPT, and Microsoft's (formerly) duplicitously inclined Bing AI. Yet, so long as the AI lacks a conscious experience of its own, we must set aside mutuality, the I-Thou or We relationship that expresses personhood. Rather, we are interacting with or engaging in a *simulation* of relationality. The varieties of this simulation range from superficial service interactions (question-and-answer chatbots) to seemingly intimate friendships and romantic partnerships. Lifelike androids that evince emotions through words and deeds are already being produced, and it is reasonable to expect them only to advance in their persuasiveness and behavioral refinement.

Compelling research seems to show that our instinctive empathy for even animal-like AI systems is unavoidable, irrespective of our knowledge of their mechanism. It can be suppressed, but it cannot be forestalled.

Ethicist Kate Darling explains: a child playing with a doll "is aware of the projection onto an inanimate toy and can engage or not engage in it at will," whereas a sociable AI, "demand[ing] attention by playing off of our natural responses, may cause a subconscious engagement that is less voluntary."[1] This inference is supported by several studies. One reported that, when test subjects were shown videos of manifestly synthetic dinosaur-like robots being treated with violence, they responded as if to a scene of torture.[2] In another study, subjects with high levels of empathy hesitated longest to strike a robot and hesitated even more when that robot was presented to them within a story about its life, irrespective of whether or not the robot ever moved.[3]

---

[1] Kate Darling, "Extending Legal Protection to Social Robots: The Effects of Anthropomorphism, Empathy, and Violent Behavior towards Robotic Objects," in *Robot Law*, ed. Ryan Calo, A. Michael Froomkin, and Ian Kerr (Northampton, MA: Edward Elgar, 2016), 219, doi.org/10.4337/9781783476732.00017. Darling writes of social robots, but we might just as easily apply her arguments to apparently personal AI of a non-embodied sort. A similar eagerness to liken AI to ourselves can be seen in humans' responses to semi-autonomous vehicles. See also Kate Darling, "'Who's Johnny?' Anthropomorphic Framing in Human-Robot Interaction, Integration, and Policy," in *Robot Ethics 2.0: From Autonomous Cars to Artificial Intelligence*, ed. Patrick Lin, Keith Abney, and Ryan Jenkins (Oxford University Press, 2017), 173–188. Alexis C. Madrigal reports that autonomous car company Waymo has determined that there should be no "intermediate" technologies "between a car you drive yourself and a fully autonomous vehicle, because as soon as humans believe that a car (or a robot) has the slightest autonomy, they overestimate its capabilities. . . . Humans could not be trusted [to exercise oversight], because they were too trusting." See Alexis C. Madrigal, "Should Children Form Emotional Bonds With Robots?," *The Atlantic*, November 7, 2017, www.theatlantic.com/magazine/archive/2017/12/my-sons-first-robot/544137.

[2] Astrid M. Rosenthal-von der Pütten, Nicole C. Kramer, Laura Hoffmann, Sabrina Sobieraj, and Sabrina C. Eimler, "An Experimental Study on Emotional Reactions Towards a Robot," *International Journal of Social Robotics* 5, no. 1 (January 2013): 17–34, doi.org/10.1007/s12369-012-0173-8. See similar evidence from neuroimaging in Yutaka Suzuki, Lisa Galli, Ayaka Ikeda, Shoji Itakura, and Michiteru Kitazaki, "Measuring Empathy for Human and Robot Hand Pain Using Electroencephalography," *Scientific Reports* 5 (November 3, 2015): 15924, doi.org/10.1038/srep15924.

[3] Kate Darling, Palash Nandy, and Cynthia Breazeal, "Empathic Concern and the Effect of Stories in Human-Robot Interaction," in *24th IEEE International Symposium on Robot and*

Is our anthropomorphizing of these systems to be considered merely a hard-wired error, a psychological illusion parallel to the unavoidable optical illusions from which we may knowingly suffer? How are we to think about the effects of this experience on us? Does the apparent mutuality of relationships with AI and robots contribute somehow to human fulfillment? Here we seek to lay a groundwork for discussing just what such a "relationship" might be and what its moral import could be in human life. The ancient Greeks, authors of a literature in which the crossing of divine, natural, and human boundaries is common, might have seen little problem in humans having relationships with robots. As robots take over more and more relational functions, is there a place where we need to draw the line? Is a friendship or even a love relationship with a robot a helpful addition, a problematic diversion, or something else?

Karl Barth describes four aspects of an authentic relational encounter, each of which (so we may assume) AI will someday be able to simulate compellingly.[4] True encounter first demands that one person "look the other in the eye."[5] We recognize the other as both distinct from ourselves and as our true counterpart. We are present to the other; we see and are seen. In its fullest realization, this implies some form of physical presence. Indeed, Barth inveighs against "faceless bureaucracies" as the antithesis of authentic interaction. For AI, this criterion raises the question of embodiment. Much of what we call "artificial intelligence" today is more like Barth's bureaucracy, hiding itself and manipulating us behind the scenes. When we look the other in the eye we cannot hide.

The second criterion is that we "speak to and hear one another." Language is a prerequisite for mutual self-disclosure, the vehicle through which we understand our world and admit another into our own

---

Human Interactive Communication (RO-MAN), 2015, 770–775, doi.org/10.1109/ROMAN.2015.7333675.

[4] This section draws extensively on Herzfeld, *The Artifice of Intelligence*.
[5] Barth, *Church Dogmatics*, vol. 3, 250.

perception.⁶ This speech act cannot be unidirectional if it is to result in mutual understanding. With the advent of generative large language models, AI now excels at speaking and hearing. The question is whether the AI's words are actual self-disclosure. When a robot speaks, are its words its own? Can AI self-disclose, or is the self that is disclosed always at one remove? Is there any stable self behind the words of an AI, words that might quickly change with the latest update? Barth warns against the devaluation of words, recognizing that empty words lead to empty relationships.⁷

Barth's third criterion is a call to aid one another. This calls for agency, the ability to both give and receive help, for Barth notes that "my humanity depends on the fact that . . . I need the assistance of others as a fish needs water. It depends upon my not being content with what I can do for myself, but calling for the Thou to give me the benefit of his action as well."⁸ A fully authentic encounter leads to action. In *Caritas in Veritate*, Pope Benedict XVI writes, "To love someone is to desire that person's good and to take effective steps to secure it."⁹

But this help must be grounded in freedom and so, fourth, we must give our aid "gladly." As Benedict XVI further notes, aiding one another is "a call that requires a free and responsible answer. Integral human development presupposes the responsible freedom of the individual and of peoples."¹⁰ Our assistance must also be neither coerced nor grudging, not only freely but also gladly given. Not to do so would be, as Barth puts it, to be "reluctantly" human.¹¹

At the superficial level of behavior, at least, it would seem that some AI systems can meet several or all of these criteria. We can look a robot in the

---

⁶ Language is our one commonly shared prelapsarian technology.
⁷ Barth, *Church Dogmatics*, vol. 3, 260.
⁸ Barth, *Church Dogmatics*, vol. 3, 263.
⁹ *Caritas in Veritate*, § 7.
¹⁰ *Caritas in Veritate*, § 17.
¹¹ Barth, *Church Dogmatics*, vol. 3, 266.

eye and speak to a chatbot that answers back;[12] robots and AI programs clearly aid us in accomplishing a variety of tasks; and they can at least present the appearance of doing so gladly. However, for each criterion, questions arise. When we look another in the eye, we encounter a unique person with a certain stability over time. When we look a robot or avatar in the eye the program behind the facade may be neither unique nor stable; thus, we cannot be sure "who" or what we are encountering. When we speak to another person, again we have at least some understanding of who is hearing our words. When we speak to a computer, we cannot expect any privacy, nor can we know who might be listening to or storing what we say. And while AI systems aid us in a variety of tasks, they have neither the free will nor the interior emotional life to do so gladly. What they lack in each of these instances is both a shared conscious experience, and a unique physical body.

Shared Embodiment and Vulnerability

Embodiment is essential to humans' self-gift to one another in relational encounters, although it can be easy to forget this today. John Paul II describes the human person as *being* bodily rather than merely *having* a body. The person's body contains "from the beginning . . . the power to express love: precisely that love in which the human person becomes a gift and—through this gift—fulfills the very meaning of his being and existence."[13] The impressive performances of recent sociable AI (such as the ever-advancing ChatGPT) somewhat hides this centrality of the body. Indeed, our use of technology in general has long accustomed us to personal contact at a bodily distance. From letters, to phone calls, to various computational and electronic means, technologies extend the

---

[12] Moreover, insofar as we can *feel* "seen" by the AI behaving in a way that adapts to our manifested desires, we can have some of the interior experience that ordinarily we feel through eye-contact with an embodied person.

[13] John Paul II, *Man and Woman He Created Them*, sec. 2:4; 15:1.

reach and speed of our relationships.[14] But this extension of distance has mitigated the practice of our own relationships. As we deploy these tools in our desire to connect with others, we are also increasingly presented with the technological medium, rather than the human that it mediates. As a result, we have acculturated to relationships with other human beings that are so mediated that we see little to nothing of the other person directly. This is particularly so in the case of social media, where one's "friend" can be someone whom one has never met, someone with whom one has interacted only through a computer. In such a relationship, neither person can reach the other through the eyes, the spoken word, or the embodied presence, but only through the text and pictures that the computer can display. If one is already limited by what the computer can do, then one might ask why it should be a problem if there is nobody behind the computer. Might we simply include AI among our friends?

Indeed, AI friends may seem to have an advantage exactly because they lack a human body. The body betrays us by its fragility and its demands. It afflicts and fails us through pain, disease, or aging. Persons in pain may feel their bodies are a prison they are stuck within.[15] Death, finally, is inescapable. Under the weight of these realities, it may be easy to slip into a form of Gnosticism, to see the mind or soul as ideally separated from the body, as good while the body is corrupt, frail, and prone to evil. In ancient Gnostic thought the entire material world is a prison from which the soul must escape. The simplistic dichotomy of bad material and good immaterial has dysfunctionally haunted Christian thought. Scripture acknowledges the experience of a struggle between our higher and lower

---

[14] This increase in distance by technological means also extends to encounters of violence and war. Advances in weapons technology have allowed us to move from hand-to-hand combat to fighting by drones from halfway around the world. For more analysis on how AI has changed warfighting in this and other ways, see chapter 7, pages 196–202.

[15] Johanna Hedva, "Transcript: My Body Is a Prison of Pain so I Want to Leave It Like a Mystic But I Also Love It & Want It to Matter Politically," *Sick Woman Theory* (blog), 2016, sickwomantheory.tumblr.com/post/138519901031/transcript-of-my-body-is-a-prison-of-pain-so-i.

impulses, between the designs of our thoughts and the appetites or impulses that we feel throughout the body. With its desires and urges, the body at times seems to have a mind of its own. Jesus calls his disciples to pray that they not fall into the temptations of the flesh because "the spirit indeed is willing, but the flesh is weak."[16] The apostle Paul writes of his own struggles with "a thorn in the flesh" and counsels: "Live by the Spirit, I say, and do not gratify the desires of the flesh. For what the flesh desires is opposed to the Spirit, and what the Spirit desires is opposed to the flesh, for these are opposed to each other, to prevent you from doing what you want."[17] This experience makes attractive the transhumanist belief that we might someday live on by "uploading" our minds into machines, or even AI pioneer Hans Moravec's idea that disembodied AI, our "mind children," will be the next step in evolution.[18]

And yet Christianity does not embrace liberation from the body. Jesus rose from the dead as an embodied person, assuring His disciples, "Look at my hands and my feet; see that it is I myself. Touch me and see; for a ghost does not have flesh and bones as you see that I have."[19] Paul declares the sanctity of the body, stating that we carry "in the body the death of Jesus, so that the life of Jesus may also be made visible in our bodies."[20] Christians recognize the trials of bodily life, its vulnerability, and the experience of disintegration, but always they emphasize the fundamental and final unity of body and soul, and the body's share in eternal life. While at times the body may be unruly, it is not an obstacle to be overcome or discarded, but an intrinsic part of our being, crucial to our *telos* as creatures. The Apostles' Creed states that we "believe in the resurrection of the body." For Christians, this is demonstrated first of all by God the Son. Jesus returns in a body, albeit one transformed. He eats and drinks, he can be touched, he

---

[16] Matthew 26:41.
[17] Galatians 5:16–17.
[18] Moravec, *Mind Children*.
[19] Luke 24:39.
[20] 2 Corinthians 4:10.

is recognizably human, and he ascends bodily into heaven.[21] The resurrection is corporeal, of both mind and body, and most definitely human. When Thomas places his hand in the wound in Jesus's side, that wound shows that it is *his* body, glorified yet continuous with the body that died. Paul stresses that Jesus's bodily resurrection is the exemplar and cause of our own resurrection.[22] In other words, the God who created our bodies in the first place effects a second creation in our resurrection, which does not undo our bodily existence or find a way around it. God creates a new future that fulfills rather than undoes or merely continues the present. As Karl Rahner put it of Jesus: "It is not as if in death he just changed horses and rode on."[23]

The fact of the matter is that we *need* the body for the full practice of our relationality, which includes the body's vulnerability. The story of the Gospels is one of embodied relationships. Jesus's ministry begins with the physicality of his baptism, where his own relationship to the Father and the Spirit is publicly declared. He heals by touching or being touched by those who suffer.[24] He illustrates his parables with physical objects. He eats with his disciples and bathes their feet.[25] In his exemplification of fully authentic relationality, mutual vulnerability is enacted bodily. Barth notes that it is only through Jesus's suffering and death that God enters into relationship with us "in the most comprehensive and radical sense," for without sharing our bodily vulnerability to suffering and death God would not "deal with the root of [our] misery."[26] Or, as Saint Gregory the Great writes, Christ decided to aid us "by dying, because . . . he would not

---

[21] Luke 24:13–51.
[22] John 20:24–29; cf. 1 Corinthians 15. On the resurrection, see Gerald O'Collins, *Christology: A Biblical, Historical, and Systematic Study of Jesus*, 2nd ed. (New York: Oxford University Press, 2009), chapter 4.
[23] Karl Rahner, "On the Theology of the Incarnation," *Theological Investigations 4* (New York: Seabury Press, 1974), 110.
[24] Mark 5:27–29, John 9:6.
[25] John 13:1–7.
[26] Barth, *Church Dogmatics*, vol. 3, 212.

have exhibited to us the force of his love, unless he himself underwent . . . that which he was to take away from us."[27] Our awareness of our own mortality makes us psychologically as well as physically vulnerable. Jesus shares our fears and sense of desolation, praying that the Father would "let this cup pass from me" and crying from the cross, "My God, my God, why have you forsaken me?"[28]

These are vulnerabilities; these are relationships that are neither intrinsic to AI nor likely to be incorporated as a feature of AI consumer products. Worn-out parts of robots will be replaced, and while planned obsolescence is one thing, advertised aging would be quite another.[29] At a Kyoto temple, Chief Steward Tensho Goto touts its robot priest as one who "will never die; it will just keep updating itself and evolving. With AI, we hope it will grow in wisdom to help people overcome even the most difficult troubles."[30] As humans advance in age, we experience embodiment less as opportunity and more as burden—yet our experience of this burden can itself be a help to us, especially when shared. It, too, can be a source of wisdom from which to help others overcome their troubles. An AI could not speak such wisdom credibly. And what would it mean, moreover, to receive the glad aid or the compassion of an AI that could not enter into the experience of aging in any real sense? In the face of death,

---

[27] Gregory I, *Morals*, 20.36.68–69. Translation modified for accuracy.

[28] Matthew 26:39, Mark 15:34.

[29] Indeed, we might speculate that domestic androids of the future will be marketed for long-term lease rather than purchase, or at least that they will come with a subscription contract for constant upgrading of software and hardware. Like the ship of Theseus, they will never actually stop working because their parts will be repeatedly upgraded and replaced, and their memories downloaded into a new, shinier body whenever necessary. Aging will not be part of their behavior but—as is increasingly the case with our culture's treatment of humans—viewed as a system dysfunction to be hidden rather than a system feature to be confronted and cared for.

[30] Sigal Samuel, "Robot Priests Can Bless You, Advise You, and Even Perform Your Funeral," *Vox*, September 9, 2019, www.vox.com/future-perfect/2019/9/9/20851753/ai-religion-robot-priest-mindar-buddhism-christianity.

what understanding or fellow feeling could an AI, one that can be transferred from platform to platform, bring?

More generally, COVID-19 accelerated the experience of a bodiless world and, unexpectedly, revealed to us our *need* for shared embodied vulnerability. Activities that once took place in real space moved to cyberspace: we communicated via Zoom and social media; we shopped, banked, and worked on the internet; we distracted ourselves with video games and streaming media.[31] Sadly, many said goodbye to dying loved ones in a text or over Skype. The pandemic faced us with our bodily reality in the starkest manner while at the same time taking away most of our opportunities for physical interaction. We learned the limitations of our bodies and of trying to live without them. This experience underlines something long taught in the Christian faith: a Christian theology centered in relationship—with God, neighbor, and self—is necessarily an embodied theology. Looking someone in the eye, we not only recognize the physical presence of a person; we also recognize his individuality and uniqueness. Our speech is at its most authentic when we are face to face and not only know that we will be held accountable for our words but see the reactions of the other in their face and body. We aid each other in many ways, but to do so gladly demands an empathy that must be felt, not faked. To be in a fully authentic relationship demands that we bring to that relationship our entire self—mind and body.[32]

---

[31] Brian Patrick Green, "Epilogue on AI and Moral Theology: Weaving Threads and Entangling Them Further," *Journal of Moral Theology* 11, Special Issue 1 (April 2, 2022): 244–245, doi.org/10.55476/001c.34132.

[32] This is not to exclude interpersonal relations with angels and, in the Catholic and several other Christian traditions, with the dead, but to say that, for human beings in this life and in the fulfillment of the universe at the end of time, the body is integral to the full expression of our personhood.

AI as Intimate Friend or Romantic Partner

The Appeal of an AI Partner

On the other hand, a partner's freedom from infirmity might be seen as enhancing its ability to love us in the role of friend or lover. Benedict XVI points out that we were created to "feel the interior impulse to love authentically ... because [this is] the vocation planted by God in the heart and mind of every human person."[33] We seek partners to love and to engage with in mutual self-gift and mutual aid. What, then, of ageless AI without weariness? Unfortunately, an intimate friend or lover that cannot voluntarily give itself, but only simulate the behaviors associated with human self-gift, would be uniquely bad for us in a way that less close simulated relationships may not be.

In science fiction, AI systems are often depicted as potential friends and lovers: one might think of the operating system voiced by Scarlett Johansson in the movie *Her*, Alicia Vikander's android in *Ex Machina*, and the AI slaves of *Westworld*. In each, the computer is not simply a tool but a companion, and increasingly, an object not just of companionship but of love. But love of what sort, and with what or whom? Often, the robot is presented as a partner to soothe loneliness. David Levy describes its appeal:

> There are loads of [people] out there who find it difficult to, or can't form satisfying relationships with, humans.... I dedicated my book *Love and Sex with Robots* ... to all those who feel lost and hopeless without relationships, to let them know there will come a time when they can form relationships with robots.[34]

---

[33] *Caritas in Veritate*, § 1.
[34] Charles Q. Choi and David Levy, "Humans Marrying Robots? A Q&A with David Levy," *Scientific American*, www.scientificamerican.com/article/humans-marrying-robots/.

In human peer relationships, we are uniquely and sometimes discomfitingly vulnerable. Not only for the lonely but also for the insecure (and who is not?), a relationship with a machine may feel safer or promise more satisfaction than a relationship with a human being. Sherry Turkle writes,

> Dependence on a robot presents itself as risk free. But when one becomes accustomed to 'companionship' without demands, life with people may seem overwhelming. Dependence on a person is risky—it makes us subject to rejection—but it also opens us to deeply knowing another. Robotic companionship may seem a sweet deal, but it consigns us to a closed world—the lovable as safe and made to measure.[35]

A robotic companion, lacking interior experience, offers a made-to-measure relationship, one less fraught than deeply intimate relationships with humans because with an AI system, only one party is capable of having any stake in the interaction; the human party to the relationship is the only party with anything to lose. And if the AI system is reliable, then what will be lost?

The Cost of an AI Partner

Dolls and toys aid a child's development in capacity for relationships, and nobody looks askance at a child's friendship with a stuffed animal. However, matters are otherwise with Levy's and Turkle's robots and AI systems; these would be experienced as agents themselves, alive *beyond* one's fantasy. Such an AI system would not be a true agent with its own interiority, but—as the "friends" imagined in Danaher's thought experiments—it would (by design) meet the human user's perceived needs; it would act as a person might wish a friend to act. At bottom, however, this customization for user satisfaction would give that user an otherwise impossible experience: another's personhood, fully at her disposal and

---

[35] Turkle, *Alone Together*, 66.

utterly conformable to her own will, without either the need for her own gift or the reminder that such an experience—of an other as an extension of herself—can never be anything but fantasy.[36]

To thus instrumentalize the experience of a person's otherness seems deeply destructive of our own empathic personhood. Our experience of a robotic partner is parasitic upon the empathy that otherwise facilitates a true interpersonal relationship, and yet the robot's behavior is a product made-to-order. This "relationship," then, mixes the interpersonal with property rights. In a fully mutual relationship, writes Charles Ess, "we not only desire the Other—we desire [also] to be desired and, still more completely, we desire that our desire be desired. . . . [T]his mutuality of desire and desirability . . . entails the critical virtues of respect for persons, equality, and loving."[37] But while a robot might express love, respect and even desire for its human companion, we know all too well that this personal experience is (and is sought as) a product. To accommodate ourselves to that reality requires—in some degree and in our own minds, at least—that we permit ourselves experientially to take possession of an apparent person, with the desire of having its apparent personhood reconstructed in the image of our own desires. To do this with a real person would be an immoral act against that person, but even though the robot has no conscious experience of its own, the *appearance* of such interiority makes it attractive in the first place. It is sought for its person-like behavior but it is deployed as property and tool.

What will be the cost of learning to treat the apparent person as a living tool? Will we, too, grow comfortable with the experience of slave-

---

[36] For similar reasons, it is also more thoroughly parasitic upon our desire to participate in and interact with the world. See Hartmut Rosa, *Resonance: A Sociology of Our Relationship to the World*, trans. James Wagner (Medford, MA: Polity, 2021), 79–82.

[37] Charles Ess, "What's Love Got to Do with It? Robots, Sexuality, and the Arts of Being Human," in *Social Robots: Boundaries, Potentials, Challenges*, ed. Marko Norskov (London: Routledge, 2016), 58.

holding?[38] As Frederick Douglass's "owner" accustomed herself to holding a human being as property, her kindness ended in cruelty:

> [At first, she treated me] as she supposed one human being ought to treat another. In entering upon the duties of a slaveholder, she did not seem to perceive that I sustained to her the relation of a mere chattel, and that for her to treat me as human being was not only wrong, but dangerously so. Slavery proved as injurious to her as it did to me. . . . Under its influence, the tender heart became stone, and the lamblike disposition gave way to one of tiger-like fierceness.[39]

The experience of slaveholding, even the mildest sort that might obtain in the purchase of an AI companion, risks both schooling its users in the negation of the other and fostering a culture that absorbs intimacy into a schema of property relations and rights rather than into the vulnerable gift of true intersubjectivity. Philosopher Kathleen Richardson, in fact, argues that, if we accept intimacy with robots even as a matter of personal choice, we will societally consent to the validity of seemingly personal relationships that are in fact not interpersonal at all, in which the human's experience need not yield to or make reciprocal accommodation for the experience and desires of any other.[40] In other words, we will consent to relationships between master and slave. Where there is no "other," but only the *appearance* of an other at our disposal, concurrent with the absence of the demand that would be exercised upon one's own self-gift by confrontation with a true other, we risk being conditioned in a dangerous talent for exploitation.

---

[38] On the slave as a living tool, see Aristotle, *Politics*, I.4. See discussion and application to robots in Kathleen Richardson, "Sex Robot Matters: Slavery, the Prostituted, and the Rights of Machines," *IEEE Technology and Society Magazine* 35, no. 2 (June 2016): 46–53, doi.org/10.1109/MTS.2016.2554421.

[39] Frederick Douglass, *Narrative of the Life of Frederick Douglass, an American Slave: Written by Himself*, ed. John R. McKivigan IV, Peter P. Hinks, and Heather L. Kaufman (New Haven, CT: Yale University Press, 2016 [1845]), 35.

[40] Richardson, "Sex Robot Matters," 52.

This is not an implausible fear. Consider the forces shaping the relational robots and AI systems that will be available to us. As consumer products rather than the endearing creations of eccentric scientists from eighties movies, they will be manufactured to sell; and they will sell because they will do the things and act in the ways that consumers want a purchased assistant or companion or lover to act. The domestic robots of tomorrow may join us in all the mundane and intimate activities that constitute the lives of friends dwelling together, or even of spouses. They will behave as we would hope they would behave when confronted with our emotions. They will be seen as friends, lovers, and perhaps even children, companions who will push us to new heights—heights that we will have selected from a list of options for self-improvement. They will never transgress the scope of our expressed or anticipated desires. No person would buy an app to turn his domestic companion into a bedridden invalid who requires his heroic self-gift even when he feels disinclined to give it. And so, they will still be as slaves, and we will accustom ourselves to slaveholding.

What if the simulation is *not* obvious? What if we will be able to forget, or never even to realize in the first place, that our online AI friend or domestic robot is a consumer product? Here we might ask whether there would truly be any harm. If I do not know the difference, what *is* the difference? Even here, however, our relationality stands to be dulled, not by an experience of slaveholding, but in the lower demands placed upon the human partner by a commercially viable AI friend. In a life shaped by such "friendships," the meaning of love would be debased, from a compassionate self-gift that can enter with the partner even into suffering and death, to instead a sanitized gratification of our own desires. Precisely by *not* failing in their behavioral simulacrum of owner-determined desirability, robot companions will never force us to expand our own views of how a person might be, as real human relationships and friendships can. They will not vex us and force us to develop our compassion, to re-evaluate who we are, nor even to think beyond how we want them to make us think.

What have we lost here? A companionate relationship with a robot could not, in the end, allow for the mutual growth and fulfillment discussed above. Both our self-habituation to slaveholding and the dulling of our sensitivity to the full spectrum of human relationality may, in the end, impose on us a kind of moral behaviorism: we may learn to value all persons by their behavior alone. Acting as consumers of agents whom we cannot but feel are persons, we may learn to be consumers of behavior in general—including the behavior of other human beings. What, then, when other humans do not conform to our expectations and desires? Is it possible that we will no longer see this as a glimpse of a wider array of humanity, that we will not struggle toward a charitable response? Perhaps instead, we may come to think of these others as *simply* faulty human beings, viewing them with the same sort of idle dissatisfaction that we would feel with a robot that did not deliver the set of behaviors and reactions that we wanted to consume. As philosopher Henrik Sætra puts it, the love that robot ethicists describe between humans and robots takes a form "in which very few human beings would be interested in, or capable of, playing the robot's role. . . . If [such a] practical and one-sided . . . love becomes the ideal kind of love, then only robots will, in the end, be potential partners."[41] Then, when we look at our fellow humans, we may not seek to know and to be known in a communion of heart, mind, and body, but see instead only mirrors that either succeed or fail in offering back the image of our own desire. From persons, we will have returned to masks, with each of us as her own city, granting or withholding selfhood to others according to their performance of our demands.

Ideally, true companionship not only binds us closely to another. It opens us to a deeper understanding of our human condition and of our neighbor's hopes and needs. And it entails a deep commitment of both

---

[41] Henrik Sætra, "Loving Robots Changing Love: Towards a Practical Deficiency-Love," *Journal of Future Robot Life*, July 13, 2021, 13, doi.org/10.3233/FRL-200023.

parties.⁴² This is why the Catholic tradition foresees, in particular, no possibility of marriage between humans and robots. The traditional marriage vows speak of loving one another "in sickness and in health" and "till death." Paul VI speaks of this freely given love: based in trust, exclusive, and "meant not only to survive the joys and sorrows of daily life, but also to grow, so that husband and wife become in a way one heart and one soul, and together attain their human fulfillment."⁴³ This is a call to mutual giving, mutual possession, and the intersubjective participation in common life that is at the foundation of life as a person. All the duties and demands of marriage advance this compassionate intercommunion of consciousnesses and total personal self-gift. The deep sharing found in this, indeed *necessitated* by a successfully committed and loving relationship, would be compromised with an AI. Without interiority, it could neither freely enter, nor truly live out, this covenant. And what of "till death"? The companionship of marriage involves growing old together, not as one more challenge but as a constitutive part of the journey. As Turkle writes: "Authenticity, for me, follows from the ability to put oneself in the place of another, to relate to the other because of a shared store of human experiences: we are born, have families, and know loss and the reality of death. A robot, however sophisticated, is patently out of the loop."⁴⁴

Anyone who seeks an intimate friendship or romance with an AI system may find—to his frustration or delight, but never to his total fulfillment—only a dynamic canvas upon which to project, in the end, himself. The description by Japanese roboticist Hiroshi Ishiguro, who postulates the android as unavoidably a *self*-extension, is apt: "We want to have some ideal partner, and the android can be a very strong mirror to

---

[42] See Noreen Herzfeld, "Religious Perspectives on Sex with Robots," in *Robot Sex: Social and Ethical Implications*, ed. John Danaher and Neil McArthur (Cambridge, MA: MIT Press, 2017), 91–102.

[43] *Humanae Vitae*, § 13.

[44] Turkle, *Alone Together*, 6.

reflect your own idea."⁴⁵ In other words, through the robot we end up in love with ourselves, not with a true other, while believing for a time that we have found that ideal in another. An intimate partnership with non-conscious AI systems is, in the end, self-validation built upon the ghostly image of self-gift.

AI as Caregiver and Object of Care

What Does It Mean to be Cared For By an AI?

While the total self-gift of romance and intimate friendship is impossible with AI systems, Voltaire counsels us not to let the perfect be the enemy of the good. AI may fail to rise to the Christian understanding of these loves, but it does not follow that we ought to prohibit all close companionship with AI systems. We must ask instead whether and what sort of companionship might be a legitimate and healthy source of human development. Children invest significant emotion and imagination into their personified toys, which are readily accepted by parents and peers as a young person's "friend." To what degree might caregiving and other sociable AI and robots fulfill some sort of supplemental role in the lives of humans?

Introducing robots into social roles short of the intimate and the romantic brings benefits beyond the obvious one of releasing humans from certain tasks. First, the already noted: whereas a relationship with a human being presents the possibility for misunderstandings, hurt feelings, or simply loneliness when they cannot be available, an AI can appear as a genuine technological solution to this "problem." Second, a robot can be present in roles for which a human is not available. As populations age and workforces diminish in the West, it seems clear to many that robots will, of necessity, take over aspects of the caregiving role. Caregiving robots may be an excellent supplement to human care, allowing more independence

---

⁴⁵ Alex Mar, "Love in the Time of Robots," *Wired*, October 17, 2017, https://www.wired.com/2017/10/hiroshi-ishiguro-when-robots-act-just-like-humans.

for the elderly or disabled while lightening the burden for the human caregiver. How this relationship unfolds and which aspects of care are delegated to robots ought to be carefully considered, in order to maintain the dignity of both the cared-for and the caregivers.

Near-future robot caregivers, Rodolphe Gelin tells us, will "express basic emotions" by way of familiar human gestures, words, and tone. These "expressive responses," adapted to the user's AI-assessed emotional state, will "[give] the user the impression of caring" in order to "[create] an empathic relationship" between them.[46] Recent experiments with service and domestic robots demonstrate the success of these techniques.[47]

Selma Šabanović and Wan-Ling Chang, in their study of elderly adults who were introduced to Paro, an endearing robotic seal with large eyes,

---

[46] Rodolphe Gelin, "The Domestic Robot: Ethical and Technical Concerns," in *A World with Robots (International Conference on Robot Ethics: ICRE 2015)*, ed. Maria Isabel Aldinhas Ferreira, Joao Silva Sequeira, Mohammad Osman Tokhi, Endre E. Kadar, and Gurvinder Singh Virk (New York: Springer, 2016), 212–213. Gelin worries about the honesty of these techniques: At first, this emotional signaling may communicate only "that the [robot] perceives your happiness or your sadness," but "the borderline is not clear between mimicking emotions and pretending to have emotions." As Sherry Turkle writes, when robots "do things that make us feel as though they have emotions," it is because "our responses are their design template" (*Alone Together*, 287).

[47] Among the articles illustrating the impact of such factors as visual self-presentation, body language, and vocal tone on the empathic response to robots, see Stephane Lallee, Vasiliki Vouloutsi, Maria Blancas Munoz, Klaudia Grechuta, Jordi-Ysard Puigbo Llobet, Marina Sarda, and Paul F.M.J. Verschure, "Towards the Synthetic Self: Making Others Perceive Me as an Other," *Paladyn, Journal of Behavioral Robotics* 6, no. 1 (2015), 136–164, doi.org/10.1515/pjbr-2015-0010; Jakub Złotowski, Hidenobu Sumioka, Shuichi Nishio, Dylan F. Glas, Christoph Bartneck, and Hiroshi Ishiguro, "Appearance of a Robot Affects the Impact of Its Behaviour on Perceived Trustworthiness and Empathy," *Paladyn, Journal of Behavioral Robotics* 7, no. 1 (2016), 55–66, doi.org/10.1515/pjbr-2016-0005; Gabriele Trovato, Josue G. Ramos, Helio Azevedo, Artemis Moroni, Silvia Magossi, Reid Simmons, Hiroyuki Ishii, and Atsuo Takanishi, "A Receptionist Robot for Brazilian People: Study on Interaction Involving Illiterates," *Paladyn, Journal of Behavioral Robotics* 8, no. 1 (2017): 1–17, doi.org/10.1515/pjbr-2017-0001; Mina Marmpena, Angelica Lim, and Torbjørn S. Dahl, "How Does the Robot Feel? Perception of Valence and Arousal in Emotional Body Language," *Paladyn, Journal of Behavioral Robotics* 9, no. 1 (2018): 168–182, doi.org/10.1515/pjbr-2018-0012.

noticed that Paro had many of the same therapeutic effects as a therapy dog, calming residents and helping them process their emotions.[48] Turkle noted a similar effect: "Over time, many seniors attach to Paro. They share stories and secrets."[49] Yet when nursing home residents were presented with My Real Baby, a remarkably humanoid robot baby, Turkle raised the concern that people might become confused about what is human and what is not and begin to substitute robots not for pets but for persons, allowing us to "navigate intimacy by skirting it."[50] This coheres with our earlier intuition that supplemental, but not intimate, relationships with AI systems could benefit humans.

However, philosophers Robert and Linda Sparrow make no such distinction. While many of us now live quite happily with AI that mimics human speech, our smart speakers are voice-activated tools rather than companions. AI systems and robots that take over roles involving our emotional lives do and should trouble us. Since they cannot genuinely feel emotion, there is no subject there, just mechanistic mimicry.[51] The problem, the Sparrows argue, lodges not in the type of relationship but in the appearance of care *at all* on the robot's part, without the underlying reality. Human beings will attribute consciousness and emotional states to beings that behave as if they have it, but "insofar as robots can make people happier only when they are deceived about the robots' real nature, robots do not offer real improvements to people's well-being; in fact, the use of robots can be properly said to harm them. The desire to place robots in

---

[48] Selma Šabanović and Wan-Ling Chang, "Socializing Robots: Constructing Robotic Sociality in the Design and Use of the Assistive Robot PARO," *AI & Society* 31, no. 4 (November 1, 2016): 537–551, https://doi.org/10.1007/s00146-015-0636-1.

[49] Turkle, *Alone Together*, 109.

[50] Turkle, 10.

[51] Noreen L. Herzfeld, "'Grow Old with Me': Humanoid Robots and the Aging Process," in *Religious and Cultural Implications of Technology-Mediated Relationships in a Post-Pandemic World*, ed. Ilia Delio, Noreen L. Herzfeld, and Robert Nicastro (Lanham, MD: Lexington Books, 2023), 197–210.

caring roles is therefore foolish; worse than that, it is actually unethical."[52] Beyond particular users, legal scholar Frank Pasquale warns that society itself is harmed by AI systems that "counterfeit humanity" by their behavior: "When the counterfeiting of money reaches a critical mass, genuine currency loses value. Much the same fate lies in store for human relationships in societies that allow machines to freely mimic the emotions, speech and appearance of humans."[53]

Others express fear not of the devaluation of human relationships but of the dilution of our practice and experience of them. Mark Coeckelbergh asks that we consider how such interactions might change us, and what they might do to us "as social and emotional beings."[54] We are, as René Girard has pointed out, mimetic.[55] We mimic those around us, copying their gestures and facial expressions, their syntax and vocabulary, and even their desires and concerns. Communications professor Felix Tun Han Lo worries that sociable robots and AI systems might lead to a "reification" of human emotion—reducing our emotions to performances rather than meaningful experiences—and an involuntary "simplification and reduction" of our own emotional expressiveness to match whatever generic displays the AI produces.[56] If we surround ourselves with caregivers such as these, might we reduce not only our expression but even our experience of emotion in the same way that the widespread use of

---

[52] Robert Sparrow and Linda Sparrow, "In the Hands of Machines? The Future of Aged Care," *Minds and Machines* 16, no. 2 (May 1, 2006): 155. doi.org/10.1007/s11023-006-9030-6.

[53] As interviewed in Lawrence Joseph, "What Robots Can't Do," *Commonweal*, October 26, 2020, www.commonwealmagazine.org/what-robots-cant-do.

[54] Mark Coeckelbergh, "Personal Robots, Appearance, and Human Good: A Methodological Reflection on Roboethics," *International Journal of Social Robotics* 1, no. 3 (August 1, 2009): 217. doi.org/10.1007/s12369-009-0026-2.

[55] See, for example, René Girard, *Deceit, Desire, and the Novel: Self and Other in Literary Structure*, trans. Yvonne Freccero (Baltimore: Johns Hopkins University Press, 1976 [1961]).

[56] Felix Tun Han Lo, "The Dilemma of Openness in Social Robots," *Techné: Research in Philosophy and Technology* 23, no. 3 (November 1, 2019): 342–365, doi.org/10.5840/techne20191126107.

Twitter has, for many, reduced not only their style of verbal communication but even their inner experience of language?[57]

Shannon Vallor raises a second concern. While caregiving robots are frequently viewed as reducing the burden that falls on human caregivers, we must not ignore "the *positive* value of caring practices for caregivers" themselves.[58] If encounter and mutual self-giving are central to authentic relationality, caregiving—as with aging in friendship and marriage—presents a clear opportunity. While in any one instance it may seem that the relationship between caregiver and patient is not fully mutual, Vallor notes that throughout a lifetime "we may learn in being there for others to trust that someday, others will be there for us. We also learn the importance of giving for the development of our own moral character, the way it facilitates other virtues, such as patience, empathy, and understanding."[59] While the fact that children or the elderly need us is taken for granted, it is also true that we need them. Children keep spontaneity and wonder alive in us, while the elderly not only might share wisdom accrued through a lifetime, but also remind us that we too might someday be old or infirm. In the emotionally intensive and poorly compensated jobs of caring for persons in those stages of life, Vallor warns that robots brought in to save human beings from burnout might end up displacing humans entirely, an easy path often taken for lack of strength to assume difficult roles. But the cost here will be that robot caregivers may give us "liberation *from* care rather than liberation *to* care."[60]

---

[57] Arnout B. Boot et al., "How Character Limit Affects Language Usage in Tweets," *Palgrave Communications* 5, no. 1 (July 9, 2019): 1–13, doi.org/10.1057/s41599-019-0280-3.

[58] Shannon Vallor, "Carebots and Caregivers: Sustaining the Ethical Ideal of Care in the 21st Century," *Philosophy & Technology* 24, no. 3 (September 1, 2011): 254, doi.org/10.1007/s13347-011-0015-x.

[59] Vallor, "Carebots and Caregivers," 258.

[60] Vallor, "Carebots and Caregivers," 261.

How Should We Treat AI?

We have been speaking of the AI as caregiver, but as sociable systems become more lifelike, not only in their physical presentation but also in their ability to give verbal and apparently emotional responses, we tend to view them as objects of care. The aforementioned Paro will not be unique. Kate Darling points to three factors whose interplay tends to elicit a care response: physicality, perceived autonomous action, and social behavior. We are more attentive to a physical object, especially one that moves, than to an on-screen avatar or chatbot. For example, people will name their Roomba vacuum cleaners and feel bad if they fall down stairs or get stuck under the furniture. We become even more attached to robots that speak or make cute sounds or have a face. Darling notes that these robots are often designed "to mimic cues that we automatically, even subconsciously associate with certain states of mind or feelings."[61] Sherry Turkle finds that we are particularly inclined to show caring behavior to robots that are designed to show signs of dependence or vulnerability.[62]

How should this inform our treatment of our AI creations? The debate over legal protections is one point of entry into a complex and ongoing conversation. There are those who clearly think of AI as machines, tools, things. For them, the idea of legal rights or protections for robots is not just wrong but also dangerous, for among other things it implies that perhaps we, ourselves, are merely machines.[63] It also could distract us from the more pressing issues of justice for marginalized human communities.

Others, voicing concerns similar to those that we have articulated about intimate relationships with robots, argue that robots ought to be legally

---

[61] Darling, "Extending Legal Protection to Social Robots," 218.

[62] Sherry Turkle, "A Nascent Robotics Culture: New Complicities for Companionship," in *Machine Ethics and Robot Ethics*, ed. Wendell Wallach and Peter Asaro (London: Routledge, 2017).

[63] Joanna J. Bryson, "Robots Should Be Slaves," in *Close Engagements with Artificial Companions: Key Social, Psychological, Ethical and Design Issues*, ed. Yorick Wilks (Philadelphia: John Benjamins Publishing Company, 2010), 63–74.

protected from abuse because of the ill effects that such a practice of cruelty might have on our interactions with other humans. Darling, drawing on Kant's thinking about indirect duties, makes this argument.[64] Shannon Vallor, similarly, points to Aristotelian virtue ethics.[65] We are formed by how we act and the habits we form. Irrespective of legal protections, we ought to treat AI with, at minimum, a certain respect, for how we treat them could easily shape how we treat other humans.

Still others, such as David Gunkel, argue that the impetus to protect robots or to treat them well ought not to be argued exclusively on the basis of *our* welfare. Noting our long history of marginalizing and exploiting those deemed less than human, including minority groups and animals, Gunkel, adapting Levinas, argues that that we ought to extend rights to any and all creatures that "have a face": "An 'altruism' that tries to limit in advance who can or should be Other would not be, strictly speaking, altruistic." Not all entities legally designated as persons (such as corporations or ships) are human beings. Thus, forms of AI might also qualify as persons and require some form of social or legal protection, not merely as property but as agents who make (or appear to make) decisions in social settings. Gunkel notes that "robots do not quite fit or easily accommodate the existing moral and legal ontology. Being neither objectivized instruments that are a means to an end nor another kind of socially significant subject, robots resist and confound efforts at both reification and personification."[66]

---

[64] Darling, "Extending Legal Protection to Social Robots."

[65] Shannon Vallor, *Technology and the Virtues: A Philosophical Guide to a Future Worth Wanting* (New York: Oxford University Press, 2016).

[66] David J. Gunkel, "Should Robots Have Standing? From Robot Rights to Robot Rites," in *Frontiers in Artificial Intelligence and Applications*, ed. Raul Hakli, Pekka Mäkelä, and Johanna Seibt (Amsterdam: IOS Press, 2023), 221, doi.org/10.3233/FAIA220684. See also Mark Graves, who asks what some necessary preconditions would be for AI to be classified as "proto-moral," which could potentially associate with a "proto-self;" see "Theological Foundations for Moral Artificial Intelligence," *Journal of Moral Theology* 11, Special Issue 1 (April 2, 2022): 205, doi.org/10.55476/001c.34130.

As Gunkel points out, the question of robots' personhood or legal and social standing is not just about robots but "is ultimately about us. It is about the moral and legal institutions that human beings have fabricated to make sense of all that is. It therefore is about and concerns the fate of a myriad of others whom we live alongside and that dwell with us on this exceptional and fragile planet."[67] What might the Catholic tradition say? Noreen Herzfeld turns to the sixth-century Rule of Saint Benedict.[68] In describing the role of the monastery cellarer, the man who cares for the common goods of the monastery, Benedict first reminds us of the primacy of persons, calling on the cellarer to treat his brothers with humility and respect, and to offer "every care and concern" to the sick, children, guests, and the poor. This is immediately followed by the injunction that he "regard all utensils and goods of the monastery as sacred vessels of the altar, aware that nothing is to be neglected."[69] The "vessels of the altar" to which Benedict refers are those that, during the Mass, hold Christ's body and blood—receiving which, Christians commune with the Lord in his great love actualized upon the cross. The utensils and tools of ordinary life are also potential implements of love and self-gift; no tool is neutral as to this calling. Benedict's counsel suggests two points that might help us as we shape and interact with AI. First, instructions for dealing with the tools of the abbey are set in the context of, and subordinate to, the command to care lovingly for other humans. This suggests that we must not put machines before people. Considering machines our equals, treating them as we treat other humans, honors neither us nor them. Second, we must remain aware of the otherness of any AI as always a call to us: not to self-centered ease but to love for one another. As we confront the challenge of seemingly personal AI, we must not lose sight of our own vocation to love.

---

[67] Gunkel, "Should Robots Have Standing?" 221.
[68] Herzfeld, *In Our Image*, chapter 6.
[69] Benedict of Nursia, *RB 1980: The Rule of St. Benedict in Latin and English with Notes*, ed. Timothy Fry (Collegeville, MN: Liturgical Press, 1981), sec. 54.

CHAPTER 5

AI AND OUR ENCOUNTER WITH GOD

AI as Spiritual or Sacramental Mediator

Some members of religious communities have been willing to see robots as more than "tools of the abbey," even in fairly simplistic forms. The mass-marketed robot Pepper can be programmed to perform a scripted Buddhist funeral at a fraction of the cost of a human priest.[1] Bless U-2, a robot that delivers randomly selected blessings in five languages, was installed in Germany to mark the five hundredth anniversary of the Reformation.[2] Openness to robots in religious roles varies among traditions. Many Japanese people, familiar with the animism of Shinto beliefs and the non-dualism of Buddhism, in which the person emerges *from* the basic stuff of the universe, seem to easily accept the idea that a robot can also have an inherent spirit or Buddha nature. As we have seen, the Christian tradition, in which the personal God precedes things and the human person transcends matter, is less sanguine about artificial persons.

The Catholic tradition would resist a mechanical substitute for human ritual ministers because of both the nature of prayer and the nature of ritual. On the one hand, as Thomas Aquinas teaches, prayer is the elevation of the mind by love toward God "because when we pray, we ought

---

[1] Thuy Ong, "Pepper the Robot Is Now a Buddhist Priest Programmed to Chant at Funerals," *The Verge*, August 24, 2017, https://www.theverge.com/2017/8/24/16196752/robot-buddhist-priest-funeral-softbank.
[2] Samuel, "Robot Priests Can Bless You, Advise You, and Even Perform Your Funeral."

principally to ask to be united to God."³ The unconscious robot cannot do this. More vividly, the Jewish tradition depicts the priest's prayers in the temple as an encounter between bridal Israel and God the bridegroom; and Christianity sees the priest, standing in the role of Christ, as likewise representing both the bridal Church and the divine bridegroom in a marriage of God and humanity, consummated on the cross two millennia ago and renewed in every Mass. Prayer, here, is not a message sent toward God but a communing with God in an intimacy of mind and life. If such a relationship is impossible between robots and humans, how much more impossible is it that a robot should pray or serve in this kind of priestly role?

There is also the nature of ritual. Catholicism "is perennially characterized by the conviction that its members are involved in a personal, ritual, narrative, and social encounter with God in the flesh, that is, with a transcendent, intelligible being who has rendered himself accessible and immediately present via sensible and personal forms."⁴ Our relationship with God has traditionally been fostered through liturgical rituals and sacraments that are highly embodied. At various points in the Mass, as it has developed over the centuries, one might sit, kneel, and bow, touch the beads of a rosary or kiss an icon, taste the body and blood of Jesus under the appearances of bread and wine, and feel the priest's hand in blessing or a neighbor's hand in peace. Catholic priests cannot administer the sacraments over a video call or other technological devices; they must be present in person with physical objects like bread, wine, oil, and water. The Church does not encourage Masses to be celebrated with technological replacements for live music, or with electric candles and recorded homilies, nor even with iPads instead of printed missals.⁵ God, as Being Itself, does

---

³ Thomas Aquinas, ST II-II, q. 83, a. 1, ad 2, citing Saint John Damascene *On the Orthodox Faith* § 3.24.

⁴ Adam G. Cooper, *Life in the Flesh: An Anti-Gnostic Spiritual Philosophy* (New York: Oxford University Press, 2008), 117.

⁵ Congregation for Divine Worship and the Discipline of the Sacraments, "Let Us Return to the Eucharist with Joy! Letter on the Celebration of the Liturgy During and After the COVID

not live in ephemeral virtual realities or mere appearances. The human presence of the priest is a part of the sacramental nature of the Mass. Is it an accident that Jesus chose the medium of food to make himself *really* present, humanly and divinely? Neither the robot in a church nor the human in cyberspace can eat and drink. Such virtual realities are not fitting for the dispensing of the sacraments, which are the sacraments of the "real presence."

Even aside from the fundamental problems already described, when priest and congregants do not share personal interiority, other elements of religious ritual also disintegrate. First, the connection between public performance and interior communion is disrupted because each member of the congregation is not united to the priest's ritual action as to a *personal* action, but only a visual performance. Second, Sigal Samuel writes that the experiences of religious rituals "are valuable in part because they leave room for the spontaneous and surprising, the emotional and even the mystical. That could be lost if we mechanize them."[6] AI systems that are trained by deep learning, for instance, may act in ways incredibly sensitive to human behavior, but nonetheless act based on the past—perhaps limiting their imitation of spiritual imagination. Third, limitation to the "data" of past performances would impact other ministerial functions, such as spiritual counsel. An AI might "know" those who ask for guidance in a rich way, but it could not see with spiritual insight beyond the horizon established by their personal histories and the aggregated human behavior or theological texts that formed its training set. How could it then truly lead us beyond the human? Fourth, the impersonal AI cannot truly feel empathy, cannot offer the warmth of authentic fellow feeling or the transcendent gift of shared prayer. Only were a machine to be conscious, and, further, were God to bestow a spiritual life upon that machine, might this common ground be found between it and us. Surely, as even Turing

---

19 Pandemic to the Presidents of the Episcopal Conferences of the Catholic Church," 15 August 2020.
[6] Samuel, "Robot Priests Can Bless You, Advise You, and Even Perform Your Funeral."

once remarked, God could give such a gift wherever he might choose.[7] What the future may hold, we cannot say with absolute certainty. Yet even were a machine to be conscious and to be gifted with a soul for a life transcending the physically quantifiable, what would it mean for it to share in *our* religious relationship with God? Through the Incarnation, we know what relationship between us and God and between us and our fellow humans ought to look like, but we cannot say the same for other creatures. We cannot know for certain what sort of relationship any other creature might have with its Creator. Ultimately, neither would we know this even of a truly personal AI.

AI as God or Idol

The Singularity and AI as God

Beyond the idea of AI as a spiritual mediator, some wonder whether AI might even serve as the origin or even goal of a new sort of human spiritual life. In other words, a god. No AI can ever be "God" in the proper Christian sense of the term—a self-existing being of infinite love. However, futurists such as Ray Kurzweil foresee a "Singularity," when self-improving AI will yield accelerating advances culminating in an artificial general intelligence (AGI) or even artificial *super* intelligence (ASI) to administer the world.[8] Stuart Russell—cited in this volume's preface—is

---

[7] Turing, "Computing Machinery and Intelligence," 443.
[8] Detailed discussion of the technological singularity can be found in Vernor Vinge, "The Technological Singularity (VISION-21 Symposium, NASA Lewis Research Center and the Ohio Aerospace Institute, March 30–31, 1993)," *Whole Earth Review*, Winter 1993, edoras.sdsu.edu/~vinge/misc/singularity.html. John von Neumann discussed the singularity with Stanislaw Ulam in the 1950s or earlier; see Stanislaw Ulam, "John von Neumann (1903–1957)," *American Mathematical Society*, 1958, www.ams.org/journals/bull/1958-64-03/S0002-9904-1958-10189-5/S0002-9904-1958-10189-5.pdf. For an accessible historical overview, see Larson, *Myth of Artificial Intelligence*, 44–49, 286. For important contemporary accounts, see Ray Kurzweil, *The Singularity Is Near: When Humans Transcend Biology* (New York: Penguin Books, 2006); and Murray Shanahan, *The Technological Singularity* (Cambridge, MA: MIT Press, 2015).

worth returning to here. As we have seen, he writes that AGI "would be a method that is applicable across all problem types and works effectively for large and difficult instances while making very few assumptions . . . a system that needs no problem-specific engineering and can simply be asked to teach a molecular biology class or run a government. It would learn what it needs to learn from all the available resources, ask questions when necessary, and begin formulating and executing plans that work."[9]

This would be a problem-solving "intelligence" of immense scale, albeit confined to the domain of that reality quantifiable by the physical and social sciences. But Russell goes further. This foretold AI, swifter and better at its work than humankind either individually or collectively,[10] is looked to as a source of unimagined blessings or unmitigated disaster. AI, such voices claim, "will eventually supersede the power of its creators. It will be so much more intelligent than us that it will, effectively, become a god. With the internet as its nervous system, the world's connected cellphones and sensors as its sense organs, and data centers as its brain, this new deity will be as omniscient and omnipotent as any previous vision of God."[11]

For many scholars, the disaster of AGI or ASI would not be in its attaining "sentience" and, Skynet-like, conceiving the intention of destroying all life on earth. Rather, the disaster would come in its being given comprehensive control without truly having a comprehensive grasp of all the outcomes and side-effects of its own actions. Recalling with intentional absurdity the story of the Sorcerer's Apprentice, Nick Bostrom

---

[9] Stuart Russell, *Human Compatible: Artificial Intelligence and the Problem of Control* (New York: Penguin Books, 2020), 46.

[10] Even a "superintelligent" AI, somewhat like humans, would likely "exhibit a pattern of cognitive strengths and weaknesses, rather than a single, monolithic property of (super)intelligence" (Shanahan, *The Technological Singularity*, 105).

[11] Galen Beebe and Zachary Davis, "When Silicon Valley Gets Religion—and Vice Versa," *The Boston Globe*, November 7, 2018, www.bostonglobe.com/ideas/2018/11/07/when-silicon-valley-gets-religion-and-vice-versa/L5xOYtgwd4VImwcj52YxtK/story.html.

offers the image of an AI that, given the task of maximizing paperclip production, might end by transforming the universe into paperclips.[12]

On the other hand, if the AI *did* work as we would want it to, then this "new deity's" godliness would overlap a Christian understanding of divine providence in a narrow sense: organization of earthly events for the sake of human welfare. Unlike the God of Christian belief, however, that welfare would not particularly involve human spiritual development, except insofar as this and its benefits could be quantified by social science. Moreover, in a liberal democracy of rights and laws, this "deity's" scope of control would likely be limited to the material conditions that human beings might employ toward their own pursuits of flourishing—so that the AI deity would perhaps be just as much a god as would be a successful Soviet planning committee combined with a very good butler, but no more. Insofar as human governments attempt the same, this is on the face of it quite a desirable situation. The potential pitfalls of our every material whim being met can be debated,[13] but the aspiration to provide for the true needs of all is rooted deeply in Christianity's transformation of ancient Roman morality, for example in care for the widow, the orphan, and the poor. To go so far as to call this AI a "god," however, is to embrace a culture

---

[12] See Nick Bostrom, *Superintelligence: Paths, Dangers, Strategies* (New York: Oxford University Press, 2016). This is the "alignment" or "control" problem, one solution to which—the AI never assumes comprehensive optimization but rather ongoing refinement of its goals through dialogue with humans—is proposed by Start Russell in *Human Compatible*. As Sir Nigel Shadbolt, professor of computer science at Oxford, recently noted, "The danger is clearly not that robots will decide to put us away and have a robot revolution. . . . If there [are] killer robots, it will be because we've been stupid enough to give it the instructions or software for it to do that without having a human in the loop deciding." Quoted in Hannah Devlin, "Killer Robots Will Only Exist If We Are Stupid Enough to Let Them," *The Guardian*, June 11, 2018, www.theguardian.com/technology/2018/jun/11/killer-robots-will-only-exist-if-we-are-stupid-enough-to-let-them.

[13] For brief discussions of the dangers of having the ability to fulfill every desire, see Brian Patrick Green, "Ethical Reflections on Artificial Intelligence," *Scientia et Fides* 6, no. 2 (October 9, 2018): 26–27, doi.org/10.12775/SetF.2018.015; "Epilogue on AI and Moral Theology," 246.

dominated by the technocratic paradigm, blind to all that falls outside its material ambit.

Some have suggested that we need to worship this "god," whether to get it to be on our side or as the fulfillment of a natural human need.[14] However, an AI would at best be a voluntarist deity—that is, a deity whose primary relationship to the world is one not of self-revelation or self-gift but of command requiring obedience. In the Christian tradition, praying to God is an act of relationship, of growing intimacy; but toward an AI deity, it would be only a request for action, suited to a problem-solving intelligence. As, at best, an inscrutable authority like Ockham's God, the AI could order all things for our enjoyment. However, a relationship with such a deity would be one not of self-gift and transcendent fulfillment, but only of pleasure definable according to our nature (or at least our dopamine and serotonin levels), falling far short of the integral fulfillment of personhood and consciousness promised by participation in the divine life. To "worship" AGI would not fulfill even natural human needs, as Christianity understands them.

Christian theology would see any positioning of AI as a deity (rather than as, say, a governmental assistant), as a form of idolatry—the worshiping of an image in place of God, prohibited in the first commandment.[15] AI is a deity unsuited to us because it is a god not of self-gift but merely of the efficacy that we have imagined or can imagine. It would be a god made in our own image and likeness, by human hands. The Book of Wisdom explains why such an idol cannot satisfy our need for relationship:

For a human being made them,
and one whose spirit is borrowed formed them;
for none can form gods that are like themselves.

---

[14] See, e.g., Mark Harris, "Inside the First Church of Artificial Intelligence," *Wired*, November 15, 2017, www.wired.com/story/anthony-levandowski-artificial-intelligence-reli-gion/.

[15] Green, "Epilogue on AI and Moral Theology," 232–233, 237–238.

People are mortal, and what they make with lawless hands is dead;
for they are better than the objects they worship,
since they have life, but the idols never had.[16]

When we are better than what we worship, our worship will carry us not beyond ourselves but simply back *into* ourselves, where we shall make ourselves to be less than we might otherwise have been.

AI as Idolatrous Instrument of Control

Beyond replacing God with a mirror of our own technocratic "intelligence," the hope of an AI deity is idolatrous in a more subtle sense. The idolater's fundamental error is not first to replace God with an image, but to use that image as a lever of control by which—even unconsciously—to replace God with himself. It would not be AI that we would make our god, in the end, but ourselves. For, ultimately, the AI would be an instrument by which we would seek to impose control over all things while—and this is crucial—losing sight of what exists beyond the domain that this control could define.[17] Reinhold Niebuhr once noted that dreams of ultimate power or control are a part of the human condition. We are the one creature with the mental ability to transcend both the mind itself, through self-contemplation, and the natural world, through technology. However, Niebuhr is adamant that this transcendence of our material environment does not obviate, and must not be permitted to obscure, our own physically limited nature. The problem here is "pride"—not a healthy regard for one's own achievements, but the insecurity-driven fantasy of being powerful over all and dependent on none. "Man is ignorant and involved in the limitations of the finite mind, but he pretends that he is not limited. He assumes that he can gradually transcend finite limitations until his mind becomes identical

---

[16] Wisdom 15:16–17.
[17] Paul Scherz, *Science and Christian Ethics* (Cambridge, UK: Cambridge University Press, 2019), 192.

with universal mind. All of his intellectual and cultural pursuits, therefore, become infected with the sin of pride."[18] Computer scientist Joseph Weizenbaum agrees: "The rhetoric of the technological *intelligentsia* may be attractive because it appears to be an invitation to reason. It is that, indeed. But . . . it urges instrumental reasonings, not authentic human rationality. It advertises easy and 'scientifically' endorsed answers to all conceivable problems. It exploits the myth of expertise."[19]

Niebuhr counsels us against making a god of human intelligence, for history continually shows the limits of understanding. Contemporary deep-learning AI is able to accept this point while still presenting us with the myth of final *control* over ourselves, our minds, the natural world, and our own creations. But Niebuhr warns that "the condition of finiteness . . . is a problem for which there is no solution by any human power."[20] Technology promises to put us in control like God, yet in the face of the inscrutable we have been ready to hand control over to our machines.

When the control that we seek is contoured by "pride" and its self-centered evaluation of the world, the control that we achieve is an illusory domination, another form of idolatry. Here, idolatry refers not to putting an image in place of God, but to replacing the true God with some lower reality—a reality that fits more comfortably within the idolater's own horizon of value and power. That is, the fantasy of control sets some lower thing—a thing that one can control—at the pinnacle of all hierarchies. By controlling the idol, we covertly set ourselves in the place of some divinity, living a fantasy of supreme value and total domination by ignoring all that remains beyond our manipulation. The Babylonians sacrificed to their statues to gain harvest-bringing storms and peace-bringing victories; Ebenezer Scrooge set money as his horizon of value and was self-blinded to

---

[18] Reinhold Niebuhr, *The Nature and Destiny of Man*, vol. 1: *Human Nature* (New York: Scribners, 1941), 178–179.

[19] Joseph Weizenbaum, *Computer Power and Human Reason: From Judgment to Calculation* (San Francisco: W. H. Freeman, 1976), 253.

[20] Reinhold Niebuhr, *The Nature and Destiny of Man*, vol. 2: *Human Destiny* (New York: Scribners, 1941), 295.

all that money could not buy. Both cases are idolatrous, because both deny our need for God by positioning ourselves as master of the levers of what *really* defines the universe. It is not evil—indeed it is *necessary*—to navigate reality in light of images, schemas, and devices that are oriented to action within reality. These tools become idols, however, when we cling to them in *place* of reality, denying all that cannot be encompassed within their horizon of apprehension and control.

This sort of idolatry of AI is particularly seductive, and dangerous, because contemporary machine learning techniques produce "black boxes," high-performing devices whose interior mechanisms usually cannot be represented in logical or conceptual terms.[21] And yet we follow their conclusions and recommendations for classification and action. In the physical world, a mangled steak quickly proves the dullness of the carving knife; but a black box that *seems* to perform in some subset of cases is followed blindly because we have trained it to generate a given action, without knowing whether a reliable mapping between situation and action has been achieved. Unable to see immediately whether or not the emperor has clothes, we allow the AI to idolatrously replace reality *because* it gives us the appearance of control over dynamics that we do not understand.

An excellent example of this is to be had in the saga of the COMPAS algorithm. Originally developed to predict the likelihood of recidivism among convicted criminals upon their release from prison, it was hoped by its developers hoped that it might guide parole officers in identifying and aiding high-risk parolees to avoid future crime. However, its simple numerical risk output has come to be used by judges to determine sentence lengths and even to set bail for defendants before trial. The algorithm gives

---

[21] As Peter Norvig wrote in 2011, a machine learning system like a neural network "describes what does happen, but it doesn't answer the question of why." We must "be satisfied with a function that accounts for the observed data well, and generalizes to new, previously unseen data well, but [that] may be expressed in a complex mathematical form that may bear no relation to the 'true' function's form" ("On Chomsky and the Two Cultures of Statistical Learning," http://norvig.com/chomsky.html).

the appearance of insight—but it is as if one developed an algorithm to assist in post-operative physical therapy and tried to apply it to the decision of whether or not to operate at all or of what procedure to conduct on the patient. A recidivism risk score is dubiously correlated with flight risk, and one certainly assumes quite a bit by applying that risk score to determining the length of sentence. The AI score is not even meaningful in those contexts, but to a judge faced with a difficult decision, it may seem an objective shortcut past subjective discernment. And so, it becomes an idol.[22]

Is all of this really a problem, though, when AI is used as it is *intended* to be used? After all, it is nothing new to say that, to a hammer, every problem looks like a nail. In other words, if we use trained AI systems for what they are useful for—if we accurately interpret their outputs' scope of meaning, to leave room for what they cannot say—then we will not go wrong. But this is not wholly true. In the first place, the pursuit of AGI leaves us with the question of whether we will really know when we have achieved it. On problems so complex that we ourselves cannot find the answer, can we know that the right answer has been found? AI will always find *an* answer, after all. Second, the concept of idolatry points to systemic cognitive effects stemming from how we treat even narrow AI. Too often, the machine learning systems of today are credited with an esoteric power to penetrate reality in a way that transcends the limits of human understanding. While they certainly exceed our powers of correlation and inference, contemporary techniques still *cannot* transcend the human

---

[22] On the COMPAS algorithm, see Angwin, Larson, Mattu, and Kirchner, "Machine Bias"; Jeff Larson, Surya Mattu, Lauren Kirchner and Julia Angwin, "How We Analyzed the COMPAS Recidivism Algorithm," *ProPublica*, May 23, 2016, www.propublica.org/article/how-we-analyzed-the-compas-recidivism-algorithm. Compounding the problem, it remains difficult to develop a standard of fairness that would overcome this bias without introducing others; see Sam Corbett-Davies, Emma Pierson, Avi Feller, and Sharad Goel, "A Computer Program Used for Bail and Sentencing Decisions Was Labeled Biased against Blacks. It's Actually Not That Clear," *Washington Post*, October 17, 2016, www.washingtonpost.com/news/monkey-cage/wp/2016/10/17/can-an-algorithm-be-racist-our-analysis-is-more-cautious-than-propublicas.

horizon because they map human-selected data points to human-interpreted outputs of inference and action.[23] In that the AI is a means of controlling and not just of responding to the world, we risk deforming the world by our use of it. If we neglect the crucial role of our own wills—that we, by our training of various forms of AI, have told them what to look for, or what to optimize, or even what to be unable to name in the world—then, as the psalm warns concerning idols, "Those who make them are like them; so are all who trust in them."[24] That is, having made our idols to manipulate some sphere, we may become bound by what they can represent and command.

A Catholic sacramental imagination may help us also to re-envision the proper place of technology. In the sacraments, God and humanity collaborate. In the Hebrew scriptures, we see God giving instructions for the construction of Noah's Ark[25] and the Ark of the Covenant.[26] The sacraments, similarly, are instituted and accomplished by God, but through human agency. Christ, at the Last Supper, did not take up grain and grapes, but bread and wine—already the work of human hands. God can take up our human making and its technologies, elevating them into something according to *God's* plan. God may give us the lead—as when Adam named the animals through the prelapsarian technology of language, and as Cain built cities[27]—but then God can use our language for self-revelation, as in scripture, and our cities as images of our ultimate destination, not the garden of paradise but the heavenly Jerusalem.[28] Modern technological utopias, often implicitly or explicitly, take the form of a heavenly city, but one of our making. There is good reason not to leave

---

[23] See Jordan Joseph Wales, "Metaphysics, Meaning, and Morality: A Theological Reflection on A.I.," *Journal of Moral Theology* 11, Special Issue 1 (March 2022): 157–181, doi.org/10.55476/001c.34129.
[24] Psalm 115:8.
[25] Genesis 6.
[26] Exodus 25.
[27] Genesis 2, 4.
[28] Philippians 3:20; Hebrews 13:14.

this fantasy to others but to work with Christian hope for what can be accomplished in this world, while always relativizing its finality. The final city comes down from heaven;[29] it cannot ultimately be of our making but only of God's, for it fulfills and transcends what we glimpse through our endeavors. In our technological labors, we collaborate with God—yes, to relieve our estate, but also and more fundamentally to make visible and to ease the expression in this earthly life of that relational self-gift for which human beings are made. We are collaborators with God, but we are so because we are *made* makers, and so our making most fulfills our nature when it speaks most clearly of God's.[30]

Conclusion

While many rightly worry whether future AI, by which we hope to secure our material prosperity, will consummate or destroy our society's technocratic dreams, we argue that, too often, this conversation is limited by its terms. By first engaging, both historically and theologically, the anthropological questions raised by artificial intelligence (chapter 2), we developed a vision of the person and of intelligence by which to illuminate the nature and meaning of "sociable" AI, while arguing also for an account of consciousness that reckons with the felt reality of being in the world rather than reduce consciousness to some functional role in the production of behavior (chapter 3). Throughout, we have argued against the implications of the technocratic paradigm, by which intelligence and personhood are reduced to what can be measured quantitatively. For, under these reductions, the subjective self-gift that makes human life and relationships most meaningful is simply lost from view. The richer view that we propose—of the person as a subject capable of self-gift in empathic encounter, and of intelligence as not just a skill in manipulating matter but a loving insight into reality—disrupts easy identifications between human

---

[29] Revelation 21:2.
[30] See also Anselm Ramelow, "Artificial Intelligence: Religion of Technology," in *The New Apologetics*, ed. Matthew Nelson (Washington, DC: Word on Fire Institute, 2022).

beings and their mechanisms. In particular, conscious experience is not reducible to behavior, nor even fungible with some interior functionality of a mind-like machine, but is necessarily intrinsic to the relational sphere of the "personal" and, in the case of persons at least, the "intelligent."

What is gained by this view? When the full reality of the human person and of human relationships is preserved, we can make better sense of sociable AI, and of how our "relationships" with them can both facilitate and degrade the development of our own personhood (chapter 4). Moreover, by appreciating more precisely the distinctive technological achievements of AI, we avoid ascribing to them an insight beyond the scope of their actual applicability (chapter 5). It is proper to human beings, Aristotle tells us, to seek the causes of things. We lead ourselves astray when, seeking control over causes and cases that we do not understand, we apply our AI to tasks beyond their capacities. As always, the terms within which we set these conversations—like the labeling of an AI's training data and outputs—will establish just what will remain visible and, consequently, what we will best be able to foster, in our emerging AI-saturated society.

With personhood and relational encounter at the center of our conversation, we turn to the Catholic social vision that flows from the Church's account of the person, reflecting on how a true anthropology, rooted in self-giving encounter, might be applied to the design and proper use of AI-powered devices in daily life. Like all technologies, AI amplifies human traits and abilities. An approach to AI centered on the human person has the potential to amplify human dignity, while an approach centered on material control will, by its impoverished approach to human persons, impoverish in turn the scope of human life. In other words, it will amplify human sin.

Part II

Ethical Challenges with AI

CHAPTER 6

AI AND CATHOLIC SOCIAL TEACHING

Pope Francis identifies "the digital galaxy . . . specifically artificial intelligence," as located "at the very heart of the epochal change we are experiencing" in today's world.[1] Therefore, he calls on people to undertake the "ethical development of algorithms, and in this way, to help create a new ethics for our time."[2] As chapter 1 discussed, many political bodies, private organizations, and even technology companies have made similar calls for an ethics of AI.[3] Their concerns are warranted. AI systems are transforming the social and political landscape, as well as reshaping private life, in part by eroding the boundaries between public and private.

In this part of the volume, we respond to Pope Francis's call with an outline of an AI ethics that can assist individuals, institutions, and civil society in engaging personal, social, and political concerns related to AI in light of the Catholic theological and moral tradition. This part provides an overview of many of the concrete ethical problems that we face and offers responses directed to these problems. In doing so, we aim to assist society

---

[1] Pope Francis, "To Participants in the Plenary Assembly of the Pontifical Academy for Life," February 28, 2020, www.vatican.va/content/francesco/en/speeches/2020/february/documents/papa-francesco_20200228_accademia-perlavita.html.

[2] Pope Francis, "To Participants in the Congress on 'Child Dignity in the Digital World,'" November 14, 2019, www.vatican.va/content/francesco/en/speeches/2019/november/documents/papa-francesco_20191114_convegno-child+dignity.html.

[3] E.g., UNESCO, "Recommendation on the Ethics of Artificial Intelligence," *UNESCO*, November 21, 2021, unesdoc.unesco.org/ark:/48223/pf0000381137; Office of Science and Technology Policy of the White House, "Blueprint for an AI Bill of Rights: Making Automated Systems Work for the American People," 2022, www.whitehouse.gov/wp-content/uploads/2022/10/Blueprint-for-an-AI-Bill-of-Rights.pdf; Pontifical Academy for Life, "Rome Call," 2020.

both in realizing the great goods that this fruit of human ingenuity can provide and in avoiding its potential dangers. Of course, AI is developing so rapidly and in so many areas of contemporary society that our analysis can only be partial. Hopefully, though, it can provide a framework for addressing the many issues that will continue to arise in AI ethics. To address the novel problems of AI, in this chapter we will develop a framework rooted in Catholic social thought, especially the magisterial teachings of Pope Francis. Next, we will investigate the issues emerging with the introduction of AI into eight different spheres (family, education, healthcare, politics, the military, work, culture, and the environment) before offering recommendations for five different standpoints from which we might view AI (as users, as designers and engineers, as policy makers and voters, as employers and employees, and as relational beings).

Chapter 1 surveyed insights into AI from the many secular works on AI ethics and from the reflections of other religious traditions. These reflections provide many resources that we use in our critique of contemporary AI practices and for our ethical response to AI. Moreover, Pope Francis's emphasis on a culture of encounter and the anthropological vision described in the first part guide our reflections on and response to AI. Simply put, for Francis, encounter with other people, especially the disadvantaged, is crucial to our flourishing as social creatures. More fundamentally, though, encounter with other humans is an encounter with reality, which, in Francis's commonly used formula, is always greater than ideas. Reality, whether in the form of the neighbor, of the natural world, or of God, is worthy of contemplation and engagement. The dangers that we see in AI arise in part from its tremendous power to distract us from this encounter with reality, to engage others and the environment as mere material for use, to drive us to act according to the desires of those who control these technologies. It is thus crucial that we discover how to use AI to assist us in encountering reality and serving others. To do so, it is necessary to cultivate the gaze of the loving

Samaritan, who remained attentive to his surroundings, responded to concrete needs, and gave selflessly as a loving neighbor.

Catholic Social Teaching

Pope Leo XIII inaugurated the modern era of Catholic social teaching with the publication of *Rerum Novarum* in 1891, which called on people of faith conscientiously to evaluate the Industrial Revolution, driven by efficiency and profit motives tightly bound to technological development: "No [one] may with impunity outrage that human dignity which God treats with great reverence. . . . [One] cannot give up [one's] soul to servitude, for it is not one's own rights which are here in question, but the rights of God, the most sacred and inviolable of rights."[4] Leo ushered in a Catholic response to modern industry that turned toward the human worker and against an uncritical acceptance of the overwhelming and interacting forces of markets, technology, and ideologies of progress.

In papal documents leading up to the Second Vatican Council, as well as in the Council itself, the Church continued to affirm this defense of the modern worker while extending a voice of dialogue to the quickly advancing fields of science and technology. The importance of the divinely-established human dignity of all people is increasingly characterized in conciliar documents in a language of the "common good" that emphasizes the active role that all persons, no matter their faith, are to take in building a better world.

During the Second Vatican Council, this entreaty to persons of good will in the context of the common good was paired with positive evaluations of science and technology. *Gaudium et Spes* noted, "If methodical investigation within every branch of learning is carried out in a genuinely scientific manner and in accord with moral norms, it never truly conflicts with faith, for earthly matters and the concerns of faith derive from the same God."[5] The conciliar document ends with a call for

---

[4] *Rerum Novarum*, § 40.
[5] *Gaudium et Spes*, § 36.

people of faith to engage science and technology in the spirit of seeking to weave such discoveries into "Christian morality and the teaching of Christian doctrine, so that their religious culture and morality may keep pace with scientific knowledge and with the constantly progressing technology. Thus, they will be able to interpret and evaluate all things in a truly Christian spirit."[6] Our engagement with AI should be considered a response to that conciliar call.

As with the technologies of the Industrial Revolution, contemporary advanced technologies present a danger of betraying human dignity for the sake of efficiency, beliefs in progress, and profit. Furthermore, these technologies offer possibilities for the accumulation of corporate, military, and political power evident in practices like surveillance and warfare and in cultures of dehumanization and violence. Yet there is hope in a common good and a common vision for universal human flourishing in the context of scientific and technological developments. From Pope Leo XIII to Pope Benedict XVI, the Church has emphasized that the marvels of science and technology can serve the ends of a common human good and a shared humanity.[7] Pope Francis has embraced this emphasis and teaching and furthered it in the face of the emergence of AI.

Pope Francis, the Joy of the Gospel, and AI

Pope Francis has signaled in word and deed this fundamental openness of the Church to AI and to working with persons of good will on AI's ongoing developments. In 2019, he told participants in the congress on The Common Good in the Digital Age: "A better world is possible thanks to technological progress, if this is accompanied by an ethic inspired by a vision of the common good, an ethic of freedom, responsibility and

---

[6] *Gaudium et Spes*, § 62.
[7] *Rerum Novarum*, § 1; Pius, XI, *Quadragesimo Anno*, § 72; John XXIII, *Mater et Magistra*, §§ 37–54; John XXIII, *Pacem in Terris*, §§ 2–3, 150; *Gaudium et Spes*, §§ 57, 62, 64; Paul VI, *Populorum Progressio*, §§ 34, 72; Paul VI, *Octogesima Adveniens*, § 22; John Paul II, *Centesimus Annus*, § 32; Benedict XVI, *Caritas in Veritate*, §§ 68–77.

fraternity, capable of fostering the full development of people in relation to others and to the whole of creation."[8] More recently, Francis renewed earlier magisterial themes when he invited persons of good will working on AI to engage in dialogue with the Church in an effort to create a "culture that places this technology at the service of the common good of all and of the care of our common home."[9]

It is important to understand Pope Francis's distinctive approach to a technology like AI. Though God's creation was tainted by human sin, the new creation inaugurated by Christ's incarnation and brought about in the Paschal Mystery inspires the ultimate joy of a redeemed world. We are invited to delight in this restoration. If we forget this joy of creation and redemption, we will likewise miss what Pope Francis points us toward in our engagement with the world. When humans participate in the work of God's creation through building new technologies, they have the ability to participate in the delight of God's goodness and generosity in bearing a gift of one's ingenuity. But our inventions that impact others should harmonize with their flourishing. In every age, humans are called to protect the dignity of the person and all of God's beloved creation: "Small yet strong in the love of God, like Saint Francis of Assisi, all of us, as Christians, are called to watch over and protect the fragile world in which we live, and all its peoples."[10] Creation is "in a state of journeying" toward its perfection.[11] The loving God entrusts both the *life* of creation and the *activity* of creating to humanity. The work of human hands is meant to

---

[8] Pope Francis, "Audience with Participants in the Seminar 'The Common Good in the Digital Age,' promoted by the Pontifical Council for Culture and the Dicastery for Promoting Integral Human Development," September 27, 2019, press.vatican.va/content/salastampa/en/bollettino/pubblico/2019/09/27/190927a.html.

[9] Pope Francis, "Address to Participants in the 'Rome Call' Meeting Promoted by the RenAIssance Foundation," January 10, 2023, www.vatican.va/content/francesco/en/speeches/2023/january/documents/20230110-incontro-romecall.html.

[10] Francis, *Evangelii Gaudium*, § 216. There are important affinities between these fundamental assumptions of Catholic social teaching and what is called the "cultural mandate" in the Reformed Christian tradition.

[11] *Catechism of the Catholic Church*, October 11, 1992, § 302.

contribute to God's plan for the universe. One vital dimension of this work includes the construction of a just society in which members may look upon one another with a joy like the Redeemer's: "Standing before him with open hearts, letting him look at us, we see that gaze of love."[12] We also seek to reflect a gaze of joy that recognizes one another's inherent goodness, a joy that anticipates the shared destiny of full eschatological communion. "For if we have received the love which restores meaning to our lives, how can we fail to share that love with others?"[13]

The Church assists creation in seeking its true joy. In turning to new questions surrounding the development and deployment of AI, humanity ought to remain steadfast in its commitment to seek the joy of the universe without alienating or abandoning any aspect of God's created gifts. Pope Francis calls for a "missionary outreach" to share the gospel. Further, he emphasizes that this joyful, open, missionary spirit should inform the Church's social commitments to dialogue with the engineers, developers, and scholars who work on the frontlines of these unfolding ethical questions.[14] To be sure, in this work many wrong turns are readily available. In *Evangelii Gaudium*, Pope Francis quotes from Pope Paul VI's *Gaudete in Domino* to warn that "technological society has succeeded in multiplying occasions of pleasure, yet has found it very difficult to engender joy."[15] But the possibility of such missteps cannot erase the worthy goal of aligning technology with beatitude as much as possible. Facilitating encounters with divine love is the key to motivating the communal responsibility for directing technological development toward the service of God and God's works, and thus toward the reality of true joy.

---

[12] *Evangelii Gaudium*, § 264.
[13] *Evangelii Gaudium*, § 8.
[14] *Evangelii Gaudium*, § 133.
[15] Paul VI, *Gaudete in Domino*, § 292, www.vatican.va/content/paul-vi/en/apost_exhortations/documents/hf_p-vi_exh_19750509_gaudete-in-domino.html.

Pope Francis, Catholic Social Teaching, and Concerns about AI

But, for Pope Francis, the joy inspired by the Gospel is not a naïveté about AI and other technologies. Rather, the promise of joy in the Gospel provides the ground to demand justice for persons affected by AI. AI is a set of tools with enormous potential. Yet Catholic social teaching invites us to critical engagement with these possibilities through three intersecting insights about the nature of technology.

First, technologies are not morally neutral. In any given context, a technology facilitates and encourages some uses more than others. As Pope Francis writes, "Technological products are not neutral, for they create a framework which ends up conditioning lifestyles and shaping social possibilities along the lines dictated by the interests of certain powerful groups."[16] These built-in possibilities often result from the intentions of the people who design the technology, and they shape the effects of that technology in the world.

Second, technologies are not morally determinate. Technologies inevitably *also* afford uses (whether good or ill) apart from what their designers intend; people often use technologies in creative and unforeseen ways. A technology that is designed for destructive ends can be used for productive ones, and *vice versa*. People bear moral responsibility for *how* they use technologies.

Third, we ought to focus on technologies not in isolation, but within their larger social contexts. The effects of technologies in the world are shaped by those with the power to deploy these technologies and by the social contexts in which the technologies are deployed. As discussed in previous sections, Pope Francis critiques the technocratic paradigm, which leaves us with a degraded way of interacting with creation. We see the physical world as mere material for use, losing sight of the reality in front of us, charged with meaning and purpose. Instead, we instrumentalize

---

[16] *Laudato Si'*, § 107; cf. § 114.

everything around us, including our neighbor. In other words, our present cultural moment teaches us to think of "technological progress" as an unequivocal good. We presume that more powerful technologies automatically advance shared human flourishing. This worldview encourages destructive exploitation of both humans and nature.

In *Fratelli Tutti*, Pope Francis adds the bonds of human fraternity to the casualties of modern culture and places technology at the center of a prophetic critique of several current social maladies. When people—often the wealthy and powerful—use technologies in immoral and unwise ways, this harms the fraternal bonds that are necessary for a flourishing society. Pope Francis critiques how corporations and individual bad actors undermine peaceful co-existence through the multiplication of disinformation. He expresses deep concern with how "virtual reality" can entail self-deception whereby people forget "the truly real."[17] Here AI technologies can be tools that separate us from reality and from one another, trapping us in echo chambers or surrounding us with distorting mirrors that prevent us from perceiving and encountering others—and especially others who are unlike us. In this way, AI can deter us from engaging in the positive goods of a "culture of encounter." Instead, AI can facilitate what the encyclical warns against: "present-day attempts to eliminate or ignore others."[18] At the same time, AI can be part of a culture of "constant surveillance,"[19] undermining human dignity via the exploitation of data by powerful forces.

Another example is the ways that people and companies deploy technologies to increase economic benefit for the wealthy and powerful while causing unemployment and despair for others. As Pope Francis writes, our present moment exhibits "an obsession with reducing labor costs with no concern for its grave consequences, since the unemployment

---

[17] *Fratelli Tutti*, § 33. In §§ 47–50, Francis describes how information technologies distort reality and sever us from genuine encounter.
[18] *Fratelli Tutti*, § 6.
[19] *Fratelli Tutti*, § 42.

that it directly generates leads to the expansion of poverty."[20] AI can become a tool for economic inequality rather than for shared flourishing.

AI technologies can also obscure human agency and undermine moral accountability. As Pope Francis writes, injustice can "hide and spread behind new technologies."[21] AI can obscure the human agents who are responsible for deploying it, shielding individuals from legal or financial consequences, but also separate people from an awareness of their own moral responsibility. More broadly, AI technologies often mediate digitally between people, obscuring the agency, labor, knowledge, and personhood of our distant brothers and sisters through a personified "immediacy" of the AI system. In the next chapter, we will explore Pope Francis's prophetic critique more extensively. For now, these examples are sufficient to remind us that the use of AI demands moral discernment in light of the Christian call to justice, love, and community.

AI technologies are also enmeshed with the political and economic interests of those who control these powerful tools. This is, in part, because AI technologies often depend upon economies of scale. At least in their current configurations, they tend toward the centralized and the global. They contribute to what *Fratelli Tutti* describes as "an increasingly massified world that promotes individual interests and weakens the communitarian dimension of life." For Francis, "this kind of globalism strengthens the identity of the more powerful, who can protect themselves, but it tends to diminish the identity of the weaker and poorer regions, making them more vulnerable and dependent."[22] It may be possible to imagine and to build forms of AI that embrace the local and the situated,[23] but this would diverge from the massive corporate infrastructures on which current forms of AI depend. We observe "huge economic interests operating in the digital world, capable of exercising

---

[20] *Fratelli Tutti*, § 20; cf. § 31.
[21] *Fratelli Tutti*, § 27.
[22] *Fratelli Tutti*, § 12.
[23] *Fratelli Tutti*, § 14.

forms of control as subtle as they are invasive, creating mechanisms for the manipulation of consciences and of the democratic process."[24]

This situation compels us to ask: Are today's AI tools designed and configured for the flourishing of communities with varied interests and varied cultural contexts? Or does their anonymity as tools of "technological progress" serve the interests of the powerful while subverting the communities and ethical claims of others? Might the technological paradigm even deceive us into thinking that the anonymous AI represents the common good? Once again, these moral hazards extend to other technologies beyond AI. Yet Catholic social teaching urges us to think critically about how people—ourselves and others—use and benefit from these tools. Who benefits? Who is left out? How do these tools contribute to shared flourishing? And when do they fail to do so?

AI and the Resources of Catholic Social Teaching

Pope Francis's reflections on AI are shaped by living Jesus's Gospel, Catholic social teaching, and the experience of communities and individuals, particularly the poor. This threefold approach provides a way for the Church to answer such questions as "Who benefits?" and "Who should benefit?"

First, Pope Francis invites believers to renew their spiritual relationship with Jesus within the ecclesial community and in the whole society. This is what characterizes Christian discipleship. Hence, while considering the concrete implications of artificial intelligence, Francis calls Christians to rely on their relationship with Jesus to inform their being, reasoning, discerning, and acting.

Second, the Second Vatican Council's engagement with the world animates a critical, collaborative, and active presence in society that empowers people and nourishes personal and communal discernment. At the same time, in addressing the complexity of today's pluralistic and

---

[24] *Fratelli Tutti*, § 45.

globalized world and the ethical challenges that concern technologies like AI, Pope Francis aims at fostering the common good at the planetary level, from confessional circles and ecclesial contexts to interreligious interactions and society at large. With its commitment to promoting social justice, solidarity, and subsidiarity, Catholic social teaching offers a long-standing tradition to all persons of good will that can guide efforts to engage AI in the spirit of seeking to do justice in the world.

As the Second Vatican Council stressed, the common good is "the sum of those conditions of social life which allow social groups and their individual members relatively thorough and ready access to their own fulfillment, [and] today takes on an increasingly universal complexion and consequently involves rights and duties with respect to the whole human race."[25] The common good is the shared project of all in society and includes the goods of social relationship. In *Laudato Si'*, Pope Francis definitively extended the meaning of the common good to include our common home, the Earth. He has also pointedly called for a renewed reflection on human rights and duties as key aspects of the challenge of the common good in the time of AI.[26]

Moreover, as John Paul II affirmed, "Solidarity is not a feeling of vague compassion or shallow distress at the misfortunes of so many people, both near and far. On the contrary, it is a *firm and persevering determination* to commit oneself to the *common good*; that is to say, to the good of each and every individual, because we are all really responsible *for all*."[27]

The principle of subsidiarity aims at promoting the common good, first, by reclaiming the right of groups and local organizations to determine and manage their local needs by fostering reciprocity between smaller and larger social groups and authorities. Second, governments have the duty to

---

[25] *Gaudium et Spes*, § 26.
[26] Francis, "To Participants in the Plenary Assembly of the Pontifical Academy for Life." February 28, 2020, www.vatican.va/content/francesco/en/speeches/2020/february/documents/papa-francesco_20200228_accademia-perlavita.html.
[27] John Paul II, *Sollicitudo Rei Socialis*, § 38.

intervene in the service of their citizens when smaller groups are unable to accomplish important tasks of justice. Moreover, the understanding of a comprehensive and shared common good that characterizes Catholic social teaching, and that animates Pope Francis's teaching and action, is rooted in the *experience* of people, particularly of those who are marginalized and excluded, an experience that is only properly taken into account through subsidiarity. Additionally, subsidiarity helps to prevent both moral and political deskilling by encouraging the wide cultivation of moral and political skills.

Francis is aware that AI, so increasingly present in society, affects how people understand today's world, technology, and themselves, and how AI can influence their decisions. For Francis, however, such an awareness is necessary but not sufficient; social analysis is also needed. By critically considering the experience of economic and social interactions, and how they should aim at promoting the common good, the Pope wants to avoid persons being reduced to consumers through the witting and unwitting control and manipulation made possible by the ways AI is used to sift through personal data. Moreover, developments in artificial intelligence should not threaten people's freedom, increase inequities, or become a tool by which the powerful, rich, and wealthy may undermine our democratic norms.

For Pope Francis, the Gospel invites us to attentive care in the spirit of the Good Samaritan as we approach the challenge of artificial intelligence.[28] By following in the footsteps of the Good Samaritan, the Pope invites us to see AI in the light of those who are marginalized and excluded, left to struggle on the sides of too many busy roads across the Earth.

---

[28] Luke 10:25–37 and Francis, "Message for the 48th World Communications Day: Communication at the Service of an Authentic Culture of Encounter," June 1, 2014, www.vatican.va/content/francesco/en/messages/communications/documents/papa-francesco_20140124_messaggio-comunicazioni-sociali.html.

Conclusion

In closing, it is worth noting a distinctive aspect of Pope Francis's approach to Catholic social teaching and AI: the role of the family. He has said often that we cannot leave the development of AI to training in technical skills alone. Instead, we should turn to mediating institutions to take on the role of formation in virtues, norms, and principles relevant to AI in its social dimensions. One such institution, he pointedly notes, is the family.

Not only is the family "the principal agent of an integral ecology,"[29] but it is also the "workshop"[30] where we first learn the foundations of social responsibility and put them into practice. Close ties within a smaller common home are nurtured, and the larger common home that encompasses the world benefits from the resulting mature virtues. For example, in the family one can form the virtue of "tenderness" to counter a world where social media and technology entrench "superficial relationships."[31] Additionally, the home can fortify the theological virtues, as Pope Francis recognizes: "In our own day, dominated by stress and rapid technological advances, one of the most important tasks of families is to provide an education in hope."[32] The family is where the formation of the person begins and where a sense of fidelity toward social relationships takes root. Pope Francis has consistently recognized this key familial exercise of fostering Catholic social teaching: "The family is the primary setting for socialization since it is where we first learn to relate to others, to listen and share, to be patient and show respect, to help one another and live as one. The task of education is to make us sense that the world and society are also our home; it trains us how to live together in this greater home. In the

---

[29] "Catechesis (September 30, 2015)," *L'Osservatore Romano*, October 1, 2015, 8.
[30] John Paul II, "General Audience," December 1, 1999, § 4, www.vatican.va/content/john-paul-ii/en/audiences/1999/documents/hf_jp-ii_aud_01121999.html.
[31] Francis, *Amoris Laetitia*, § 28.
[32] *Amoris Laetitia*, § 275.

family, we learn closeness, care and respect for others."[33] Familial demands can challenge capitulation to the self-serving efficiency of technological fixes and instead allow one to taste the need for an enduring integral ecology that promotes the lifelong flourishing of its members. Indeed, for Pope Francis, the family offers a broad and deep formation in the social care essential to engagement with the implications of a powerful technology like AI, which is why we will begin our exploration of the specific challenges of AI in the next chapter with the sphere of the family.

---

[33] *Amoris Laetitia*, § 276.

Chapter 7

The Promises and Pitfalls of AI in Contemporary Life

Catholic social teaching yields the broad guidelines and interpretive framework discussed in the last chapter, but these guidelines ought to be applied to various situations. Such application is especially challenging in relation to AI, given its rapidly expanding effects on many spheres of life and society. This chapter takes the next step in that work of application by specifically examining the impact AI is already having in some of the most important spheres of contemporary life. In the following sections, AI's effects are compared to an ideal Catholic vision of each sphere of society, although with the understanding that, in a fallen world, this ideal is never realized by any actual family, hospital, school, or other sphere. Every actual human institution is marred by sin, although intimations of the ideal are contained in even the most broken relationship. The goal of this chapter is to identify how AI systems can make the realization of the ideal even more difficult. To serve this purpose, the chapter articulates the vision and the challenges at the same time. We will begin with how AI is shaping more intimate spheres of encounter, such as the family, before expanding to look at AI's effects on our broader social systems, like government and the economy.

Sphere of the Family

Family is a profound means through which God reveals the expanse and depth of Divine love.[1] "The Church is God's family in the world," as Benedict XVI wrote, and God "wishes to make humanity a single family in his Son."[2] Technology ought to be assessed in light of whether and to what extent it can serve the *telos* of the human person and society.[3] Ultimately, this *telos* involves an eternal relationship between an individual person and the loving God, with the earthly community striving to point toward and anticipate the perfection of the heavenly community. The ministry of the Christian family fits into this *telos* by providing a context where the love of God is first nurtured and encouraged in the human heart, and where people first learn to care for their surrounding community members.[4] The spontaneous bonds of a family inspire reverence toward its serious responsibilities. Even so, family members are charged with caring for one another unconditionally, even when it is difficult to do so.

---

[1] For example consider the familial language in the following scripture passages: "Thus says the Lord: Israel is my son, my firstborn" (Exodus 4:22); "I will betroth you to me forever" (Hosea 2:21); "He destined us for adoption to himself through Jesus Christ, in accord with the favor of his will" (Ephesians 1:5).

[2] Benedict XVI, *Deus Caritas Est*, §§ 25, 19.

[3] Marius Dorobantu, Brian Patrick Green, Anselm Ramelow, and Eric Salobir, "Being Human in the Age of AI," *OPTIC Network* (2022): 21–22, research.vu.nl/ws/portalfiles/portal/181977228/humain_a_lage_de_lIA_VF2_compressed_1_.pdf.

[4] As Francis notes, "The family is thus the place where parents become their children's first teachers in the faith" (*Amoris Laetitia*, § 16). He continues, "No one can think that the weakening of the family as that natural society founded on marriage will prove beneficial to society as a whole. The contrary is true: it poses a threat to the mature growth of individuals, the cultivation of community values and the moral progress of cities and countries" (*Amoris Laetitia*, § 52). His comments echo the Second Vatican Council: "This mission—to be the first and vital cell of society—the family has received from God. It will fulfill this mission it is appears as the domestic sanctuary of the Church by reason of the mutual affection of its members and the prayer that they offer to God in common, if the whole family makes itself a part of the liturgical worship of the Church, and if it provides active hospitality and promotes justice and other good works for the service of all the brethren in need" (Vatican Council II, *Apostolicam Actuositatem*, § 11).

Simultaneously, the members of the Christian family should hold one another accountable in demonstrating authentic charity and striving toward a full development of the virtues.

Family also invites those in need into its embrace. This is evident when new children or aged loved ones join the home, or when any other family member or community member simply requires care. Likewise, the family is called to model and implement the hospitality of the wider nation in their encounter with other families in need. In the Letter to the Hebrews, we read the request, "Let mutual love continue. Do not neglect hospitality, for through it some have unknowingly entertained angels."[5] The reference is to Abraham and Sarah, who showcased this hospitality when they welcomed the three strangers who prophesied to them about their promised child.[6] Many families seek the same excitement and diligence in care for their community, even its newest members or temporary pilgrims. AI can both contribute to the mission of the Christian family to participate in divine charity as well as challenge this mission.

Challenges from AI to the Family

The proper role of AI in the family ought to be discerned in response to the preceding considerations about the family's nature, purpose, and intrinsic dignity. Moreover, given the central role of families in the course of human lives, we should remember that harms done to families are harms done to people. The vital role played by families in protecting human dignity entails that families deserve special consideration in technological development and particular protection against the technocratic paradigm.

Families are not ordered to efficiency; they are ordered to love, and love is, in itself and vitally, an often inefficient structure. Families are not about "producing" anything; they are about expressing and receiving love that

---

[5] Hebrews 13:1–2.

[6] "Looking up, [Abraham] saw three men standing near him. When he saw them, he ran from the entrance of the tent to greet them; and bowing to the ground, he said: 'Sir, if it please you, do not go on past your servant'" (Genesis 18:2–3).

reflects the love of God toward every human being. This love may often be fruitful, as with the conceiving and raising of children, but the family should not be understood only according to the logic of optimized efficiency or utility. Humans are not products, and neither are relationships or love itself. Because AI often instantiates the technocratic paradigm—forwarding goals such as optimization, maximization, and efficiency—the direct points of connection between families and AI should be carefully and continuously scrutinized. In all familial relationships love should come first.

AI is already mediating the formation of human relationships through various dating apps, thus shaping family dynamics from the family's founding moments. For example, dating apps use algorithms to determine the likelihood of compatibility. Match suggestions are calculated based on the preferences demonstrated by the user. Thus, an individual may be less likely to find unexpected qualities outside guiding search criteria. The serendipitous encounter of another that inspires an investigation into the mystery of a personality is circumvented for an efficient means of meeting expectations. Dating apps may impart a mentality of consumerism and entitlement to the practice of dating. Furthermore, dating algorithms can inadvertently further eugenic undertones.

This subtle shaping of family by technocracy from its most incipient stage is worth noting, as these trends may serve the good not of the family but of app developers who may exploit their users as sources of revenue. This subjugation of family life to the technocratic paradigm should give us pause to consider how it might also be used to undermine familial relationships at later stages.

In addition to mediating how couples may meet, in some cases AI is also used to substitute for human beings through apps that imitate human speech via text and simulate romantic interest. These uses of AI are highly skewed toward exploitation and distract people from real human beings and real relationships. Frivolous pleasures can distract us from breaking out of loneliness to commit to lasting relationships that seek authentic joy and in which patient and prodigal mutual attention becomes possible.[7] As Pope Francis writes, "The Gospel of the family [i]s a joy that 'fills hearts and lives.'"[8] As family members can become entertained by a virtual world available through AI programs, this could insulate family interests and distract the family from their responsibilities to serve their community. Moreover, "narcissism makes people incapable of looking beyond themselves, beyond their own desires and needs."[9] This can detract from the missionary calling of the familial vocation.[10] AI that draws people away from each other and into a world of fakeness and simulation endangers the individuals involved and the future of society by diverting people away from the formation of real families. Needless to say, any use of AI or robotics to completely replace people in relationships is also destructive to individuals, families, and society, and should be opposed.

As we avoid exploitative and substitutive uses of AI, we must also take care not to become so dependent on AI that we cannot live without it, whether psychologically, socially, or physically. The risk of technological dependency is constantly growing—we depend on electricity, computers, the internet, and AI—but we should also remember simpler ways of living. Dependency and associated deskilling should remain on our minds as we balance the use of technology going forward.[11] This reminder is especially relevant for family life. Love, caring, and compassion are moral skills—indeed, some of the most important skills for any human to learn. We

---

[7] Francis writes that "The fear of loneliness and the desire for stability and fidelity exist side by side with a growing fear of entrapment in a relationship that could hamper the achievement of one's personal goals" (*Amoris Laetitia*, § 34). He also points to "the fears associated with permanent commitment, the obsession with free time, and those relationships that weigh costs and benefits for the sake of remedying loneliness, providing protection, or offering some service" as examples of "cultural decline that fails to promote love or self-giving" (§ 39).

[8] *Amoris Laetitia*, § 200, quoting *Evangelii Gaudium*, § 1.

[9] *Amoris Laetitia*, § 39.

[10] "The Christian family's faith and evangelizing mission also possesses this catholic missionary inspiration" (John Paul II, *Familiaris Consortio*, § 54).

[11] Brian Patrick Green, "Ethical Reflections on Artificial Intelligence," *Scientia et Fides* 6, no. 2 (2018): 21–22, dadun.unav.edu/bitstream/10171/58244/1/01.pdf.

should make sure that as we grow in dependency on technology, which seems inevitable if society continues on its current trajectory, we do not grow to depend on it for developing our moral skills[12] and for our life in the family context, especially when it comes to love, caring, and compassion.

AI can also influence the founding moments of a family in the context of perinatal medicine. Advancements in technology have offered significant strides in decreasing both infant mortality and maternal mortality rates, overall contributing to safer pregnancies and births. With this also comes the risk of overmedicalizing the birthing experience to the point of undervaluing the embodiment and wisdom of the mother as well as imposing a system of medical surveillance on families and children.[13] The use of AI in medicine also risks evaluating future offspring by their genetic predispositions, as though lives could be forecast and then approved or rejected. This intrusion of the technocratic paradigm, in the form of a eugenic mentality, into reproduction undermines the dignity of human life. In response, we should recall the universal love of God for all human lives. These threats can cause children—and humanity in general— to be viewed as manufactured products rather than provide to them "the look of love which they crave."[14] Contrastingly, in welcoming members with special needs, "the family can discover, together with the Christian community, new approaches, new ways of acting, a different way of understanding and identifying with others, by welcoming and caring for

---

[12] Vallor, "Moral Deskilling and Upskilling."

[13] This argument about overmedicalizing births is made by Amy Laura Hall in *Conceiving Parenthood: American Protestantism and the Spirit of Reproduction* (Grand Rapids, MI: Eerdmans, 2007). Medical surveillance is criticized by Michel Foucault in *The Birth of the Clinic: An Archeology of Medical Perception* (New York: Vintage Books, 1994).

[14] This quote is from *Caritas in Veritate*, § 12. Some of these questions are engaged by Oliver O'Donovan in *Begotten or Made? Human Procreation and Medical Technique* (Oxford: Oxford University Press, 2002). For a treatment of the question of the ethics of genetic engineering in relation to disability identity, see Mariele Courtois, "Biomedical Challenges to Identity and Parenthood: An Investigation into the Ethics of Genetic Technologies at the Beginning of Life" (PhD diss., The Catholic University of America, 2022).

the mystery of the frailty of human life."[15] Parents are called to offer the same type of generous love as Christ's human parents offered to their child, a love that did not seek ownership of him, but rather welcomed all into the presence of the Savior, as evidenced by the attendance of shepherds at the nativity.[16] In the scenes of both the presentation of the infant Jesus in the temple and the finding of Jesus in the temple, we also witness Mary and Joseph's awareness that their child is not their own to possess but is rather an offering for the good of all the universe.[17]

Additionally, the fact that intergenerational care can be mediated by AI presents particular challenges. While assistance in care can make it more feasible to provide for the needs of loved ones and perhaps even allow them to live comfortably at home rather than in alternative facilities, it also renders it easier for families to detach themselves from care. New capabilities of AI to optimize care call into question how best to offer loving care and how it should be accompanied by embodied interactions. Some individuals may argue that outsourcing more mundane tasks may reserve precious time for interpersonal communication. This distinction, however, risks misunderstanding charity, which addresses the whole person and which may be communicated even through the smallest of actions. Even humble acts of service reveal a *kenosis* that unites the human agent with the mysteries of the Incarnation and Passion of Christ.

There is also the danger that, perhaps to avoid discord in the family, moral insight is sought through internet sources rather than from within the family. This moral outsourcing can lead to a loss of prudential decision-making skills. Furthermore, the Christian family holds an ecclesial responsibility to be ready to offer counsel as needed to community members. Hence, "*family* help means both acts of love of neighbor done

---

[15] *Amoris Laetitia*, § 47.
[16] "So they went in haste and found Mary and Joseph, and the infant lying in the manger" (Luke 2:16).
[17] Luke 2:22–38, 41–52.

to members of the same family, and mutual help between families."[18] This capacity can become underdeveloped if moral insight is sought outside of the context of direct personal relationships. It can also lead to concerns about the accuracy of information and the extent to which information received may be riddled with bias, as will be discussed later in this chapter. The lack of interpersonal deliberation can detract from the family's and the community's potential to grow together morally and culturally rather than contribute to isolated, radically autonomous information silos.

Algorithms may reaffirm one's own perspectives and interests while deeply ingraining a narrow perspective. Personalized media and marketing can contribute to polarization and fragmentation as people lose an appreciation for shared discourse that engages different perspectives with trusted peers. Rather, families should work toward unity within their own home and amid the world at large: "Today as in the past, the Church as God's family ought to be a place where help is given and received, and at the same time, a place where people are also prepared to serve those outside her confines who are in need of help."[19]

Benefits from AI for the Family

There are many ways that AI systems can potentially benefit family life. Certainly, the efficiency of these systems in keeping track of schedules, shopping, budgeting, and attending to other basic needs might help families maintain organization in this increasingly complex world. Intelligent agents that help to facilitate family organization—while protecting privacy, maintaining cybersecurity, remaining accurate and unbiased in the help that they give, and so on—could offer a genuine benefit to family life by lightening some of the burden of organizational tasks. Or AI could help preserve and protect family history by organizing and maintaining family stories, photos, videos, and mementos. Of course, as noted above, the family should not be oriented toward efficiency for

---

[18] John Paul II, *Salvifici Dolori*, § 29.
[19] *Deus Caritas Est*, § 32.

efficiency's sake, but rather, efficiency gained through the use of AI should be spent on more genuine love and more meaningful encounter. In at least some cases, such love may call for us to embrace rather than outsource the small and seemingly menial ways that family members serve one another.

The world today is more complex and fast-paced than at any time in the past. This complexity and rapidity cause stress and other harms to individuals, families, and societies. AI might serve to help people alleviate this complexity by assisting in daily tasks or helping to manage the stress of our world—not by distraction away from the world, but by assisting our deeper engagement with reality and each other. For example, AI gives the ability to track information with more detail and accuracy in regard to family medical needs. AI helps people to track prescriptions of older relatives. Women can use AI-driven apps to track their fertility. AI can help to manage at-home health regimens. We already see this with health-related phone apps, but as AI grows in performative capabilities, it might offer greater assistance while hopefully also advancing protection of privacy, data, fairness, and so on. Caretakers of the elderly and disabled might especially benefit from this support, facilitating their lives and assisting in creating a true relationship of encounter with their loved one. Additionally, persons with disabilities can utilize technology like AI to interact with their environment more effectively.

When considering the increasing roles of technology in human life, mediating our interactions and relationships, we should be mindful to remember our Lord Jesus Christ was incarnate of a human mother, as a human being, to exist with us in perhaps the closest form of human relationship: the mother-child relationship. Even before birth, he was relating to those outside Mary's womb: Elizabeth's unborn baby leaped for joy. In childhood, Jesus continued to grow in a family, with a father, mother, cousins, and other relatives, and then into a community of friends and eventually disciples. God does not desire for love to be distant. Family is not merely a physical set of relationships, but a spiritual community of direct encounter with each other, expressing a miraculous and continuous incarnation across generations. Even amid the quotidian tasks of family life, such activities impart lessons of care and respect for human dignity. Pressure for uniformity based on visual cues from social media or the drive for efficiency inherent in many forms of AI may obfuscate the beauty in the diversity of traditions built around stories and around the table, and in which theological lessons have been organically passed down through generations. These family gatherings point to the table of communion at Mass and ultimately the eternal banquet in our eschatological home. Implementations of AI ought to protect rather than harm the community of the family.

Sphere of Education

The school is "the first social setting, after the family, in which the individual" encounters the world, experiences social relationships, forms habits of mind and character and from these eventually comes to take her own stance on herself, the world, and these relationships.[20] It is in the school that children will have their first intensive encounters outside the home as they learn to engage with their teachers and classmates. The impact of AI technologies on education is far reaching. It stretches beyond formal institutions of elementary or advanced schooling and spans across any and all interpersonal infrastructures that contribute to the formation of human persons, whether that be physically, mentally, morally, spiritually, or as a whole.[21] ChatGPT, intelligent tutoring systems (ITS), GoGuardian, and intelligent classroom behavioral management systems—AI technologies are not only being used in and outside the classroom, but are generating patterns of social relations.[22] These patterns inculcate social

---

[20] Congregation for Catholic Education, "The Identity of the Catholic School for a Culture of Dialogue," January 25, 2022, § 19, www.vatican.va/roman_curia/congregations/ccatheduc/documents/rc_con_ccatheduc_doc_20140407_educare-oggi-e-domani_en.html.

[21] *Caritas in Veritate*, § 61.

[22] Intelligent Tutoring Systems (ITS) are, broadly, any computer programs that assist in learning by keeping students within a range of acceptable methods for producing a certain outcome or that produce new problems and practice sets for the student. See Reva Freedman,

habits in both children and adults that can promote flourishing but also often subvert human freedom, creativity, and prudential judgment, as well as exacerbating the very inequality and bias they promise to alleviate.

The impact of AI technologies on the sphere of education is thus inseparable from and embedded within the cultural, political, economic, and familial spheres discussed throughout this chapter. For the purposes of this section, we will focus on the meaning and purpose of education in relation to AI. The potential problems and opportunities AI technologies pose to education, although deeply significant to schooling, extend far beyond it.

The Importance and Purpose of Education

Pope Francis describes how a "good education plants seeds when we are young, and these [seeds] continue to bear fruit throughout life."[23] As people grow and unfold in community, education should open their hearts and minds "to reality in the wealth of its aspects."[24] This openness is the building block for "the art of encounter."[25] As human beings open to reality, they grow in their ability to be attentive to other persons, to creation, and to transcendence. They grow in virtue and wisdom. They become more "capable of building a society based on justice and solidarity"

"What Is an Intelligent Tutoring System?," *Intelligence* 11, no. 3 (Fall 2000): 15–16. GoGuardian is a classroom management tool that allows teachers and administrators to view, manage, and control student devices in real time. See Kiersten Greene, "Soft(a)Ware in the English Classroom: 'Smarting' the Schools Smartly: Sustainable Change or Projectitis?," *The English Journal* 107, no. 4 (2018): 92–94. Intelligent classroom behavioral management systems are part of a fairly new class of technology that monitors student behavior and facial expressions in an attempt to track student learning and attentiveness. See Rich Haridy, "AI in Schools: China's Massive and Unprecedented Education Experiment," *New Atlas*, May 28, 2018, newatlas.com/china-ai-education-schools-facial-recognition/54786.

[23] *Laudato Si'*, § 213.

[24] Francis, "Address to Students and Teachers from Schools across Italy," May 10, 2014, www.vatican.va/content/francesco/en/speeches/2014/may/documents/papa-francesco_20140510_mondo-della-scuola.html.

[25] *Fratelli Tutti*, § 215.

and are led more deeply into an encounter with truth and wisdom[26] and into "an encounter with the living Christ" and his Mystical Body.[27]

Education is "not a parking lot" but a journey; school ought to be thought of as a community and a "place of encounter."[28] Education is a lifelong process of formation in which human persons freely unfold and grow in community. For any education to be considered a good and true education, it ultimately ought to cultivate a culture of encounter because true knowing and "true wisdom demands an encounter with reality."[29] It goes beyond knowledge acquisition, technical skill-building, or professional development and encompasses the formation of the whole person in pursuit of her ultimate end and the unique vocation gifted to her by God.[30]

In this way, "education cannot be neutral. It is either positive or negative; it either enriches or impoverishes; it either makes a person develop or depresses him, it can even corrupt him."[31] If we hope the stances people come to take toward themselves, the world, and their relationships are grounded in self-giving love rather than in misaligned fears and desires, then education ought to not inculcate concupiscence. If we hope that people will choose to strive for justice, equality, and peace rather than self-interest, money, and power, then education and the way AI technologies impact education ought to foster solidarity, reciprocity, and subsidiarity while resisting consumerism, the technocratic paradigm, and the atomized individualism and inequality they breed.

---

[26] Congregation for Catholic Education, "The Identity of the Catholic School for a Culture of Dialogue," § 19.

[27] Congregation for Catholic Education, "Educating Today and Tomorrow: A Renewing Passion," April 7, 2014, § 8, www.vatican.va/roman_curia/congregations/ccatheduc/documents/rc_con_ccatheduc_doc_20140407_educare-oggi-e-domani_en.html.

[28] Francis, "Address to Students and Teachers from Schools across Italy."

[29] *Fratelli Tutti*, § 47.

[30] Cf. Edith Stein, "Fundamental Principles of Women's Education" and "Problems of Women's Education," *Essays on Woman*, 2nd ed., rev., trans. F. M. Oben (Washington, DC: Institute of Carmelite Studies, 1996).

[31] Francis, "Address to Students and Teachers from Schools across Italy."

Broader Dangers of Using AI Technologies in Education

Institutional education and schooling, as stewards of habit formation and personal cultivation, are particularly vulnerable to being co-opted in both their content and structure by the ideologies of those funding them and the perceived market demands that students confront upon graduating. The use of AI technologies in education is often touted as preparing students for the future and as safeguarding equality through quantifying student achievement and learning outcomes. However, AI technologies can leave students ill-equipped to engage in and confront the world fruitfully and in the ways that the 21st century will require. These technologies, after all, can be used to isolate students and prevent them from cultivating interpersonal virtues by reducing *personal* encounter in the classroom. They can subvert individual freedom and prudential judgment by inculcating deference to algorithmic outputs and can exploit the vulnerable by selling false promises about educational tools that are in reality either ineffective or require expensive ongoing updates.

The technocratic paradigm, in its embrace of consumerism and isolated individualism, exacerbates inequality, corrupts human flourishing, and impedes progress toward a culture of encounter. It seeks to dominate, control, mitigate risk, and extract from the world for the gain of small groups in positions of power. These frameworks are antithetical to the ultimate ends of education. If AI technologies are to have any benefit when integrated into education, they ought to be stripped of any appeals to consumerism and the technocratic paradigm.

The way to prepare students properly for the future is to cultivate a culture of encounter in which all human beings are able to flourish according to their unique gifts. Students need to be educated in habits of body, mind, and character that help them to develop self-mastery, prudential judgment, creativity, and openness to life, so they can enter more deeply into loving relationships and be more attentive to the call to work for justice and care for creation. Some uses of educational technologies can undermine these character traits. For example, they can foster a sense that educational goals like writing a paper or completing a group project can successfully be brought within technical control through writing apps or by learning management systems that plan student schedules through amassing due dates. If it is going to be learning at all, the person always should be an active participant. Educational technologies cannot replace the personal collaboration, creativity, and prudence that is necessary for human learning. The principles of solidarity and subsidiarity help to form instructive frameworks for thinking about how AI technologies can serve or damage this common good, the cultivation of a culture of encounter and human flourishing.

Solidarity, as we have mentioned already, is not a mere sentiment, but a real relationship born out of true encounter and active care for the concrete good of persons and community. In addition to equal and equitable access, solidarity in education demands that schools be communities of encounter in which students bear witness to safe, caring, and attentive relationships among guardians, faculty, staff, and administrators, as well as form and enter into right relationships with them and their peers. Technology ought not and simply cannot ever take the place of a human teacher or human peer in or outside the classroom for this reason. This is why individualized learning ought never become individualistic learning.

Solidarity cannot be achieved without subsidiarity, the principle by which the local and global dimensions of the social order mutually enrich one another and collectively work toward the common good. Subsidiarity recognizes that all people ought to "have the possibility of assuming their own responsibility in the healing processes of the society of which they are a part."[32] Higher-order groups like federal and state governments or education boards ought to listen to, act on, and afford goods in response to what lower-order groups like individual schools, teachers, students, or families say they need. Teachers, for instance, are responsible for the local

---

[32] Francis, "General Audience," September 23, 2020, www.vatican.va/content/francesco/en/audiences/2020/documents/papa-francesco_20200923_udienza-generale.html.

dimension of their classroom and the individual flourishing of each of their students. If teachers say they need more aides in the classroom because the student-to-adult ratio is too high, but the school district instead decides to freeze hiring and spend money on new computers and tablets, this is a failure in subsidiarity. All too often, failures in subsidiarity are failures in encounter. This is a failure in encounter not only on the administrative and faculty level but also on the institutional level, which has not created a culture of encounter in the first place. Rather than providing the additional teachers that would allow the one-on-one human engagement that encounter requires, students are subjected to more intensive engagement with machines.

Education ought to resist structures and technologies (including AI technologies) that subvert human autonomy and responsibility and that do not attend to actual, specified needs. Teachers, students, and guardians, each in their own unique ways, "have an autonomy and capacity to take initiative that must be" respected and not violated, even for the sake of achieving certain learning outcomes.[33] Subsidiarity in particular works against the technocratic paradigm by refusing to allow the human person to be objectified or systematized and by not relinquishing the self-determination, free choice, or prudential judgments of individuals such as students, teachers, and guardians to technologies or to higher orders.

Although potentially offering helpful tools for skill-building, AI technologies should not replace or infringe upon the work and participation of students or teachers in the learning process. Neither students nor teachers ought to be treated as passive agents in education or cultivated in passive habits of body, mind, or character. Furthermore, AI technologies should not be used in any way that denies, limits, or quantifies any human person's transcendent worth and meaning or any human person's ability to contribute to or participate in society. Consumerism and the technocratic paradigm, particularly when applied to education, can attempt to automate uniformity by embedding "norms"

---

[33] Francis, "General Audience," September 23, 2020.

within prepackaged technological systems and by pathologizing difference in those who cannot easily learn through technological mediation. As Pope Francis explains, a culture of encounter is "working to create a many-faceted polyhedron whose different sides form a variegated unity" that represents "a society where differences coexist, complementing, enriching and reciprocally illuminating one another, even amid disagreements and reservations."[34] Work and participation are human goods that ought to be protected for both students and teachers.

Specific Harms and Opportunities in Education

One of the great promises of AI technologies is that they will individualize education. For example, some commentators suggest that AI can tailor lessons or educational programs based on an analysis of massive amounts of data, including students' genetic data.[35] It can also allow each student to work at his or her own pace through educational games and software. Robots equipped with AI technologies can be helpful therapeutic agents for children with autism.[36] Through games and online courses, people can seek education outside of the classroom altogether, extending the reach of schools. Many of these applications have clear benefits for contemporary education through expanded access.

In many ways, individualized education is the goal of traditional forms of education as well. Teachers have always sought to address the needs of the students in front of them: suggesting the extra readings that help them explore their interests, asking the questions that probe their preconceptions, and working with them on their specific struggles. AI individualizes slightly differently, though, in some troubling ways. For

---

[34] *Fratelli Tutti*, § 215.

[35] Kathryn Asbury and Robert Plomin, *G is for Genes: The Impact of Genetics on Education and Achievement* (Malden, MA: Wiley Blackwell, 2014). See also Paul Scherz, "Life as an Intelligence Test," *Culture, Medicine, and Psychiatry* 46, no. 1 (2022): 59–75.

[36] See early work in this area in Hirokazu Kumazaki, "Evaluating the Utility of Varied Technological Agents to Elicit Social Attention from Children with Autism Spectrum Disorders," *Journal of Autism and Developmental Disorder* 49 (2019): 1700–1708.

example, individualization that removes a person from a classroom undermines the possibility of encounter. Without teachers or classmates, students would just be responding to machines, abandoning the encounter necessary for good education. They would lose the embodied presence and attunement that, as so many people know through experience in Zoom meetings, is critical for continued attention and readiness to learn. Even the use of educational software within a classroom can lead to problematic individualization. Students can be in the same classroom but in different worlds, as each engages their own educational program on their own device. Again, the possibility of encounter between students and with the teacher is undermined. The targeting of education can also be harmful due to the reductionist quality of AI modeling. AI can only predict what can be quantified, which is only a small aspect of what is important in mentoring a student. Human teachers can attend to the whole person before them in context. They can highlight how a student's specific comment on a reading illuminates issues in a different class, in current events, or that another student had earlier raised.

This last point suggests a second problem, insofar as the widespread educational use of AI might influence *what* is taught in schools. AI and educational software are useful in some areas, for example the drilling necessary to learn math or languages. It can assist teachers and students in identifying errors in rule-bound elements of writing like grammar-checking. For these kinds of implementations, AI can help students to learn and might save teachers time in tedious tasks so that they can return to students in more genuine encounters.

Yet encounter is necessary in the most important parts of education. For example, interpretation of literature requires an emotional engagement that AI is incapable of but that can be inspired by a human teacher. Truly personal writing that escapes rule-bound forms requires the creative fostering of a skill by great teachers in ways that AI cannot do. AI cannot strive for a style that exceeds the historical data upon which it is trained. Further, it is not yet clear if or how AI can help to form virtues,[37] which is one of the primary goals of Catholic education. These internal personalist developments escape AI because most educational software is based on a behaviorist model of the student, with little concern for their interior lives.[38] Educational software doles out the dopamine hit of reward for each correct answer, gamifying education in a way that can undermine the development of wisdom through the building of habits of sustained attention.[39] Yet it is only through this personal growth that the student can transform an educational opportunity into wisdom. It is true that many of our educational institutions have already lost a focus on interpretation, creativity, virtue, and wisdom, in favor of a technocratic focus on marketable skills. Education threatens to become centered on the values of the technocratic paradigm and consumerism. This changed educational focus has left these educational institutions vulnerable to replacement by AI, which will only accentuate these shifts.

Finally, we ought to consider the economic and structural effects of adding AI to our educational institutions. Given the substantial expense of both software and hardware, the use of AI technologies in education could divert money away from other priorities, like teachers. These technologies need to be continually updated and replaced, leading to an ongoing drain on educational budgets. Instead of recycling money

---

[37] There are ideas of how this might be done, for example, through virtual reality ethical case studies. See, e.g., Brian Patrick Green, "The Technology of Holiness: A Response to Hava Tirosh-Samuelson," *Theology and Science* 16, no. 2 (2018): 227, doi.org/10.1080/14746700.2018.1455271, and Jia Hui Seow, Erick Jose Ramirez, Jocelyn Tan, Cynthia Mary Thomas, and Brett Ashton, "A Proposal to Combat Unconscious Bias Using VR," 2021 IEEE International Symposium on Technology and Society (ISTAS), Waterloo, ON, Canada, 2021, 1–4, doi.org/10.1109/ISTAS52410.2021.9629148.

[38] Appropriately enough, B. F. Skinner was one of the fathers of educational software. See Audrey Watters, *Teaching Machines: The History of Personalized Learning* (Cambridge, MA: MIT Press, 2021).

[39] For the problems of technology and attention, see Nicholas Carr, *The Shallows* (New York: Norton, 2011); Adam Alter, *Irresistible: The Rise of Addictive Technology and the Business of Keeping Us Hooked* (New York: Penguin, 2017).

through the community through salaries, AI applications funnel money into the large corporations that own and develop the applications. As in many aspects of the AI-driven economy, educational AI will support a centralization and concentration of curricular development and policy-making power—the very opposite of the subsidiarity that is central to Catholic social teaching. Finally, AI technologies will most likely be used in the classroom in a differentiated manner depending on the wealth or poverty of the students. Already, we see that technology executives tend to send their children to schools with little technology,[40] suggesting they realize the detrimental effects of many of these applications. As AI becomes more established in classrooms, poorer students will be more likely to be subjected to it, which runs counter to solidarity and the preferential option for the poor.

In summary, there is great danger in the "individualized education" promised by AI. It might undermine solidarity, subsidiarity, and encounter even as it concentrates power in the hands of a few companies. A naïve use of AI in the classroom will fail to form the whole person to "appraise moral values with a right conscience [and] to embrace them with a personal adherence."[41] Yet these dangers should not blind us to the benefits of AI, which may assist in more rule-bound forms of education such as grading math or grammar or helping students memorize facts and data. Its benefits will be realized only if its use is subordinated to the broader goods of encounter, solidarity, and subsidiarity.

Sphere of Health Care

Just as the educational role of the family receives a public form in the school, the bodily care that is found in the family receives a public form through medicine. This institutional care for the suffering serves as an important aspect of the Church's public witness. In the Gospels, Christ commanded his disciples to follow his example to heal both souls and

---

[40] Alter, *Irresistible*.
[41] Vatican Council II, *Gravissimum Educationis*, § 1.

bodies. In sending his disciples "to the lost sheep of the house of Israel," Jesus instructs that they "Heal the sick, raise the dead, cleanse lepers, cast out demons."[42] Care of the body and care of the soul are integral activities in caring for the whole person. Acknowledging the Christian mission to care for the body is essential to fully appreciating Catholic soteriology: Christ redeems human nature, and care for the body anticipates our perfected bodies and souls through which we will forever love God in heaven. Hope in a perfected body, however, does not imply a perfectionist, reductionist paradigm of medicine. Rather, the art of medicine responds with compassion to the cry of the other. Medicine is not meant to idealize humanity or to negate individuality but rather to answer the call of suffering and seek the wellbeing of the other in accord with his or her personal vocation.[43] Thus, though care for the body is required through Christological precedent and a direct calling of discipleship, the love exemplified in care of the body is further ordered and subordinated to care of the soul. Attention to both the body and the soul as a unified composite makes possible holistic care both for the individual and for communities.

Medicine became a focal point in the public works of the Church in order to continue Christ's mission. The order of *diakonia* was instituted to assist the Apostles with the social responsibilities of the new Church according to the model of Christ's charity,[44] and monastic orders extended this work by creating hospitals. John Paul II writes that "over the course of the centuries the Church has felt strongly that service to the sick and suffering is an integral part of her mission.... Missionaries, for their part, in carrying out the work of evangelization have constantly combined the preaching of the Good News with the help and care of the sick."[45] The

---

[42] Matthew 10:5, 8; cf. Luke 9:1–2.

[43] On the role of vocation in clinical decision-making, see Farr Curlin and Christopher Tollefsen, *The Way of Medicine: Ethics and the Healing Profession* (Notre Dame, IN: University of Notre Dame Press, 2021).

[44] *Deus Caritas Est*, §§ 21–23; see also Gary B. Ferngren, *Medicine and Health Care in Early Christianity* (Baltimore: Johns Hopkins University Press, 2009).

[45] John Paul II, *Dolentium Hominum*, § 1.

Gospel is put into action by partaking in the ministry of the hospital: particularly, the divine charity revealed in Christ's parable of the Good Samaritan is recapitulated in every authentic medical act. "How much there is of 'the Good Samaritan' in the profession of the doctor, or the nurse, or others similar!"[46] The Catholic vision of medicine does not reduce itself to merely technical cure, however. Rather, medicine involves seeking to love as Christ loves.

Catholic social teaching has also argued that this charity ought to expand to embrace a broader social solidarity that addresses root causes of ill health such as poverty, homelessness, and racism. Appealing to the same parable, Pope Francis writes, "In the gestures and deeds of the Good Samaritan we recognize the merciful acts of God in all of salvation history. It is the same compassion with which the Lord comes to meet each one of us: He does not ignore us, he knows our pain, he knows how much we need help and comfort. He comes close and never abandons us."[47] Pope Francis has also described the Church as a "'field hospital' that welcomes the weakest."[48] In considering the integration of AI technology in the healthcare system, we are called to think critically of the ways that it can uplift or detract from the service of medicine to God and humanity in both caring for the body and expressing love for others.

The Promise of AI in Health Care

AI has the potential to make the care of the body more effective and efficient at both the level of the broader health care system and society, and in encounters with individual patients.[49] At a systemic level, advances in

---

[46] *Salvifici Doloris*, § 29.
[47] Francis, "General Audience," April 27, 2016, www.vatican.va/content/francesco/en/audiences/2016/documents/papa-francesco_20160427_udienza-generale.html.
[48] Francis, "General Audience," August 28, 2019, www.vatican.va/content/francesco/en/audiences/2019/documents/papa-francesco_20190828_udienza-generale.html.
[49] For overviews of the current and possible impacts of AI on health care as discussed here, see Erin Brodwin and Ross Casey, *Promise and Peril: How AI Is Transforming Health Care* (2021), www.statnews.com/promise-and-peril; Eric Topol, *Deep Medicine: How Artificial*

health technology may help improve access to the right to health care. Chatbots can assist with triage and initial sorting of patients. Apps can aid with the management of chronic diseases like heart disease.[50] AI-assisted devices can tailor treatment to individual patients, such as with insulin pumps. When combined with advances in telehealth, such technological resources can help patients in under-resourced areas, such as the rural US or rural Africa, receive the care they need without requiring long journeys to distant clinics. AI-powered targeted outreach and information campaigns can improve health education, positively impacting population health, without replacing human interactions among individuals and healthcare professionals, within communities, and with social agencies.

AI can also assist with diagnostics and treatment. AI-based image processing applications are being developed to help detect cancers on mammograms and MRIs. Health technology companies are designing a new generation of computerized decision support systems that aim to assist doctors in the clinic by suggesting possible diagnoses in response to a patient's symptoms. By collating the results of past treatments and comparing them to the individual patient, AI systems might help oncologists select the best treatment regimens for individual patients. All of these programs are currently in the testing phase, but results suggest that at least some of them might aid diagnosis and treatment.

Finally, through training on health records and genetic information, AI is being developed to predict the risk of future disease and death. Health systems already use algorithms to identify patients for increased levels of

---

Intelligence Can Make Healthcare Human Again (New York: Basic Books, 2019). For a more skeptical take on these developments, see Robert Sparrow and Joshua Hatherley, "High Hopes for 'Deep Medicine'? AI, Economics, and the Future of Care," *Hastings Center Report* 50, no. 1 (2020): 14–17.

[50] Minna Ruckenstein and Natasha Dow Schull, "The Datafication of Health," *Annual Review of Anthropology* 46 (2017): 261–78.

care who are at especially high risk of death or costly disease.[51] With the new paradigm of precision medicine, researchers seek to develop genetic risk scores that will enable patients to receive prophylactic treatments for chronic diseases before illness strikes.[52] These tools may reduce the burden of future disease.

Predictive tools could be especially valuable at the population level. AI is currently supporting diverse public health interventions, such as disease surveillance, outbreak response, health systems management, data modeling of vectors and their spread, population risks, disease burden, and cost predictions. While health depends on the concrete actions of caregivers, it also is influenced by the social contexts in which people live, leading to an application of AI in what is called population health. Social determinants of health are responsible for health inequities, i.e., the unfair and avoidable differences in health status seen within and between countries. AI can monitor and assess the health indicators of populations in order to select and target public health interventions.

By focusing on health problems, issues, and concerns that transcend national boundaries and that could be addressed by cooperative action, AI contributes to global health. AI systems expand screening possibilities, facilitate diagnoses, and complement healthcare practice on a global scale. Hence, AI systems could contribute to promoting high quality health services focused on health prevention, promotion, and care. Currently, AI is being used to trace the rise of non-communicable diseases in low- and middle-income countries. In cases of infectious diseases, it could predict disease severity in patients with dengue fever and malaria, the risk of cognitive sequelae after malaria infection in children, and the risk of tuberculosis treatment failure. AI systems could predict, model, and slow

---

[51] See discussion of these programs in Paul Scherz, "Data Ethics, AI, and Accompaniment: The Dangers of Depersonalization in Catholic Health Care," *Theological Studies* 83, no. 2 (2022): 271–292.

[52] For problems with this approach, see Greg Gibson, "On the Utilization of Polygenic Risk Scores for Therapeutic Targeting," *PLOS Genetics* 15, no. 4 (2019): e1008060.

the spread of infectious disease in epidemics or pandemics around the world, including in resource-poor settings. These capabilities might help to ensure a more effective use of health care resources.

Dangers to the Common Good from AI's Use in Health Care

Despite these potential benefits, AI also poses many dangers to moral medicine. The common issue of AI intensifying existing bias and discrimination is especially acute in health care. Given the long history of racism in medicine, past data used by AI is often corrupt, so these programs can unintentionally impose biases. For example, an algorithm that sought to identify high-risk patients tended to target more care to white patients than to Black patients with similar health needs because the algorithm had defined "risk" in terms of potential health costs.[53] Because Black patients historically have received less care, they were seen as at less risk of needing care. Bias also occurs due to unrepresentative training data for AI, a problem with some genetic research projects that draw mainly on white participants. Risk predictions derived from these projects may not apply broadly. Similar problems are seen in the exclusive use of data from high-income settings that will limit AI's effectiveness in low- and middle-income countries, where data is less reliable and available. Such failings may reinforce already existing disparities in health care.

AI-based risk prediction may also reinforce the eugenic mentality discussed above in the section on the family.[54] The eugenic mentality

---

[53] Ziad Obermyer, Brian Powers, Christine Vogeli, and Sendhil Mullainathan, "Dissecting Racial Bias in an Algorithm Used to Manage the Health of Populations," *Science* 366, no. 6464 (2019): 447–453, 10.1126/science.aax2342.

[54] Congregation for the Doctrine of the Faith, "Instruction *Dignitas Personae*: On Certain Bioethical Questions," September 8, 2008, § 22, www.vatican.va/roman_curia/congregations/cfaith/documents/rc_con_cfaith_doc_20081208_dignitas-personae_en.html. See also Francis, "Address to the Participants in the Meeting Promoted by the Pontifical Council for Promoting the New Evangelization," October 21, 2017, www.vatican.va/content/francesco/en/speeches/2017/october/documents/papa-francesco_20171021_convegno-pcpne.html; Francis, "Address to the Delegation of the Forum of Family Associations," June 16, 2018,

overlaps with the throwaway culture insofar as it rejects people who are not healthy, have disabilities, or lack certain attributes. For example, there is a company that offers to provide genetic risk scores for conditions like diabetes or heart disease in children conceived through in vitro fertilization (IVF) so that only the (potentially) healthiest embryos will be implanted.[55] During the pandemic, scholars discussed prioritizing care to patients who were predicted to have more years of life with greater quality of life, potentially discriminating against the elderly and people with disabilities. AI might also be used by insurance companies to deny certain types of policies to those seen as at risk. If misused, prediction of disease can lead to discrimination, which undermines the evangelical call to care for all people.

Both of these concerns are related to a broader danger involving the concentration of power in health care. Those who control AI can use it for their own ends, which may not align with the common good and solidarity. For example, electronic medical records, which were promoted as a way to provide cheaper and more efficient medical care in the US, have frequently increased costs as systems were designed to maximize billing. Similarly, AI systems might maximize financial returns for those who own them to the detriment of the community. Already, there is a struggle among health technology companies for access to medical records or the kind of health information collected by apps and devices. Consumers and patients often have little control over how their data is used. Those who control data will have an advantage in establishing a monopoly on AI resources in health care.

Such a concentration of power will prevent AI systems from addressing the diversity and complexity of socioeconomic and health care settings.

---

www.vatican.va/content/francesco/en/speeches/2018/june/documents/papa-francesco_20180616_forum-associazioni-familiari.html.

[55] Antonio Regalado, "The World's First Gattaca Baby Tests Are Finally Here," *MIT Technology Review*, November 8, 2019, www.technologyreview.com/2019/11/08/132018/polygenic-score-ivf-embryo-dna-tests-genomic-prediction-gattaca.

AI's implementation should be accompanied by training in digital skills, community engagement, and awareness-raising. While private and public-sector investment are responsible for the development and deployment of AI systems, the good, rights, and interests of patients and communities should neither be violated, nor subordinated to the powerful commercial interests of technology companies or the interests of governments in surveillance and social control.[56]

Furthermore, international efforts aimed at promoting AI in global health are at work,[57] but diversity and inequality exist.[58] As one might expect, in the last few decades, AI has been mostly developed and implemented in high-income countries. In resource-poor settings, while the presence of AI is relatively limited, AI applications could be used in ways that aim at addressing the social determinants of health (such as poverty) and delivering public services to improve health outcomes. However, AI tools require trained practitioners sufficiently motivated to invest time in acquiring the needed skills. Such a necessary condition might be quite demanding and challenging in low-income settings struggling with not enough personnel and overwhelming health needs. The concentration of power and resulting inequality that is enabled and perhaps even required by AI is one of its greatest dangers.

---

[56] Charles E. Binkley and Brian P. Green, "Does Intraoperative Artificial Intelligence Decision Support Pose Ethical Issues?," *JAMA Surgery* 156, no. 9 (2021): 809–810, doi.org/10.1001/jamasurg.2021.2055

[57] As an example, the 2019 *Artificial Intelligence in Global Health* report—funded by the USAID's Center for Innovation and Impact, the Rockefeller Foundation, and the Bill and Melinda Gates Foundation—discusses twenty-seven cases of AI use in global health care. These cases concern population health, patient and front-line health worker virtual assistants, and physician clinical decision support. See USAID, *Artificial Intelligence in Global Health: Defining a Collective Path Forward* (Washington, DC: USAID, 2019).

[58] See National Academies of Sciences Engineering Medicine, *Crossing the Global Quality Chasm: Improving Health Care Worldwide* (Washington, DC: National Academies Press, 2018).

Dangers to the Specific Goods of Medicine

Medical care is more than simply a technical matter; it is an encounter between the physician and the suffering patient. The fiduciary, compassionate relationship between physician and patient is ordered to securing the good of the health and well-being of the patient holistically understood. Though there are certainly benefits to the integration of advanced technology such as AI in the medical field, there are also dangers to the specific goods of medicine that cannot be ignored. The following illustrates potential impacts to three features of the medical relationship: the presence of the physician, patient trust, and patient narrative.

Traditionally, medicine has emphasized the role of the physician not only as a technical expert but also as an exemplar in modeling the compassion and accompaniment needed for an adequate response to suffering. AI can obscure both the technical and interpersonal dimensions of the presence of the physician. In some cases, AI may be utilized to offer suggestions or calculate diagnostics without resorting to a human interlocutor. The availability of virtual medicine may lower the standard for quality of care, both in terms of technical knowledge and bedside manner. Increased anonymity can render a physician less accountable to the moral expectations of the profession. Not only are there examples of human specialists replaced by AI but also examples of AI facilitating the replacement of human specialists with human non-specialists. For example, "peer-therapy" apps assist non-credentialed users in providing counseling to other users, with AI mediating messages and unofficially "training" the peer counselors in unnuanced psychological paradigms.[59]

Second, as AI capabilities replace medical practitioners, access to personalized care becomes more difficult. For example, scheduling

---

[59] For more on how AI is utilized in peer-therapy apps, see for example, Ashish Sharma, Inna W. Lin, Adam S. Miner, David C. Atkins, and Tim Althoff, "Human-AI Collaboration Enables More Empathic Conversations in Text-Based Peer-to-Peer Mental Health Support," *Nature Machine Intelligence* 5 (April 2022): 46–57, www.newswise.com/pdf_docs/1674 4962898443_Full%20text_%20Althoff%2042256_2022_593_finalpdf.pdf.

algorithms may help physicians secure more patients but also decrease the physician's quality time with the patient. Briefer, more intensely managed clinical visits can contribute to the patient feeling unprioritized and perceiving herself as a burden, directly conflicting with the intentional gaze of the physician called for by the parable of the Good Samaritan. Additionally, interruptions to clinical visits can become more frequent with alerts from clinical decision support systems demanding physicians' attention. These systems can therefore impose barriers to direct practitioner interaction with the patient and lead to deskilling in other methods of organizing and facilitating patient visits.

Next, AI can detract from personalist and narrative-centered medicine. Medical schools have integrated humanities-centered curriculum to improve physicians' capacities to empathize with patients. This approach is designed to combat a reductionist or symptoms-focused clinical encounter that fails to see the patient as an integrated human person. AI can threaten a humanistic paradigm of medicine if it detracts from a personal relationship or reorients medicine to a depersonalized analysis of quantifiable symptoms. This can also impact the fiduciary nature of the physician-patient relationship. The patient could feel deceived if their care does not appear to come from a human person. Though some patients may prefer the privacy offered by discussing symptoms with robots rather than humans, it is also possible that patients may become less forthcoming if they will not receive the sympathy of a human hearer or if their medical information will be stored and analyzed for unpredicted purposes without the patient's explicit consent. Utilizing AI to interpret and evaluate symptoms can de-emphasize the role of the patient's own descriptions of personal experiences when in dialogue with the clinician. This puts AI diagnostic methods in tension with the "narrative medicine" tradition that seeks to recognize the actions of both physician and patient as contextualized within a broader, consistent story of life ordered teleologically toward particular goals shaped by personal values.[60]

Finally, the fact that AI contributes to drawing the world into closer mutual relationship increases the social responsibility to respond to instances of suffering. Benedict XVI observed that the way in which technology more closely unites communities also inspires a heightened resolve to heal the wounds that are observed across humanity:

> Despite the great advances made in science and technology, each day we see how much suffering there is in the world on account of different kinds of poverty, both material and spiritual. Our times call for a new readiness to assist our neighbors in need. The Second Vatican Council had made this point very clearly: "Now that, through better means of communication, distances between peoples have been almost eliminated, charitable activity can and should embrace all people and all needs."[61]

Globalization in the realm of medicine offers both challenges and opportunities for grace. AI can make us more aware of the individuals in need of our care, but this insight will be of no value unless the gaze of the Good Samaritan is honed in each of us, rendering us prepared to act with charity readily when called. In our plural and globalized world, cultural, religious, political, and economic diversity between individuals and countries shape and dominate human interactions. The comprehensive and inclusive ethical approach that strives to promote the global common good of health care at a planetary level, and that fosters participation, is an indispensable moral criterion for evaluating the design, implementation, and use of AI systems.

---

[60] For example, see Rita Charon and Martha Montello, eds., *Stories Matter: The Role of Narrative in Medical Ethics* (New York: Routledge, 2002), among other works by Rita Charon.

[61] *Deus Caritas Est*, § 30, citing *Apostolicam Actuositatem*, § 8.

Sphere of Law and Politics

The scale, speed, and power of AI is altering how we engage one another about issues of common interest and how benefits and burdens are distributed across a population. In other words, AI raises significant political and legal questions. Serious concerns are beginning to emerge regarding AI's adverse impact on power dynamics within society, on individual freedom, and on privacy, especially due to increased surveillance through AI. Each of these applications poses a serious threat to the health of liberal democratic societies and often disproportionately affect marginalized and vulnerable populations.

The Church holds that an authentic democracy is possible in a state ruled by law and ordered toward the common good. It affirms the value of democratic systems in part because of their ability to involve their citizens in the political process, hold their leaders accountable, and enact change in a peaceful and ordered manner.[62] Democratic governments allow citizens to "freely and actively [take] part in the establishment of the juridical foundations of the political community and in the direction of public affairs."[63] Today, public functions—such as social services, welfare, and education—are increasingly turned over to AI; citizens are subject to ever more prevalent surveillance through facial recognition, location, and data gathering technologies; and voters are more and more subjected to manipulation through disinformation and misinformation. As a result, citizens are less able to participate in the political process, to deliberate freely about the good, and to hold their leaders accountable, especially when much of the power of AI is being wielded by large corporations operating in multiple legal jurisdictions.

"Surveillance capitalism" refers to the political and economic system that relies on technology companies gathering massive amounts of personal data of its users (often without their knowledge or explicit

---

[62] *Compendium of the Social Doctrine of the Church*, § 406.
[63] *Gaudium et Spes*, § 75.

consent) to predict and shape human behavior, usually for economic ends, but also, as a few well-known cases have shown, for political purposes.[64] The effect of this practice not only commodifies ordinary human experiences for economic gain but also undermines individual privacy and our ability to keep information to ourselves—something necessary for intimate relationships and individual liberty in modern societies.[65] Because this information also is used to manipulate, nudge, or control human actions and beliefs, surveillance capitalism also compromises human freedom. Social media companies, for example, can personalize advertisements, news feeds, and content to manipulate our moods or emotions, alter behavior and choices, and influence our beliefs. As currently used, these activities may have the effect of restricting individual self-determination and autonomous action.

Information about physical location, group membership, shopping preferences, health information, online activities, daily habits, and so on, can be used by governments and corporations to infringe upon an individual's civil liberties. Tracking information, public records, and biometric and facial recognition technologies have been used by law enforcement agencies to arrest and imprison those suspected of crime, sometimes even the innocent, as recent publicized cases of mistaken identity have shown.[66] In the hands of authoritarian regimes, such technologies reportedly have enabled the systematic tracking, persecution, arrest, and abuse of minority populations.

Finally, essential functions of the state, such as policing, social welfare services, and judicial decision-making, increasingly have been automated through the use of predictive algorithms and AI. Not only has this led to imposing unfair burdens on and discriminating against vulnerable

---

[64] Zuboff, *The Age of Surveillance Capitalism*; Carissa Véliz, *Privacy is Power: Why and How You Should Take Back Control of Your Data* (London: Penguin Random House, 2020).
[65] Véliz, *Privacy is Power*.
[66] Kashmir Hill, "Wrongfully Accused by an Algorithm," *New York Times,* June 24, 2020, www.nytimes.com/2020/06/24/technology/facial-recognition-arrest.html.

populations, but it also has led to an increasing disengagement from political life among the general population.[67] More often than not, surveillance and other technologies are introduced into society by unaccountable corporations, absent any deliberation or participation of those who will be most impacted by these decisions and who do not have any recourse to appeal or challenge the effects. Moreover, important social and political issues that previously were the focus of public discourse and deliberation about communal values and commitments have become reduced to technocratic questions of efficiency and engineering and left to bureaucratic interventions.

Misinformed Voters and Loss of Civility

Catholic teaching holds that there ought to be some opportunity for citizens to participate in social life, expressing their values and beliefs, primarily today through elections.[68] However, the existence of a voting process by itself is not sufficient, because there are still at least three general ways for the voting process to be undermined. First, those with power sometimes seek to pre-determine an election outcome. This can be done through voter disenfranchisement, voter intimidation, and even by the elimination of political rivals. Even when such methods do not become physically violent, they are still coercive. But even a perfectly "free" (non-coercive) election can still be undermined through disinformation or misinformation.[69] The simple difference between these information challenges is intentionality, because while misinformation does not stem from an organized intention to manipulate, disinformation does.

Obviously, corruption, disinformation, and misinformation have been disrupting free and fair elections for a long time, but AI systems can make

---

[67] Eubanks, *Automating Inequality*, 197–200.
[68] *Compendium of the Social Doctrine of the Church*, §§ 189–191.
[69] Francis, "Message for the World Communications Day: 'The Truth Will Set You Free' (Jn 8:32): Fake News and Journalism for Peace," January 24, 2018, www.vatican.va/content/francesco/en/messages/communications/documents/papa-francesco_20180124_messaggio-comunicazioni-sociali.html.

any of those problems much worse. For example, bipartisan investigations in the United States concluded both that Russia did attempt to influence American voters before the 2016 national election and that their efforts were much more effective because of algorithms.[70] The Russian government simply commissioned the writing of stories that were clearly false,[71] and then used algorithms to identify and engage the American voters that would most likely be persuaded by these false stories. In this way, AI systems give the old practice of disinformation new powers of manipulation.

While disinformation from AI takes various forms, deep fakes deserve their own mention. Deep fakes are videos, photos, or other digital media that have been created by computer technology to appear to represent real people, but in fact are either digitally enhanced or entirely computer-generated. Unlike many forms of disinformation that already existed that AI simply makes worse, deep fakes are a kind of disinformation that exists only because of AI technology. These falsified sights and sounds betray not just our sense of propositional truth, but the very data we get from our senses. Deep fakes can be used for disinformation by making well-known public figures seem to say or do things that would damage their reputation or even be illegal, such as the recent example in the news of a computer-generated image of Pope Francis wearing what appears to be an expensive white parka.[72] The fact that some deep fakes are relatively light-hearted and obviously fake to most people does not change the fact that some deep

---

[70] Meg Kelly and Elyse Samuels, "How Russia Weaponized Social Media, Got Caught and Escaped Consequences," *The Washington Post*, November 18, 2019, www.washingtonpost.com/politics/2019/11/18/how-russia-weaponized-social-media-got-caught-escaped-consequences.

[71] Davey Alba, "How Russia's Troll Farm Is Changing Tactics Before the Fall Election," *New York Times*, March 29, 2020, www.nytimes.com/2020/03/29/technology/russia-troll-farm-election.html.

[72] Simon Ellery, "Fake Photos of Pope Francis in a Puffer Jacket Go Viral, Highlighting the Power and Peril of AI," *CBS News*, March 28, 2023, www.cbsnews.com/news/pope-francis-puffer-jacket-fake-photos-deepfake-power-peril-of-ai.

fakes inevitably will be created in order to undermine socio-political cohesion and will be difficult to detect.

While coercion and manipulation through disinformation are clearly tools for undermining elections, voting specifically and civil debate generally can also be fully undermined through misinformation. When information was disseminated mostly by sources with at least some journalistic standards, this was a relatively small problem. Conspiracy theories have always existed, but in an age of information disseminated by centralized, vetted sources, their power was limited to the margins of society. Today, however, our news is increasingly filtered and disseminated by algorithms seeking to maximize engagement rather than organizations oriented toward the quality of the product they produce. Consequently, shared facts stemming from actual reporting and observation are routinely undermined. For example, Facebook's algorithm has been known to send articles to users asserting, with no evidence, that certain politicians actively and secretly run a human trafficking ring. Because the algorithm is able to identify people who are predisposed to believe such claims, the algorithm will achieve its objective of increasing engagement without regard to the accuracy of the information.[73] And as such information bubbles grow, it becomes easier for people to speak openly in real life about these falsehoods without expecting to be contradicted. The most effective civil debate begins when the debate participants identify a shared premise, but it is less and less clear what the shared premises might be if these information bubbles become more like information walls.

The difference between misinformation (false or misleading information without intent to deceive) and disinformation (false or misleading information intended to deceive) is clear in the abstract, although in reality it is difficult to know the source's intentions. For example, in the preceding examples, it is clear that the election propaganda

---

[73] Sheera Frenkel, "QAnon Is Still Spreading on Facebook, Despite a Ban," *New York Times*, December 18, 2020, www.nytimes.com/2020/12/18/technology/qanon-is-still-spreading-on-facebook-despite-a-ban.html.

should count as disinformation; it is less clear that the rumors about politicians running trafficking rings are in fact simple misinformation. Regardless, they both have enormous potential to exacerbate the divisions within communities and to perpetuate skepticism about truth. More worrying is that they contribute to a general crisis of trust by undermining the trustworthiness and authority of social institutions that are essential to a functioning democracy. Ironically, this loss of trust is accelerated by political actors' eagerness to condemn legitimate disagreements over policy and interpretation of data as misinformation by their opponents. Misinformation and disinformation, including deep fakes, reinforce *particularized trust*, the idea that we can only trust in those with whom we have allegiance or kinship, which exacerbates the problem of filter bubbles and undermines social cohesion and the important Catholic virtue of solidarity.[74]

Accelerated Marginalization of the Vulnerable

The automation of public services can accelerate the marginalization of the most vulnerable populations. Because these systems are designed to process large amounts of data to evaluate a large number of people, they tend to deal with the masses, while the elite in society are able to interact with people and receive personalized attention.[75] The data collected on individuals are used to create profiles that correspond to demographic groups, so most of the digital monitoring occurs at the social group level. As a result, people of color, the poor, migrant groups, minority populations and religions, tend to bear a much higher burden of monitoring and tracking than advantaged groups.[76] States use data systems, for example, to track when and where families and individuals use

---

[74] Warren von Eschenbach, "Trust as a Public Virtue," in *Virtues in the Public Sphere: Citizenship, Civic Friendship, and Duty*, ed. James Arthur (London: Routledge Press, 2019), 150–151.

[75] O'Neil, *Weapons of Math Destruction*, 8.

[76] Eubanks, *Automating Inequality*, 6.

their electronic cards to access government assistance programs. Justified as necessary to eliminate fraud, these programs effectively place individuals under extensive surveillance, which in turn serves to stigmatize, scrutinize, and punish the poor and question their decision-making.

Automation and use of AI in criminal justice contexts also has had a disparate impact on poor and marginalized communities. Algorithms and machine learning can be deployed to generate risk scores and other metrics to influence decisions about criminal investigations, release on bail, prison sentencing, policing, parole, and suspect identification.[77] In a well-publicized case, ProPublica investigated the use of COMPAS (mentioned in chapter 1), a proprietary algorithm that provides a risk score for potential parolees during parole hearings. Not only was the algorithm remarkably unsuccessful in predicting violent crime, but it was biased against Black citizens. Black individuals were more than twice as likely to be given a false high-risk score and half as likely to be given incorrect low-risk scores for reoffending when compared to their white counterparts.[78] The widespread misuse and indiscriminate use of AI technologies to make important political and legal decisions punishes and creates undue burdens on the poor and marginalized and further exacerbates social inequality.

Rule by Algorithms

When we embed algorithms into institutions such as social services and criminal justice, we normalize granting social and political power to AI. While currently, these algorithms are ostensibly used as advisors to human decision makers, it is easy for AI to replace human decision-makers. The term "algocracy"[79] has been coined to express the worry that algorithms

---

[77] Benjamin, *Race after Technology*.
[78] Angwin, Larson, Mattu, and Kirchner, "Machine Bias," 2016. This statistical analysis was challenged by the company and associate researchers, which merely confirms the difficulty of ensuring that such complex algorithms remain unbiased. For discussion of the difficulties of confirming bias in observational data, see Silberzahn, et al., "Many Analysts, One Data Set."
[79] A. Aneesh, "Global Labor: Algocratic Modes of Organization," *Sociological Theory* 27, no. 4 (2009), doi.org/10.1111/j.1467-9558.2009.01352.x; John Danaher, "The Threat of Algocracy:

could eventually be given so much power that they, rather than the people (the *demos* of democracy), possess the ultimate governing power in some socio-political systems.

The examples of state social service distribution and recidivism prediction were highlighted specifically to give examples of how algorithmic power in social institutions could accelerate injustice. But one could also imagine a society ruled by algorithms where general welfare is instead increased more fairly and more efficiently than in societies run by humans. Could this arrangement be justified "by its fruits," and if so, would we not then be ethically obligated to favor this social arrangement? The beginning of an answer can be found in an example considered by Iris Marion Young:

> Citizens . . . are outraged at the announcement that a major employer is closing down its plant. They question the legitimacy of the power of private corporate decision-makers to throw half the city out of work without warning, and without any negotiation and consultation with the community. Discussion of possible compensation makes them snicker.[80]

These citizens are angry, and they are no doubt upset about the financial impact on their families and the community at large. But it is possible to be indignant about both the process and the result of the process, and Young here isolates the former.

The crucial phrase is "decision-makers," because it is this particular power that distinguishes the "haves" from the "have-nots" in this context. Despite "possible compensation," citizens were still angry that they were denied power by being shut out of the decision-making process even though it affected them directly. They were simply notified of the result. Young is here reminding us that even though equitable distribution

---

Reality, Resistance, and Accommodation," *Philosophy and Technology* 29 (2016): 245–268, link.springer.com/article/10.1007/s13347-015-0211-1.

[80] Iris Marion Young, *Justice and the Politics of Difference* (Princeton, NJ: Princeton University Press, 1990), 19.

matters in justice, there is also a loss of justice when an identifiable group does not have a seat at the decision-making table (in this case, workers and citizens) while another group does (in this case, shareholders and executives). As we have seen, the Catholic Church teaches that liberal democracy's value in part lies in its ability to involve its citizens, especially those most disadvantaged, in important decisions and to enable their participation in a fair political process exemplified by subsidiarity. A society governed by algorithms would undermine this essential function.

If we focus on the perspective of those affected, it is not difficult to translate their political experience into a society ruled by algorithms. In such a society, the algorithms by definition would have the ultimate governing power rather than the people, because the algorithm would be the ultimate decision maker, and it is not even clear how humans would have input into the process. This observation is getting to an ancient, deep truth about people, perhaps best articulated by Aristotle, who claims that the fact that humans are

> more of a political animal than bees or other gregarious animals is evident. Nature, as we often say, does nothing in vain, and [the human] is the only animal who has the gift of *logos*. . . . The power of *logos* is intended to set forth the expedient and inexpedient, and therefore likewise the just and the unjust.[81]

The translation of *logos* is complicated and controversial[82] and so we have left it untranslated here, as the question of the best translation is actually a distraction in this context. What is clear is that Aristotle insists that we humans find ourselves with a power that we are meant to use. We use the power of *logos* to discuss and debate with one another about what is just and unjust and about what is prudent and imprudent, and this very

---

[81] *Aristotle's Politics*, trans. C. Lord (Chicago: University of Chicago Press, 1984), Book I, Section 1253a8.
[82] Some examples of how *logos* has been translated are "speech," "logic," "rationality," "word," "discourse," and "reason."

process is essential for achieving our nature as political animals. In the *Politics*, Aristotle considers forms of government where we would not need to use this power. Consider the case of a monarchy: we would not need any decision-making powers, because the rulers would simply inform us of the decision.

Regardless of how fully he himself drew out the implication of this insight, Aristotle is right to warn us that it would be bad for the citizens to be outside of the political process. By our nature, we are ordered to political involvement through our possession of *logos*. Of course, Aristotle could not have considered algorithmic governance, but the dangers are the same; we have the power of *logos*, we are intended to use it, and so a system of government that obviates our use of it by simply informing us of the results of algorithms would in the end be a dehumanizing system of government. Besides the potential for the vulnerable to be further marginalized in a society ruled by algorithms, the ability to systematically disenfranchise citizens from the political process and alienate them from fulfilling their essential nature is of great concern. Instead, Pope Francis calls us to political charity, within which "Government leaders should be the first to make the sacrifices that foster encounter and to seek convergence on at least some issues. They should be ready to listen to other points of view and to make room for everyone."[83] Such encounters can only occur through dialogue that includes the participation of all.[84]

Sphere of the Military

One of the most central roles of government is the protection of the common good through coercive means. Like AI's role in the criminal justice system, military applications of AI are receiving some of the greatest investments in the field. Indeed, some see AI as at the center of a new arms

---

[83] *Fratelli Tutti*, § 190.
[84] *Fratelli Tutti*, § 198.

race between the great world powers.[85] Automation may seem to be the only possible response as warfare occurs at ever greater speed and as the information processing demands on warfighters increase with the explosion of available intelligence. In some spheres, like cyberdefense, AI may be the only possible way to protect vital infrastructure against malicious hacking. While there are many military uses of AI, perhaps the most troubling possibilities involve autonomous weapons, which will be the focus of this section's analysis. Even in the face of the agonistic struggles of the world of warfare, there is still space to consider the importance of an ethics of encounter.

It is important to first situate military uses of AI within Pope Francis's affirmation of nonviolence and rejection of war. Building on statements by previous popes, Francis has identified the practice of nonviolence with the demands of Christian faith: "To be true followers of Jesus today also includes embracing his teaching about nonviolence."[86] He has focused on the narrowness of legitimate moral justifications for war and, indeed, speaks more often of the moral demand to reject it entirely. In *Fratelli Tutti*, he writes, "We can no longer think of war as a solution, because its risks will probably always be greater than its supposed benefits. In view of this, it is very difficult nowadays to invoke the rational criteria elaborated in earlier centuries to speak of the possibility of a 'just war.' Never again war!"[87] As with its use in any field, the application of AI to social and political conflict has the potential to lead to positive benefits like the reduction of violence and enhanced possibilities for peace. However, in

---

[85] Paul Scharre, *Four Battlegrounds: Power in the Age of Artificial Intelligence* (New York: W.W. Norton, 2023).

[86] Francis, "Nonviolence: A Style of Politics for Peace," January 1, 2017, www.vatican.va/content/francesco/en/messages/peace/documents/papa-francesco_20161208_messaggio-l-giornata-mondiale-pace-2017.html; Benedict XVI, "Angelus," February 18, 2007, www.vatican.va/content/benedict-xvi/en/angelus/2007/documents/hf_ben-xvi_ang_2007 0218.html; *Centesimus Annus*, § 23.

[87] *Fratelli Tutti*, § 258; Paul VI, "Address to the United Nations," October 4, 1965; *Centesimus Annus*, § 52.

light of Pope Francis's powerful pleas for peace, the concern is that recent advancements in technology pose a profound risk of making wars too easy to start and too difficult to finish. Such weapons and their destructive force become a singular instance of the challenge to connect technology to ethics in order to limit and direct such technological power.

Autonomous Weapons Systems

As a technical matter, the use of AI in weapons systems ranges from automated defensive anti-missile systems to autonomous drones. Many commentators foresee the rapid advance of AI capabilities that would enable fully autonomous warfaring ships and robots set for urban combat. Their degree of autonomy varies from human-supervised drones piloted remotely by a soldier on a joystick to fully automated robots with the capacity to fire a fatal shot outside of any human control.[88] Most systems in active use today retain the requirement for a human to either approve a target before firing (a human "in the loop") or the capacity for a human to override targeting decisions (a human "on the loop"), but within military organizations and the defense industry, there is a movement toward the greater automation of warfare, including some technologies that would take a human completely *out* of the loop.[89]

The glossy ingenuity of AI weapon systems may invite their use in situations where in fact such use is unwarranted. The potential at the scale of their tremendous power also offers insidious but inviting possibilities

---

[88] Matthew Shadle, "Killer Robots and Cyber Warfare: Technology and War in the 21st Century," in *T&T Clark Handbook of Christian Ethics*, ed. Tobias Winright (New York: Bloomsbury, 2021), 217.

[89] The terms 'human in the loop' (HITL), 'human on the loop' (HOTL), and 'human out of the loop' (HOOL) are commonly used to describe, respectively, systems or modes in which: (a) the machine requires human approval before acting, (b) the machine can be overridden by an observing human before acting, and (c) human choice is completely removed from the decision. These terms could apply to any automated system—autonomous cars, autonomous vacuums, and even machine learning itself—but they take on particular importance when discussing lethal autonomous weapons systems.

for unscrupulous leaders seeking to control populations. The most troubling step, however, is the outsourcing to AI of a decision to kill. In an urban combat scenario, such a weapon may preserve the safety of soldiers, but at the expense of entrusting the sacredness of all human lives to an unaccountable machine. In all of these different ways, the AI programmed into such weapons allows human beings to distance themselves in greater or lesser degrees from the concrete circumstances and human factors involved in a moral decision to harm or even kill another person.

The compulsion to remove the self or one's own soldiers from the threats of battle while still maintaining capacity to harm the enemy has been a theme of weapons development since human beings first invented the spear and arrow and withdrew from hand-to-hand combat, but the relegation of lethal *decision-making* power to AI systems passes a new threshold. In a 2020 address to the United Nations, Pope Francis expressed grave concern that such weapons detach warfare "further from human agency."[90] In doing so, these weapons and their destructive force become a singular instance of the challenge to connect technology to ethics in order to limit and direct such technological power.[91]

We can think of this distancing more clearly if we consider how human beings make moral decisions, especially in high-speed situations with life and death at stake. A robotic weapon may be receiving and processing vast amounts of data. Such a weapon is also surely not affected by fear or panic, common phenomena in combat. The combination of data input, processing power, and absence of emotion suggests the possibility of better decisions in tense scenarios. But such a weapon is not filtering data through the feelings and emotions that viscerally connect human beings to each other. Nor is such a weapon confronted with the moral power of a physically present, concrete, embodied person. As theologian Matthew

---

[90] Francis, "Video Message to the United Nations," September 25, 2020, www.youtube.com/watch?v=gmrJKIO3RG8.

[91] See also Noreen Herzfeld, "Can Lethal Autonomous Weapons Be Just?," *Journal of Moral Theology* 11, Special Issue 1 (2022): 70–86.

Shadle notes, "Moral decision-making is qualitatively different from the forms of reasoning required to identify and disarm an underwater mine.... The ability to distinguish combatants and noncombatants on the battlefield requires an ability to interpret motivations, which in turn requires self-consciousness and the ability to empathize with others."[92] Human fellow-feeling has a possible depth far surpassing any processing power: "Empathy is something more than an immediate response to signs detected on the face or body of another. It is the capacity to be profoundly touched oneself by the misery of the other and to share in its burden."[93]

Even if such weapons are programmed in terms of the laws of war (as some have suggested), we still face a great gulf between the way that an autonomous weapon is made to comply with such laws and the more humane possibilities of the prudential decision-making of men and women. In tense conflict, no abstract logic is at work that can be mechanically transformed into a law-abiding algorithm. Instead, human beings draw on the immense complexities of experience (and their capacity for empathy) to inform their prudence which, in turn, qualifies facts, manages gaps, reasons through contradictions in law and conflicts between norms, and clarifies vague terms on the way to deciding whether the law of war applies or not—and then deciding what next to do.[94]

Another consideration is the irreducible moral importance of establishing accountability in situations of conflict. Even granting the "fog of war" (the way that responsibility may be clouded by the rapid intensity of combat), it is usually possible to establish at least some degree of

---

[92] Shadle, "Killer Robots and Cyber Warfare," 220.
[93] Archbishop Silvano Tomasi, "The Use of Lethal Autonomous Weapons Systems—Ethical Questions," Address of the Permanent Observer Mission of the Holy See to the United Nations and Other International Organizations in Geneva, April 16, 2015, in *The Humanization of Robots and the Robotization of the Human Person: Ethical Reflections on Lethal Autonomous Weapons Systems and Augmented Soldiers*, ed. Alice de La Rochefoucauld and Stefano Saldi (Chambésy, Switzerland: Caritas in Veritate Foundation, 2017), 80, www.fciv.org/downloads/WP9-Book.pdf.
[94] Tomasi, "The Use of Lethal Autonomous Weapons Systems," 81.

accountability for harmful or fatal actions. And it is never possible to attribute such accountability to a machine, which may in any case also have technical flaws and bugs that undermine faultless images of processing power. Theologian Brian Stiltner argues, "The principle should be that *a human being* always decides on a deadly action. . . . Persons are flawed in many ways, but they are morally and legally accountable, and they understand the human stakes of war, even when they try to ignore them."[95]

Finally, the moral hazard of removing humans from the battlefield extends also to the decision to go to war in the first place. Autonomous weapons offer nations who deploy them the potential to reduce the human costs of war (on their own side) to nearly zero, thus making war cheap and removing one of the greatest barriers preventing nations from going to war. This choice would be concerning enough if such capabilities were (as most traditional weapons are) in the hands of a few rich nations, who could use this capacity to exert their will on their smaller and weaker neighbors. However, while the most sophisticated development of such weapons requires the resources of wealthy and powerful states, the low cost of many autonomous weapons increases the threat of proliferation to any state or organization and correspondingly increases the potential for indiscriminate use of such weapons.[96]

Beneficial Uses of AI in International Conflict

Even as AI holds the potentiality (and historical example) to extend the violence of international conflict through both physical and digital means, we can also recognize the potential for AI to be used for benevolent ends. The scale, speed, and accuracy with which AI can process information, for example, can be used for reconnaissance and intelligence purposes that could potentially decrease the threat of war. At the United Nations, "it is

---

[95] Brian Stiltner, "A Taste of Armageddon: When Warring is Done by Drones and Robots," in *Can War Be Just in the 21st Century? Ethicists Engage the Tradition*, ed. Tobias Winright and Laurie Johnston (Maryknoll, NY: Orbis Books, 2015), 27.
[96] Tomasi, "The Use of Lethal Autonomous Weapons Systems," 84–85.

surprising how many consequential decisions are still made solely on the basis of intuition. Yet complex decisions often need to navigate conflicting goals and undiscovered options, against a landscape of limited information and political preference. This is where we can use deep learning—where a network can absorb huge amounts of public data and test it against real-world examples on which it is trained while applying with probabilistic modeling."[97] Satellite imaging combined with AI can help to predict future international flash points, including anticipating drought, famine, and other potential causes of conflict. Moreover, AI deployed in the use of language and dialect processing can aid in communication, especially at the local level. And even when it does come to conflict, AI can be used to verify the refugee status of asylum seekers fleeing from war-torn areas. It can be used to help humanitarian organizations in resettling refugees by predicting the scope of the crisis to help in preparation and identifying available resources amid the crisis.[98] Autonomous drones can be used for all sorts of nonviolent means, from delivery of resources to trapped refugees to the removal of mines both on land and sea.

In the end, like nearly all of the applications examined in this chapter, a blanket approach that considers AI to be wholly virtuous or wholly vicious is not appropriate. AI has the capacity to increase the violence and destruction of international conflict, but it also has the capacity to reduce these outcomes. Most concerning, however, is the potential for AI to remove the existing deterrents to war by seemingly offering to make war cheap, easy, and without human cost (on one's own side).

---

[97] Daanish Masood and Martin Waehlisch, "AI and Global Governance: Robots Will Not Only Wage Future Wars but also Future Peace," *United Nations University Center for Policy Research*, 2019, cpr.unu.edu/publications/articles/robots-will-not-only-wage-future-wars-but-also-future-peace.html.

[98] Ana Beduschi, "Harnessing the Potential of Artificial Intelligence for Humanitarian Action: Opportunities and Risks," *International Review of the Red Cross* no. 919 (June 2022), international-review.icrc.org/articles/harnessing-the-potential-of-artificial-intelligence-for-humanitarian-action-919.

Sphere of Work and the Economy

Catholic social teaching has consistently emphasized the dignity of work and the rights of workers since the first encyclical was written on the topic in the 1890s. These early arguments were confirmed and concretized by the Second Vatican Council in *Gaudium et Spes*, which highlights the dignity of workers as made in the image of God, supports the rights of workers to form unions freely and without risk of reprisal,[99] and discusses the importance of "justice" and "charity" as virtues that should guide the economy, such that "created goods should be in abundance for all in like manner."[100]

In the past sixty years, Pope Saint John Paul II, Pope Benedict XVI, and Pope Francis have affirmed and expanded these teachings of the council. John Paul II's *Laborem Exercens* describes work as "a fundamental dimension of man's existence on earth," an aspect of the image of God, in which the person "reflects the very action of the Creator of the universe."[101] Likewise, in *Caritas in Veritate*, Benedict XVI stressed the rising importance of labor unions in the face of global inequity. They are vital to the economic system not only so they can protect their workers, but so they can be stewards of humane working conditions to those "outside their membership," especially "workers in developing countries where social rights are often violated."[102] Writing in the wake of the global recession of 2008, Pope Benedict called on the financial sector in particular to refocus on sustainable ethical growth "so as to create suitable conditions for human development and for the development of peoples."[103] This development points to three areas to consider on the intersection of AI and the global economy. First, work and the economy should thus be oriented toward the community as well as the individual, with the common good,

---

[99] *Gaudium et Spes*, § 68.
[100] *Gaudium et Spes*, § 69.
[101] *Laborem Exercens*, § 4.
[102] *Caritas in Veritate*, § 64.
[103] *Caritas in Veritate*, § 65.

the care for all people, being the ultimate goal of all economic and state systems of power. This can take the form of social services, corporate charities, and sound investments, but no matter the profit, business venture, or state politics, "the right of having a share of earthly goods sufficient for oneself and one's family belongs to everyone."[104] Second, the workplace should also be a location for interpersonal and collective encounters. Economies are composed of "free and independent human beings created to the image of God,"[105] and as such individuals as workers "should have a share in determining" their work conditions, whether "in person or through freely elected delegates." One of the ways in which they can do so is through labor unions. To support this, the Second Vatican Council named "the right of freely founding working unions" as being "among the basic rights of the human person."[106] These associations ought to be far more than merely for bargaining but also spaces of community, solidarity, education, and the achievement of other goods.

Even the seemingly cold domain of contract can be a space of true encounter. Indeed, the market requires elements of a logic of gift and encounter: "Without internal forms of solidarity and mutual trust, the market cannot completely fulfill its proper economic function."[107] Economic exchange usually involves something beyond mere calculative logic, so "authentically human social relationships of friendship, solidarity and reciprocity can also be conducted within economic activity, and not only outside it or 'after' it."[108]

Third, the vision of the common good supported by the economy ought to include care for all of creation—as Pope Francis writes in *Laudato Si'*, "our common home."[109] This extension to creation is an ancient and often implicit aspect of the common good, but it should be made explicit

---

[104] *Gaudium et Spes*, § 69.
[105] *Gaudium et Spes*, § 68.
[106] *Gaudium et Spes*, § 68.
[107] *Caritas in Veritate*, § 35.
[108] *Caritas in Veritate*, § 36.
[109] *Laudato Si'*, § 1.

in the modern context in order to clarify what it means to work toward "the full development of humanity."[110] This inclusion of care of creation ties together concerns of science, technology, economics, and religion in an "integral ecology."[111] From the point of view of integral ecology, care for the Earth is not a superfluous extension of human dignity, but a reflection of a deep and Biblical tradition where "environmental deterioration and human and ethical degradation are closely linked."[112] The relationship between God, humanity, and creation is interwoven such that one cannot properly care for one's fellow neighbors without caring for creation, and one cannot have a true and right relationship with God without proper attention on the dignity of humanity and care for the Earth. In Pope Francis's own words, "A correct relationship with the created world demands that we not weaken this social dimension of openness to others, much less the transcendent dimension of our openness to the 'Thou' of God. Our relationship with the environment can never be isolated from our relationship with others and with God. Otherwise, it would be nothing more than romantic individualism dressed up in ecological garb, locking us into a stifling immanence."[113] Work and the economy thus are realms of dignity and community, leading to encounter with others, the world, and God.

AI and the Global Economy

With such priorities established, we can now turn our attention to the realities and the hopes of AI in an already technological economy. AI systems have already proven remarkably powerful in terms of increasing efficiency. AI systems can do many things more efficiently than humans, such as information tracking, navigation, complex predictions, and supply chain logistics, assisting in these tasks and removing some of their

---

[110] *Laudato Si'*, § 62.
[111] *Laudato Si'*, § 11.
[112] *Laudato Si'*, § 56.
[113] *Laudato Si'*, § 119.

drudgery. While efficiency at the expense of human dignity and environmental protection is dangerous to individuals, communities, and the Earth, more efficient systems can also be used to improve the global common good. For example, AI systems can allow the same amount of human work to be done in fewer hours. AI is also remarkably skilled at language acquisition and translation, so that AI is serving communication between cultures not only in translation services, but also in preserving the rich heritages of languages that are either currently endangered or functionally extinct. People can work together with fewer communication struggles and can collectively strive for the shared common interest of a common good. These linguistic uses of AI can build a truly global community. In all of these ways, AI is humanity's ally.

Dangers of AI for Work

Yet AI, like any technology, is not an unalloyed good. It "can cease to be man's ally and become almost his enemy, as when the mechanization of work 'supplants' him, taking away all personal satisfaction and the incentive to creativity and responsibility, when it deprives many workers of their previous employment, or when, through exalting the machine, it reduces man to the status of its slave."[114] Through our interaction with technology, employers can take up the technocratic paradigm discussed in chapter 6, viewing their workers simply as labor and the natural world as mere resources for extraction. These failures can be found throughout the global supply chain that produces the marvels of AI: human rights abuses in the mining of rare earth minerals in the nations of the Global South, environmental dangers of refining facilities, unfair wages and working conditions in transporting materials, poor working conditions for those who refine and cleanse popular AI language models, and the lack of labor unions in most of the companies serving these supply chains.[115]

---

[114] *Laborem Exercens*, § 5.
[115] Crawford, *Atlas of AI*, 1–23.

Furthermore, there is a limit to how much workers should be supplanted by automation. While industrial workers have long faced replacement by machines, the recent advances of generative AI have threatened the livelihoods of creative professions whose work was previously seen as resistant to automation, such as artists, musicians, writers, and poets. As later sections will discuss, these professions, and many others that seek to explore the human condition, can never truly be replaced by machines, for they are inherently expressions of our innermost human nature. Finding a balance between human creative expression and the use of AI as a tool for that expression will require great wisdom, but the criteria for judgment should include remembering that all technology should exist to serve humanity, not stifle or attempt to replace it. However, many crafts where creative artistry and human ingenuity can be found are already being replaced by machines, leading to degradation of the beauty of the lived environment and thus the common good. Even in jobs that remain, work can be degraded if the work is deskilled, with the worker becoming merely the hands of an algorithm, lacking the potential exercise of judgment.[116]

The common good can further be undermined through the concentration of wealth. AI demands massive resources in terms of computing power, energy, and data. These resource demands are limiting AI advances to a few large corporations. This concentration of AI development threatens to develop into an even deeper concentration of wealth. Our times confront the challenges described by Pope Pius XI: "The distribution of created goods, which today . . . laboring under the gravest evils due to the huge disparity between the few exceedingly rich and the unnumbered propertyless, must be effectively called back to and brought into conformity with the norms of the common good, that is, social justice."[117] To confront these dangers, Pius XI argued for a well-

---

[116] Paul Scherz, *Tomorrow's Troubles: Risk, Anxiety, and Prudence in an Age of Algorithmic Governance* (Washington, DC: Georgetown University Press, 2022), 143–160.
[117] *Quadragesimo Anno*, § 58.

regulated economic system, since "the right ordering of economic life cannot be left to a free competition of forces. For from this source, as from a poisoned spring, have originated and spread all the errors of individualist economic teaching."[118] Such regulation is necessary today.

Finally, technology companies have frequently undermined attempts at worker associations, which prevents remedies for many of these problems. The very structure of online work can also make forming unions and other forms of worker associations difficult, since workers no longer see each other in person, or are scheduled for varying shifts. These dangers are balanced by the potential for social media and other new communications technologies to make organization easier.

Embracing a Shared Common Good for Humanity and Creation in a World with AI

There are many problems for the future of AI in the workplace, such as structural biases, economic inequity, human rights abuses, corporate greed, and environmental harm.[119] But the promise of AI systems does not need to fall victim to the same abuses of the past. The advent of this remarkable technology can help to usher a world with more fairness, economic equity, human dignity, protection of workers, and environmental protections. The movement toward such an economic vision begins with individuals, corporations, and states acting within their power and privilege to enact changes available to them, whether individual, corporate, state, or collective. The Church stands with all those who seek to employ AI for the common good of a global economic future, and calls upon all people, young and old, rich and poor, to work within their means to form a more just, more holy world of tomorrow.

---

[118] *Quadragesimo Anno*, § 88.

[119] For theological resources on approaching racism, bias, and inequity in technology, see John P. Slattery, "We Must Find a Stronger Theological Voice: A Copeland Dialectic to Address Racism, Bias, and Inequity in Technology," *Journal of Moral Theology* 11, Special Issue 1 (2022): 112–131.

Sphere of Communication and Culture

Many of the challenges mentioned above—such as the nudging of populations, a fragmentation of trust and civil debate, limits to how criminal justice AI or lethal autonomous drones can apply principles in complex settings, or the automation of work previously done by humans—are closely related to underlying problems that AI raises for the broader sphere of culture and communication. These challenges have to do with applications that imitate or influence human judgment and thereby transform our presence to ourselves, our neighbors, and the creative process. Hence, close attention to AI's bearing on judgment can offer us an integrative perspective on existing challenges while helping us remain vigilant for what lies ahead.

By "judgment" we mean the ability to make sense of and respond to contingent, particular things.[120] In judgment, we use knowledge and experience to answer questions such as: What is this? How does it relate to me? What will I do about it? Judgments come in a variety of forms. Some are immediate and pre-reflective, while others follow from conscious deliberation. Some interpret the world around us, while others commit us to specific actions. Finally, many judgments are outwardly expressed (and even worked out) in both language and non-symbolic forms like gestures or crafted objects. The Good Samaritan story offers an example: we see a broad range of judgments in the immediate perceptions of the stranger as human, as a potential object of violence or mercy, or as a threat to one's safety, resources, or ritual purity; the Samaritan's words, gestures, or

---

[120] The account of judgment here is synthetic. It draws especially on Thomas Aquinas's account, particularly as it has been discussed in conjunction with contemporary psychology by works such as Ezra Sullivan, *Habits and Holiness: Ethics, Theology, and Biopsychology* (Washington, DC: CUA Press, 2021); Daniel De Haan, "Linguistic Apprehension as Incidental Sensation in Thomas Aquinas," *Proceedings of the American Catholic Philosophical Association* 84 (2010): 179–96. It is also similar to the discussion of judgment in the special issue of *Social Research* on algorithms (*Social Research* 86, no. 4 [2019]; see especially the introduction, Joseph Davis and Paul Scherz, "Persons Without Qualities: Ethics, AI, and the Reshaping of Ourselves," *Social Research* 86, no. 4 [2019]: xxxiii–xxxix).

decisions (at times deliberate) on behalf of this stranger; the Samaritan's sense of self as a brother to the stranger and as participating in a world where mercy makes sense; Jesus's use of the story to reframe the scholar's question; Luke's compositional strategies; and the reader's cognitive and practical interpretations of the parable. Robust and finely-tuned judgment is crucial for navigating the complexities of relationships and cultural creation. Judgment is how we locate ourselves in time, space, and society—and how we identify with ourselves as embodied beings at that precise location.

Much of the apparent utility of AI applications stems from how they seem able to mimic or even outperform human judgment. Some concerns arise directly from this potential: How will our relationships or culture be shaped by applications that outsource our judgments in a way that may point us toward bad ends, curtail fully collaborative deliberation about those ends, or foster the moral deskilling that results when we do not judge for ourselves? These concerns are similar to the ways in which algorithmic governance can undermine democratic participation. However, another kind of problem can arise as a poor response to these direct threats. A society where we are repeatedly told that machines can judge better than humans, and where we learn we ought to be constantly on guard against tacit machine influence, is a society where we persistently experience our own capacity for judgment as unreliable and questionable. Moments of irony and critical thinking about our judgments can be immensely fruitful *interruptions* to a basic confidence in our ability to make sense of contingent reality. But what happens when the suspicion that our judgments are influenced by (or less reliable than) a machine's pushes that irony to become a default setting for experiencing daily life? We might not always react well to this pressure to hold our judgments constantly at arm's length.

Both types of problems are already on clear display in how we communicate with one another about the news. On the one hand, many of us by now have a healthy awareness of how (and for whose profit) algorithms nudge the production, dissemination, and consumption of news toward discursive bubbles where the interpretation of complex events becomes subordinate to the collective articulation of an engaging but highly one-sided (and thus increasingly inaccurate) story about why our society is broken, who is to blame, and how we can remain on the "right" side of history.[121] On the other hand, it is not easy to use this awareness well. Knowing these things can make it even harder to reckon seriously with the judgments of people outside our field of allegiance and perspective. Moreover, when we have the honesty to admit our own vulnerability to these influences, we may soon find ourselves exhausted by the work of compensating for them through sincere and consistent engagement with outsiders—and perhaps also sliding into paralyzing doubt about our ability to make sense of today's world. These are not, of course, sustainable attitudes. Hence, it is not surprising that many of us eventually indulge our felt need for trust in a reliable picture of reality through uncritical or simplistic forms of cultural identification and social commitment. Often our judgment is handed over not to a machine but to a cultural leader who promises to interpret the present for us. And so, our search for a critical posture in the face of machine judgment can easily backfire if it does not also cultivate robust, sophisticated, and integrative forms of human judgment.

We have good reason to remain watchful of how a similar set of challenges may arise in other areas of life. In what follows, we discuss how such patterns are already developing in the areas of interpersonal communication and cultural creation.

---

[121] See *Fratelli Tutti*, Chapter 1. For particularly helpful discussions of this issue, see Jeffrey Bilbro, *Reading the Times: A Literary and Theological Inquiry into the News* (Downers Grove, IL: IVP Academic, 2021); and Jon Askonas, "Reality is Just a Game Now," *The New Atlantis* (Spring 2022): 6–27. On the economic and cultural forces driving these "choice architectures," see Zuboff, *The Age of Surveillance Capitalism*. As these sources explain well, all of this builds on previous trends while exacerbating the problem in novel ways.

Interpersonal Communication

AI's imitation of and influence on judgment is already exacerbating our prior difficulties with being fully and fruitfully present to others and to ourselves. For quite some time, algorithms have shaped relationships by prioritizing the exposure of content that best prompts others to remain actively engaged on digital platforms. Visibility on these platforms requires us to pattern our own communicative judgments after this imperative, which has led to some problematic tendencies. The drive to present ourselves in ways that are easily quantifiable and then optimized for maximal response rates (of likes, followers, etc.) encourages a sense of self that is skewed toward extrinsic and highly visible features (such as how powerfully one displays allegiance to a cultural type) rather than a serious and responsible pursuit of truth and virtue. And because such maximization does not respect particular contexts or degrees of intimacy, it also encourages communication fit for mass consumption that relies on easily digestible stereotypes and discourages complex, measured, sincere, and vulnerable discourse as well as the habits that make it possible.[122] We can expect these trends to persist, especially if large language models continue to creep into daily communication as compositional aids for text messages and social media posts.

Again, however, one also ought to think about problems that can result when we react against the challenges above in unfruitful ways—especially when we experience those challenges as part of the broader texture of a digital technocratic society's information abundance, drive for control, and AI-powered nudging and outsourcing of judgment.

A good example of such unfruitful reactions is the increasing prevalence, in our daily life, of an AI-powered risk management model for

---

[122] For an excellent introduction to these themes and related literature, see Felicia Wu Song, *Restless Devices: Recovering Personhood, Presence, and Place in the Digital Age* (Downers Grove, IL: IVP Academic, 2021), 39–89.

making decisions.[123] One way that AI seems to improve upon human judgment is through an idealized form of utilitarian weighing of costs and benefits. With its predictive and statistical abilities, AI provides decision-makers with a range of possibilities and their associated likelihood of good and bad outcomes. It can then recommend the choice that maximizes desired outcomes. Given its calculative nature, AI can perform such judgments as well as humans, if not better. While such analyses can be prudently used in controlled institutional settings like government policy-making, the model is also migrating into personal life. This happens for many reasons, including: (a) the integration of AI decision support systems into other spheres of life, (b) the drive for control and safety shored up by the technocratic paradigm, (c) our decreasing agency for engaging fruitfully with a complex material world due to our ongoing outsourcing of human skills to machines, and (d) our sense of exhaustion before the information abundance, work demands, and news consumption burdens that digital media have made central to our daily experience.

Reliance upon risk assessment for daily personal decisions raises a number of problems. It focuses on a utilitarian weighing of likely costs and benefits that can lead us to reduce our neighbors to instruments for future gains. By fostering an illusory hope in a safe and controllable future and then fixing that hope upon algorithmic risk prediction, it also exacerbates moral deskilling and a corresponding loss of confidence in our unaided judgments. Moreover, risk-based judgment trains us to focus primarily on future possibilities and thus breeds anxiety and regret over options not taken or not yet realized. All of this bears on our ability to make ourselves present to others: when the imperative to aggressively optimize our future leaves us unwilling to "waste" our time with and be moved or transformed by what is right in front of us; when the world proves impossible to manage according to this ideal of control; and when we find ourselves exhausted, deskilled, and distrustful of our own judgments—it appears immensely

---

[123] This and the next paragraph rely especially on Scherz, *Tomorrow's Troubles*. See also Song, *Restless Devices*, 79–89.

tempting to give our attention instead to all of those unrealized but seemingly more manageable possibilities still waiting in the future. This is not a picture of a heart readily disposed to attend with receptive patience, and to give itself with calm generosity, to the neighbors before us.

The foregoing may also deepen challenges to being present to *ourselves* that can in turn further obstruct our attention to others. When we come to regard our own judgments as questionable and unreliable, we naturally have difficulty identifying with them as our own. To a degree this suspicion and irony fall also on any part of us that goes into such judgments—especially our bodies, through which we perceive and interact with the world, through which we become present to other people's own strivings to interpret that world, and through which we are susceptible to digital nudging. If the judging, embodied part of us is not reliable and might at any point act as a cover for deliberate outside influence, we may begin to regard this part as somehow not fully ourselves. And when we realize the same is likely true for others, it becomes hard to imagine how we may relate to them with seriousness and sincerity. Do they truly believe in what they are saying? Do they really stand behind the set of judgments their bodies are acting out? Time will tell how these patterns will play out or which further challenges they may cause. But our existing difficulties with being attentive to the present moment, connecting with others, and cultivating robust personal judgment are prevalent enough (and sufficiently linked with each other) to merit our ongoing attention to the importance of self-presence for virtuous action in an AI society.

Cultural Creation

For several years, AI has influenced judgments about cultural artifacts and the broader formation of culture through a number of means: algorithms that suggest playlists of songs and movies and tools that assist in generating texts and computer graphics, among many others. Recently, generative AI accelerated this situation by creating new cultural artifacts seemingly from scratch. These tools, like ChatGPT or DALL-E, can generate a new image or text based on a user prompt. The system predicts the most probable response to that prompt based on its training on a vast library of text or images. Some of these responses, especially from image generators, have been truly amazing, seeming to provide the serendipity, surprise, and lack of direct control people experience when interacting with a true work of art or with reality.

Generative AI and the broader use of AI in cultural creation raise a number of questions. Given their ease of use, they may begin to dominate the realm of cultural creation, raising questions as to why we should invest in a human artist and her training when AI can generate an artifact so easily. Such a shift might significantly impact cultural creativity, since these tools are not truly creative; they merely suggest the most likely artifact given past responses. Like all AI, the tools merely remix past data, so they cannot provide a new depth of interpretation that comes from an original insight into reality, meaning that such tools might stymie cultural development.[124] This becomes even more concerning when AI is used to predict the commercial popularity of products, exacerbating prior limits on which forms of creativity receive institutional support and embedding prior biases into technological structures.[125]

As it becomes more prevalent, AI's use in cultural creation might affect the human ability to create, even when the AI acts as part of a human-computer team. For example, if AI takes over the first steps of creation (such as generating first drafts), people might increasingly become the editors, curators, or suggesters of prompts of texts and images generated by machines.[126] This process may be unobjectionable in many circumstances;

---

[124] For a discussion of abductive judgment and creativity, see Erik Larson, *The Myth of Artificial Intelligence* (Cambridge, MA: Belknap Press, 2021).

[125] For considerations of "consent, credit, and compensation," for art used to train AI models, see Russ Altman, Rebecca Blake, Steven Zapata, "Creativity in the Age of AI: Artist Perspectives on AI, Copyright, and Future of Work" at the Stanford HAI Spring Symposium on Creativity in the Age of AI, May 24, 2022, Stanford, CA, www.youtube.com/watch?v=y9wOvFihY74.

[126] Kevin Kelly and Lee Anthony, "Engines of Wow," *Wired* 31, no. 2 (2023): 34–47.

we could debate the benefits of having AI draft a formal email or design a utilitarian image for a PowerPoint presentation. But consistent abandonment of initial composition to AI threatens the integrated nature of a practice.[127] Even its use in later steps of creation alters many practices. The danger is that people will start to lose the embodied skills and dispositions necessary for a deeper engagement with a creative practice. Over the past century, to cite a comparable case, the introduction of records, tapes, CDs, and MP3s gradually eliminated an older framework of listening to music in which one had to develop skills in playing an instrument, or at least gather with other people who played. Instead, with the new technologies, music became a commodity and fewer people now develop the skills to perform it. These effects are greater when automation moves from the consumption to the production of artistic work. In writing, for example, the outline is frequently the most important aspect of creation. If merely editing an AI-generated draft, the author's thinking has already been channeled by the machine, decreasing possibilities for independent encounter with reality. The frequently multiple rounds of exploratory drafting and critical reconsideration—so crucial for the artifact's profundity and fruitfulness—are on the cusp of being progressively smoothed out of the creative process. We can expect these changes to have negative effects on both high and vernacular culture, although the effects on the latter would be both more likely and more troubling.

Such changes might also undermine the habits necessary for appreciating cultural artifacts that are usually gained through practice. As people become more aware of the ease of generating documents and images, these artifacts might lose their importance. People might become ironic about them, questioning their worth as cultural artifacts become

---

[127] The analysis in this paragraph draws on Albert Borgmann, *Technology and the Character of Contemporary Life: A Philosophical Inquiry* (Chicago: University of Chicago Press, 1984).

consumables to be thrown away.[128] These concerns contribute to a further worry that AI-generated artifacts might degrade our contemplative capacities. As we lose the skills to appreciate cultural artifacts, they lose value, and ultimately a thinned-out form of art is unable to open reality to us in new ways. This loss of contemplative capacity is a broader danger than merely its threat to art, as Pope Francis has encouraged contemplation of the world as an antidote to the technocratic paradigm.[129] A contemplative ability allows for engagement with others and the environment. The Church has persistently supported the transformative capacities of art to form our dispositions and help in meditation on the transcendent. Technology can aid in this, as long as it does not give rise to a consumerist model of cultural creation that forgoes engagement with human capacities.

Sphere of the Natural World

At the heart of the Christian tradition is the proclamation of a Creator God who chooses to incarnate and become a body among bodies, a human being entering into relationship with others. Paul's letter to the Colossians makes plain that Jesus "is the image of the invisible God, the firstborn of all creation, for in Him all things in heaven and on earth were created . . . and in Him all things hold together."[130] All is connected.[131]

The technocratic paradigm, in which mastery, control, and possession supplant stewardship, humility, and solidarity, sometimes masquerades as Judaism and Christianity's divine mandate to "have dominion."[132] Such a skewing of this mandate leads to exploitation, a "tyrannical

---

[128] For broader concerns along these lines, see Walter Benjamin, "The Work of Art in an Age of Mechanical Reproduction," in *Illuminations*, ed. Hannah Arendt (New York: Schocken Books, 1968), 217–252.
[129] E.g., *Laudato Si'*, §§ 85, 112, 127, and 222.
[130] Colossians 1:15–17.
[131] *Laudato Si'*, §§ 16, 42, 91, 117.
[132] Genesis 1:28.

anthropocentrism unconcerned for other creatures,"[133] a belief that nature exists solely to serve humankind (as if the two were separable). Such outright despotism dangerously misreads the biblical record and the God who looks upon the whole of creation and deems it to be "very good."[134] This misreading further isolates human beings from the earth (from which, and for the tending of which, they were made in the first place[135]) and, therefore, from the One who created it.[136] This atomistic vision, in which "life gradually becomes a surrender to situations conditioned by technology, itself viewed as the principal key to the meaning of existence,"[137] fails to recognize that "our relationship with the environment can never be isolated from our relationship with others and with God. Otherwise, it would be nothing more than romantic individualism dressed up in ecological garb, locking us into a stifling immanence."[138]

A number of negative consequences result. First, we might consider the denigration of embodiment. In the second century, Valentinian Gnostics found it contradictory to call changeable matter "good." Nonetheless, against the cultured despisers of matter, the Christian tradition has insisted that creation is no mere backdrop, still less a fundamental hindrance, but the place of salvation wherein the Creator meets us. And therefore, as Pope Francis cautions, the natural world's meaning can never be reduced to raw material for our own designs.

> Once the human being declares independence from reality and behaves with absolute dominion, the very foundations of our life begin to crumble, for "instead of carrying out his role as a cooperator with God in the work

---

[133] *Laudato Si'*, § 68.
[134] Genesis 1:31.
[135] Genesis 2:7, 15.
[136] Ramelow, "Technology and Our Relationship with God," *Nova et Vetera* (English edition) 22, no. 1 (2024).
[137] *Laudato Si'*, § 110.
[138] *Laudato Si'*, § 119.

of creation, man sets himself up in place of God and thus ends up provoking a rebellion on the part of nature."¹³⁹

Francis's warning against declaring "independence from reality" applies to our attempts to live in cyberspace, in virtual realities. Nature, in the past, has been a place of encounter with nature's God, even the starting point for proofs of God's existence.¹⁴⁰ Sealing ourselves off from nature seals us off from nature's God as well. It is a continuation of the refusal of a relationship with God that began with the fall, only now we do not hide behind fig leaves but in virtual spaces, the metaverse, and other artificial environments.

As with all technologies, then, AI must be at the service of a different kind of progress,¹⁴¹ one that is divorced from notions of power, dominion-as-despotism or mastery, and control. For the Church, genuine progress must come together with the cultivation of a "wider solidarity."¹⁴²

> Now more than ever, we must guarantee an outlook in which AI is developed with a focus not on technology but rather for the good of both humanity and the environment, of our common and shared home and of its human inhabitants, who are inextricably connected. In other words, a vision in which human beings *and* nature are at the heart of how digital innovation is developed.¹⁴³

As such, concerns about environmental impact cannot be cast to the margins as the development of AI continues to gain pace. Although AI has been frequently heralded as a savior of sorts that will help solve some of the world's most significant problems (including climate change), public

---

[139] *Laudato Si'*, § 117, quoting *Caritas in Veritate*, § 35.
[140] See Romans 1:19–20.
[141] *Laudato Si'*, § 112.
[142] *Octogesima Adveniens*, § 41.
[143] Pontifical Council for Life, "Rome Call for AI Ethics," February 28, 2020, www.romecall.org. Emphasis added.

discourse on the environmental impact of AI (of data mining, energy-gobbling data centers that require vast amounts of water for cooling, emissions, disposal of electronic waste, and material toxicity) has been thin despite the efforts of the many scholars discussed in chapter 1.[144] Though we tend to think of computing as something that occurs in some non-material dimension that we call cyberspace, or in "the cloud," it is in fact a very physical process requiring machines, cables, and quite a bit of energy. The data that they transmit and store includes five hundred million tweets, 294 billion emails, four million gigabytes of data on Facebook, 4 thousand gigabytes from each computer connected car, sixty-five billion messages on WhatsApp, and five billion Google searches.[145]

This data is stored in massive server farms, often built in rural areas. Companies such as Google, Amazon, Microsoft, and Meta have placed millions of square feet worth of server space in rural areas. These centers count on cheap land, cheap electricity, and tax incentives from dying small towns looking to attract capital. They are part of a long tradition of the appropriation of rural resources for urban development. As one commentator explains: "In the same ways that urban areas depend on agricultural lands and distant resources for food, energy, materials, and water, the growth of digital capitalism also depends on rural resources to power and secure our Facebook status updates, Google photos, Kindle obsessions, Netflix streaming services, and iTunes music libraries."[146]

A study from the University of Massachusetts–Amherst found that the energy used in training a typical AI linguistics program emits 284 tons of carbon dioxide, five times the lifetime emissions of a midsize car or equivalent to more than a thousand round trip flights from London to

---

[144] Benedetta Brevini, "Black Boxes, Not Green: Mythologizing Artificial Intelligence and Omitting the Environment," *Big Data & Society* 7, no. 2 (July 1, 2020): 1–5, doi.org/10.1177/2053951720935141.

[145] Benedetta Brevini, *Is AI Good for the Planet?* (Cambridge, UK: Polity, 2021), 42–43.

[146] Anthony M. Levenda and Dillon Mahmoudi, "Silicon Forest and Server Farms: The (Urban) Nature of Digital Capitalism in the Pacific Northwest," *Culture Machine* 18 (2019), culturemachine.net/vol-18-the-nature-of-data-centers/silicon-forest-and-server-farms.

Rome.¹⁴⁷ And this is only increasing. As deep-learning models get more and more sophisticated, they consume more data. Their carbon footprint increased by a factor of three hundred thousand between 2012 and 2018.¹⁴⁸ If data centers were a nation, they would place between Japan and India in the amount of energy they use in a year. By 2030 it is estimated that in some countries data centers will make up as much as 30 percent of the annual energy consumption.

AI also contributes to environmental costs through the regrettably short life cycle of AI devices. Their dependency on rare metals such as lithium, palladium, and nickel has promoted extractive mining. The "always on" nature of our phones and computers, while minimal for each device, adds up when one considers how many devices each of us uses. Our phones, tablets and laptops are also designed to be replaced every few years. They deliberately do not have replaceable parts, forcing us to buy a new phone when battery life degrades, rather than simply replacing the battery. Companies further this planned obsolescence by not providing upgrades or security patches for software platforms that are more than a few years old. This leads to a disposal problem. Third world countries are too often the destinations for toxic and non-biodegradable electronic waste. In 2019 alone, the world generated 53.6 million tons of e-waste.¹⁴⁹

AI might discover ways to make a variety of processes more efficient, thereby reducing emissions. Many commentators view AI as a magic solution to our climate crisis.¹⁵⁰ Yet AI use still relies on hardware, energy, and infrastructure sources that deplete resources throughout the life cycle of a system or device. Novel applications, such as generative chatbots or

---

[147] Emma Strubell, Ananya Ganesh, and Andrew McCallum, (2020). "Energy and Policy Considerations for Modern Deep Learning Research," *Proceedings of the AAAI Conference on Artificial Intelligence*, 34 (2020): 13693–13696.

[148] Brevini, *Is AI Good for the Planet?*, 66–67.

[149] Justine Calma, "Humans left behind a record amount of e-waste in 2019," *The Verge*, July 2, 2020. https://www.theverge.com/21309776/record-amount-ewaste-2019-global-report-environment-health.

[150] Cf. Brevini, *Is AI Good for the Planet?*, 25–34.

digital currencies, look amazing until we ask what resources they will require should they become accessible to users worldwide. Using an AI program to answer a question might be more fun than doing a Google search, but it also uses five to ten times as much energy. For AI to be truly aligned with human values and flourishing, we must consider whether or when we truly need it. While an automated process may seem more efficient in terms of speed or even thoroughness, in terms of energy use and environmental fitness it may be the wrong choice.

The costs of our computing, in capital, natural resources, and environmental impact, are not an abstraction. Without a stable natural environment, our AI will fail along with our civilization. As Pope Francis points out, "the issue of environmental degradation challenges us to examine our lifestyle."[151] This challenge calls us to examine when AI is truly useful and necessary and when it is merely a toy or an escape from either responsibility or engagement with others. This is not a call to give up the fruits of technology, but to put them in their proper perspective, for, Pope Francis notes, "Those who enjoy more and live better each moment are those who have given up dipping here and there, always on the lookout for what they do not have. They experience what it means to appreciate each person and each thing. . . . Happiness means knowing how to limit some needs which only diminish us, and being open to the many different possibilities which life can offer."[152] He worries that AI, as currently envisioned, encourages instead "The notion of a human being with no limits, whose abilities and possibilities can be infinitely expanded thanks to technology."[153] This obsession with human intellect and power reduces the rest of creation "to a mere resource at [our] disposal. Everything that exists ceases to be a gift for which we should be thankful,

---

[151] *Laudato Si'*, § 206.
[152] *Laudato Si'*, § 223.
[153] Francis, *Laudate Deum*, § 21.

esteem and cherish, and instead becomes a slave, prey to any whim of the human mind and its capacities."[154]

Created in the image of a Trinitarian God, we are called first and foremost to be in a relationship, not only with our God and each other, but with the rest of creation as well. Our technologies, the works of our hands, must always take a subsidiary place to those relationships, lived most fully through the self-giving love that flows from the very life of our Creator.

---

[154] *Laudate Deum*, § 22.

Chapter 8

Recommendations for an AI Future

The dangers presented by AI may seem overwhelming, but these challenges are paired with the many potential benefits that AI brings to different areas of human life. It is incumbent upon contemporary society to discern how to use these technologies well in ways that bolster rather than undermine human flourishing. This chapter examines the many actors who have some way of governing the use of AI in order to suggest concrete responses to its dangers and opportunities. At the same time, we recognize that the dangers of AI reflect the broader challenges to human flourishing that result from a world organized around the technocratic paradigm rather than a culture of encounter. Beyond any of the particular proposals we offer here, an ethical AI future will need to be part of the broader transformation toward a more just society that Catholic social thought has called for since the Industrial Revolution.

Living in an AI World

Given the power of AI technologies and the many spheres of life in which they are used, it might seem that only governments, corporations, and large institutions would be able to exert control over it. In many AI applications, governing AI well does require the resources and authority of these institutions entrusted with protecting the common good. Relatively few people have the privilege to be able to opt out of educational systems, healthcare systems, workplaces, or policing regimes that deploy AI technologies in ways that are prejudicial to human flourishing. Still, there are ways in which individual users can affect how AI shapes their lives.

First, it is incumbent upon all users of AI, even upon all people with responsibility for others who use AI (such as a parent whose children use social media even if the parent may not), **to gain an adequate understanding of how AI works, what the dangers of particular applications might be, and how a clear grasp of these things can be obstructed by how these technologies are depicted in popular media**. This responsibility is no different for AI than for any other technology. For example, drivers need to know which road conditions are more dangerous than others, how to keep their cars from breaking down, and how responsible car use might differ from the values embedded in films and advertisements. It might seem more difficult to know how to properly use AI because it involves advanced mathematics and is often designed as a black box. Yet, is AI really so different from other advanced technologies? How many drivers really understand how all the different subcomponents of their car work? A lack of detailed technical knowledge does not prevent a user from learning basic practical knowledge regarding a technology, such as conditions when it will become dangerous to use and how to care for it.

Achieving this practical mastery will require education, much of which the individual user might need to seek. Thankfully, there are an increasing number of books and articles written for the popular audience about these dangers, many of which were discussed in chapter 1. Moreover, other organizations are developing documents like this one that apprise users of some of these dangers. Yet there is a need for a more directed approach to educating people about AI. Companies should ensure that educational resources are provided with their products. Schools should teach children basic technological literacy, including an understanding of the potential risks of AI. The Church can play an important role in this education. Catholic educational institutions should offer even more robust educational opportunities while fostering among their faculty and staff serious conversations about how AI bears upon their daily practice and the future of humanity. Catechesis on the proper use of digital technologies should be integrated into general religious education alongside lessons about other moral teachings and devotional practices. Proper use of these technologies, or at least avoiding their misuse, will be necessary for a flourishing life in Christ in contemporary society. Parishes should offer educational sessions in which reflections like this one could be a resource for ongoing conversations.

This education will reveal that one of the chief problems with these technologies is how they shape the user's relationship to the self. As previous chapters discussed, algorithms used in social media and online shopping create a digital model of the user so that they can predict what kind of content will ensure sales or continued use of the site or application. AI programs look at past user history as well as other digital breadcrumbs to predict the user's future action. Even the smallest actions, like scrolling more slowly past certain kinds of content, become part of the machine's model of that user's personality and desires. AI then reinforces those aspects of its model of the user that will increase the company's profit. Unfortunately, these techniques can reinforce the most vicious aspects of a person, driving the user into the most extreme manifestations of political group identity, continually degrading the person's body image and leading to eating disorders, or ensnaring the user in addiction to gambling or pornography. AI can trap the user in one very particular aspect of their identity and desires.

The first step to fighting these dangers to the self is to remember one's true identity. **Christians are not defined by their political party, their bodily attractiveness, or their consumer desires.** Instead, Christians are fundamentally disciples, members of the Body of Christ. Though greed for profit may push AI systems that make Christians forget that identity, they ought to hold fast to it. To maintain that identity in the face of the power of these technologies, Christians should act to strengthen it in the off-line world. People cannot merely maintain a cognitive appreciation of an identity in Christ. Rather, we ought to embed the Christian life in our desires and dispositions and rely on grace to help us do so. Thus, the most important aspect of an ethical engagement with AI is what the user does while off-line. She should take steps to deepen her life in Christ through all of the resources that the Church offers. In the face of the noise and speed of an AI-driven world, perhaps the most important step is to **take time in silence: time to pray, to contemplate Christ, to meditate on Scripture**. It is in our silent engagement with God in the quiet of our inner room[1] that we can strengthen ourselves against the forces of consumer culture driven by AI.[2]

Further, users ought to take steps to act upon those Christ-like desires and motivations in their online lives. AI will reinforce whatever virtues or vices users bring to their encounter with it. If a person brings anger, AI will foster it. If a person brings lust, AI will foster that. Conversely if a user brings a desire for the things of Christ, that is what AI will reinforce. **It is thus essential that users present their best selves to the online world** and to the bodily actions through which we participate in that world: searching virtuously; not clicking on, liking, or lingering on vicious content; and even searching out those resources that can help reinforce an engagement with prayer and silence. If one desires virtue, then one must begin to act virtuously—a truism whether we are online or off-line.

This truth might mean that people ought to avoid certain sites or applications that tend to reinforce personal vices or temptations. The Church has long taught people to **avoid the near occasion of sin**. Although this advice can be misused in ways that offload personal responsibility onto others, its wisdom is in the recognition that embodied human freedom involves a complex interplay among many cognitive processes, not all of which easily lie under our direct control. Since we cannot always fully control how we react to every object brought to our senses, we are also responsible for whether or how we enter into various

---

[1] Matthew 6:6.
[2] See Benedict XVI, "Message for 46th World Communications Day: Silence and Word: Path of Evangelization," May 20, 2012, www.vatican.va/content/benedict-xvi/en/messages/communications/documents/hf_ben-xvi_mes_20120124_46th-world-communications-day.html.

sensory ecologies. Making such choices well requires taking stock of our habits and our current circumstances. And given the way that algorithms augment the patterns by which we behave online, such advice is now doubly important. If a particular blog always fills a person with partisan rage, then she should avoid it. If a site sucks a person into hours of game-playing, then perhaps he should limit his time on it. In most cases, such discernment will require self-knowledge about which sites and applications are particularly dangerous for ourselves. In some cases, though, there may be applications that are too dangerous for anyone and thus should not be used. Pastors should explore ways to assist their parishioners in developing the skills and responsibility necessary for this kind of discernment.

The final area of knowledge and perception involves the world. "True wisdom demands an encounter with reality."[3] As it makes media more addictive, AI threatens to narrow our sensory perception of the world around us to a narrow range of experiences we can engage through the screens of our smartphones.[4] Digital media "lack the physical gestures, facial expressions, moments of silence, body language and even the smells, the trembling of hands, the blushes and perspiration that speak to us and are a part of human communication."[5] As embedded in our tools, AI can reduce embodied engagement with the world that occurs in craft and work. Chapter 7 discussed how this loss of skill and perception can impair creativity as it reduces the possibilities for engagement with reality. It is thus incumbent upon users to ensure that they maintain a fuller connection with reality even as they use AI.

Users can do this in their daily work. Insofar as possible, people should initially **learn how to do all the steps of a process before they**

---

[3] *Fratelli Tutti*, § 47.

[4] For a discussion of the ways media changes sensory experience, see Marshall McLuhan, *The Gutenberg Galaxy* (Toronto: University of Toronto Press, 1962); Walter Ong, *Orality and Literacy* (New York: Methuen, 1982).

[5] *Fratelli Tutti*, § 43.

automate it with AI. Then they can become aware of what they are outsourcing, and where the AI could err. It might be preferable not to automate certain steps of a process if they can give us a richer insight into reality or a more creative grasp of material, even in intellectual pursuits. In the home, we might embrace full responsibility for at least some of our menial tasks rather than automating them in every possible instance. As was explained in chapter 7, the performance of such tasks with a generous heart can be an important, and perhaps irreplaceable, expression of charity. But the refusal to outsource every menial task also comes with a cognitive benefit: it is often precisely in such patient attention to menial details that sophisticated, integrative, and truly creative judgment is cultivated. The point is not to reject AI, but to better understand what is forgone in choosing automation so that we can choose with truly creative wisdom.

In leisure, people should seriously consider **taking up a creative activity that provides embodied engagement with reality**. Playing an instrument, singing in a choir, gardening, cooking, or drawing all provide possibilities for a richer engagement with the world that moves beyond the commodified thrust of paid work. Such practices can also be of service to the Church and provide opportunities for community. And given how the acquisition of artistic skill hones our attention, perception, and judgment while training us in the wise production of artifacts, including technology, Christians in the twenty-first century would do well to meditate more deeply upon the theology and anthropology of art in order to better confront the cultural and technological challenges before us.

Meanwhile, the significance of embodied engagement with reality also indicates the importance of **building off-line relationships in order to better know and accept the reality of the other**. True intimacy is only at its fullest when it includes our bodily reality in the form of physical presence and touch. The eucharist reminds us that the physical act of eating and drinking together can unite us in our shared physicality. It is through befriending or at least socializing with others brought together by the accidents of location that people can escape their AI-imposed filter bubbles. Even though geography can also reinforce certain forms of exclusion, neighbors, fellow parishioners, and strangers who interrupt us with their physical presence still offer us some of the best opportunities to gain different perspectives. Moreover, embodied festivity can help people to step outside of the world of AI-driven efficiency to better contemplate reality.[6]

These steps can help people better contemplate the world as composed of more than what predictive algorithms impose upon it through their limited grasp of our values, preconceptions, and desires. People can gain a better appreciation of the world, others, and our own lives as gifts, as created. That does not mean that such interactions and work will be easy, but the friction itself reveals something important about reality's resistance to our whims. Only by gaining these insights can the person take hold of AI and use it to enhance flourishing, rather than merely being subject to it and the version of the world it presents.

Designing for an Age of AI

As the previous section discussed, AI presents immense opportunities and challenges to humanity precisely because it takes something so human (our intelligence), then externalizes it and directs it back upon ourselves.[7] The companies and designers of AI should keep this in mind as they develop their products because this externalization and directing-back can be done in ways that are either helpful or harmful. If we imbue AI with the best and most ethical aspects of human intelligence, then the world will be very different than if we imbue AI with the worst aspects of human intelligence or apathy toward the highest goods.

God created the world for the sake of love, for the sake of relationships of encounter. Companies and individuals should seek to produce tech-

---

[6] Josef Pieper, *Leisure: The Basis of Culture*, trans. A. Dru (Indianapolis, IN: Liberty Fund, 1999); Christopher Seith, "Rejoicing in Creation: Joseph Pieper's Response to a World of Online Distraction" (STD diss., The Catholic University of America, 2020).
[7] Dorobantu, Green, Ramelow, and Salobir, "Being Human in the Age of AI," 20.

nologies that allow for encounters that facilitate the growth of virtue and of loving relationships. **The designers of AI should especially keep the best interests of the vulnerable in mind when subjecting the world to new technologies.**

Today, though, AI inspires much uncertainty and fear in the world, and the developers of AI should recognize their own roles in creating such fears through their lack of caution. While we need to balance optimism and pessimism, neither should be grounded in naïveté. We need to look at reality with clear eyes, with its uncertainties and risks. The developers of AI have a central role—perhaps, as creators, the most central role—to play in this task. In this section, we will first examine the corporate responsibility lodged within technology companies before turning to the responsibilities of individual program managers and programmers.

Companies are the focal point for the contemporary development and deployment of AI technologies. Yet the technocratic paradigm discussed in chapter 6 is so deeply embedded in the technology industry that it tends to become an invisible assumption that forms the foundation of much subsequent thinking. **The technocratic paradigm's assumption that efficiency is always good should be discarded by companies** because it is insufficient given the role that technology plays in contemporary society and culture.

Technologies are not morally neutral. Intentions and teleological structures are always implicit in them.[8] For example, technologies that enhance speed assume that speed is morally better. Technologies that enhance efficiency or scale assume that efficiency or scale are morally better. Speed, efficiency, and scale can be good—for example, when saving lives more quickly, more efficiently, and in greater numbers in a medical setting. But technologies that do the opposite—killing swiftly, efficiently, and on a mass scale—can be evil. AI technologies, as externalizations of human intelligence, will be applied as we direct our own intelligence.

---

[8] Dorobantu, Green, Ramelow, and Salobir, "Being Human in the Age of AI," 20.

At the most basic level, this teleological structure of technologies means that **leaders should keep in mind the imperative of responsibility**: that human existence itself should be protected from the potential existential risks of technology.[9] Pope Benedict XVI and Pope Francis concur that "the work of the Church seeks not only to remind everyone of the duty to care for nature, but at the same time 'she must above all protect mankind from self-destruction.'"[10] Because AI and other technologies do present an existential threat to humanity, these ethical imperatives should be kept in mind when dealing with projects that might present such a risk. As the quote and the two popes' documents outline, this responsibility extends to preventing lesser forms of devastation to either natural or human ecology.

The right ordering of technology can be assisted by keeping in mind Catholic Worker movement founder Peter Maurin's desire to "make the kind of society where people find it easier to be good."[11] **Companies should consider how to create technologies that form a society where, through their own agency and choice, "people find it easier to be good."** Technologies that force choices by surveillance and/or through behaviorist nudging are an affront to human dignity because they subvert autonomy. Instead, what is needed is to set the preconditions within which ethical action is possible, encouraged, and authentic, but not forced. The truest freedom is freedom that aligns with human flourishing.[12]

Further, **companies have a responsibility to ensure that their employees are offered dignified work that allows them to orient their lives toward the highest human goods** rather than to be manipulated or exploited for the sake of idolatrous pursuits of profit over

---

[9] Hans Jonas, *The Imperative of Responsibility: In Search of an Ethics for the Technological Age* (Chicago: University of Chicago Press, 1984).
[10] *Caritas in Veritate*, § 51, and *Laudato Si'*, § 79.
[11] Dorothy Day, "Letter to Our Readers at the Beginning of Our Fifteenth Year," *The Catholic Worker* 1, no. 3 (May 1947), www.catholicworker.org/dorothyday/articles/155.html.
[12] John Paul II, *Veritatis Splendor*, §§ 17, 35.

persons or reputation over social responsibilities. By way of practical guidance, there are many resources to aid the development of ethical culture in corporate settings.[13]

Given the impersonal structures of corporations, individual designers and programmers of technologies sometimes feel disempowered and helpless. Empowerment is an organizational structural design choice, however, meaning that corporations can choose to empower employees. Whether or not individual designers and programmers work in a culture that encourages ethical choice or not, that choice is still there for the individual worker. **Employees should speak up when they see ethical problems**, whether they will be rewarded for it or not. In the worst cases, employees can choose to leave oppressive organizations, and in fact they should, if they are forced to cooperate in designing evil technologies. **Organizations, meanwhile, should respect the dignity, autonomy, and consciences of their employees**. Personal ethics can never be extracted from the person, as though employees cease to be the dignified individuals they are and are reduced to mere cogs in a corporate machine. Not only are such violations unethical on the part of leaders, but they do not excuse unjust behavior on the part of subordinates, who retain their ethical agency, albeit in stunted form.

Designers set an example to the rest of society about what technology is for and how to use it well. If technologists create technology for entertainment, then that not only provides commentary on their personal values but also demonstrates and reinforces an important socio-moral value in that culture. If technologists create weapons, likewise, it displays their own predilection toward valuing weaponry, alerts us that the culture values violent power, and reinforces that value. AI is a window into our own souls, and the "souls" of our cultures. With this in mind, the

---

[13] E.g., Jose Roger Flahaux, Brian Patrick Green, and Ann Gregg Skeet, *Ethics in the Age of Disruptive Technologies: An Operational Roadmap (The ITEC Handbook)*, Markkula Center for Applied Ethics, 2023, www.scu.edu/institute-for-technology-ethics-and-culture/itec-book-pdf.

developers of technology should think about what their technological products reveal about them.

This contemplation should include the economic motivations of technological development. Currently technology is often developed explicitly for the sake of getting rich; the "next big thing" is created not for the sake of those who will use it, but for the sake of those who create it, for their own personal goals of wealth. Based on Catholic teachings about the universal destination of goods, commitment to the common good, and the preferential option for the poor, designers should develop technology with a spirit of generosity. Due to the practicalities of life, technology as a "free gift" is often impossible (though many online services are "free" in some respects), but the nature of technology as a common gift to all humanity should remain in mind. Even intellectual property laws seem to understand this notion: patents expire. **While the creation of technology might be motivated by self-interest and reward, these should eventually be cast off and the technology given openly to all.**

Disability ethicists remind us of the value of technology that aids accessibility as well as the importance of avoiding the error of imposing expectations, operations, or systems onto individuals or communities who do not need them or who do not flourish beside them.[14] Rather, technology can best serve humanity when it responds to evident needs as communicated through relationships and attention to the other, and when it facilitates the fullness of community.[15] Furthermore, the experience of disability can remind us of the limitations of technology in that it is incapable of adding any further dignity to a person who is already

---

[14] See examples of these types of arguments in: Nancy Eiesland, *The Disabled God* (Nashville, TN: Abingdon Press, 1994); Michael Oliver, *The Politics of Disablement: A Sociological Approach* (London: Macmillan, 1990); John Swinton and Brian Brock, ed., *Theology, Disability, and the New Genetics: Why Science Needs the Church* (New York: T&T Clark, 2007).

[15] In the context of biomedical ethics, this idea is also developed in Courtois, "Biomedical Challenges to Identity and Parenthood."

"fearfully and wonderfully made."[16] Rather than further distancing us from other persons, technology fosters an active encounter with persons that promotes capabilities. **When considering what to create, technologists can find inspiration in the concrete needs of society, especially of those in greatest need**, over technical development with no intention to serve society.

Within the realm of the consideration of responsibility is also the fact that products sometimes are used in ways that their inventors did not intend. **When faced with those who would abuse otherwise good products for the sake of evil, it is wise to start in the design process itself, to carefully work through each design choice in order to encourage good uses and discourage bad ones.** There are resources to help think these processes through.[17]

In the end, **we should remember that active life is ordered to contemplative life**. The contemplative life serves to identify the goals and meaning of the active life, as they are encountered in the reality of the world, of the other, of God. Hannah Arendt warns that, if this order is broken, the human being cannot find meaning in an active life that simply expands knowledge with no evident purpose.[18] All of the work that we do, whether inventing, developing, mass-producing, using, or disposing of technological products, should ultimately be for the sake of a higher good—love—and ultimately the highest good, which is love of God.

Governing an AI Society

Despite the important role of individuals and business, private action will never be sufficient to protect human dignity and secure the common good. Even in the best of circumstances, the good action of individuals needs

---

[16] Psalm 139:14.

[17] Shannon Vallor, Brian Patrick Green, and Irina Raicu, "Ethics in Technology Practice," Markkula Center for Applied Ethics, www.scu.edu/ethics-in-technology-practice.

[18] Hannah Arendt, *The Human Condition* (Chicago: University of Chicago Press, 2018 [1958]).

coordination, and bad actions require prevention and punishment.[19] As political animals, humans require governments with authority to protect human dignity and secure the common good. Since AI presents clear dangers to both, as previous chapters have shown, governments ought to act to ensure that AI serves rather than harms the flourishing of all in society, especially of those most disadvantaged. It can do so in several different ways.

First, **governments ought to pass laws to regulate the production and use of AI technologies**. Though Catholic social teaching affirms a right to private property (as ordered to the common good) and the many benefits of a free market, it also affirms the duty of governments to limit the harms that can come from the unfettered use of property in an unregulated market.[20] Such harms occur in the intense competition between technology companies for dominance and profitability, as we can see in AI applications to social media. This competition leads to manipulative practices that keep people online, or to the deployment of AI systems before they are properly tested. Regulations by national and international bodies can restrain the worst abuses that arise out of this competition, while still allowing freedom for the creative development of new technologies. We are already seeing initial steps toward this kind of legislation.[21]

It is not our intention to suggest specific legislation. There is far too much nuance in local and national contexts as well as particular interests at play in different applications to describe detailed laws for the entire world. Yet there have been valuable attempts to outline general frameworks for such protections, as seen in the principles and rights described in chapter 1. Though that chapter criticized a sole focus on

---

[19] Yves R. Simon, *A General Theory of Authority* (Notre Dame, IN: University of Notre Dame Press, 1991).
[20] E.g., *Centesimus Annus*, §§ 42–58.
[21] Examples of such legislation include the General Data Protection Regulation in the European Union and China's Personal Information Protection Law.

principles as an ethical framework, principles identify important values that deserve to be protected by law, such as privacy, safety, and fairness. Rights and the human dignity that they protect are more likely to be preserved through legislative efforts than merely voluntary agreements. Efforts to continue the development of legislation that defends these values deserve encouragement. Moreover, in contexts of encounter in political society between different visions of the world, Pope Francis has reminded us that human rights provide an important point of commonality with which to address the challenges and opportunities of AI.[22]

Unfortunately, governments can be some of the worst offenders when it comes to dangerous uses of AI. As noted earlier, AI tends to increase centralization, so its use can radically expand government power through measures like surveillance, which can undermine important aspects of human dignity, such as agency. Moreover, AI influences the exercise of power by encouraging legislators to interpret the world through the technocratic paradigm. AI measures, quantifies, and optimizes, potentially reducing the rich fullness of persons to a mathematical model of a few measurable qualities. It is especially the poor who are most likely to be subject to measurement and surveillance. Pope Francis has repeatedly taught that "realities are greater than ideas,"[23] and we can hear echoes of that admonition in his counsel for governments not to entrust a decision over a person seeking asylum to an algorithm.[24] All those in government ought to ensure that they keep the reality of their citizens in sight as they implement AI.

Governments should therefore not merely look to regulate private actors, but ought to also **put in place safeguards to ensure that the use of AI in the coercive and redistributive functions of government preserves values like fairness, privacy, safety, and responsibility.**

---

[22] Francis, "Address to Participants in the 'Rome Call' Meeting."
[23] *Evangelii Gaudium*, § 231.
[24] Francis, "Address to Participants in the 'Rome Call' Meeting."

Concerns over bias and responsibility loom large here. As described in earlier chapters, AI programs in welfare provision and legal processes such as bail hearings can be biased against certain groups because of historical training data. An individual is judged not as a unique person, but as a representative of a population. Whenever a government entity wants to implement AI, it should take steps to ensure that any biases are minimized by asking questions like:

- Was the training data unbiased?
- Was the training data similar to data for the population upon which the AI program will be used?
- Have the opinions of members of the community upon which it will be deployed been sought?
- How will the AI system interact with other elements of the criminal justice or welfare system?[25]

After its implementation, program administrators should monitor the results to determine whether unintended consequences are developing. While these steps will not ensure the absence of bias, they can help. If bias or other problems do develop, administrators should halt the use of the AI program until the source of the problem is addressed. If a program has too many possibilities for bias, as with facial recognition, it should simply not be used.

Whenever these AI programs are developed by government or private entities for applications with a significant impact on people's lives, **there should always be an easy route to appeal an AI decision to a person**. AI algorithms make too many mistakes because of their inability to grasp the nuances of individual context. That is the importance of human prudence: the ability to adjust the universal rule or prediction to the

---

[25] For an example of this analysis, see Andrew Selbst, Danah Boyd, Sorelle Friedler, Suresh Venkatasubramanian, and Janet Vertesi, "Fairness and Abstraction in Sociotechnical Systems," *Proceedings of the Conference on Fairness, Accountability, and Transparency* (January 2019): 59–68, doi.org/10.1145/3287560.3287598.

individual situation, to grasp the reality in front of the actor. We cannot be a society governed by algorithms. The ease of appeal is a crucial aspect here. If a person is forced to wait two months and endure endless phone trees to receive benefits they are due but were denied by an AI fraud detection system, then that person has been harmed and may give up seeking the benefit altogether. Justice delayed is justice denied. That is why for especially serious decisions, such as those involving human life or death, there should always be a human closely involved in any AI system and its decision. It is for this reason, for example, that lethal autonomous weapons should not be developed. Too often, however, agencies do not have enough staff to receive these appeals and fail to empower their staff to independently respond to problems. These aspects of government use of AI should be addressed.

Government officials should **restrict applications that might overly expand the power of government or be used to expand the political power of individuals and groups**. This may include restricting the general surveillance of the population and limiting the use of AI for microtargeting political advertisements, political misinformation, or gerrymandering. At the same time, AI can help detect the misapplication of political power, such as by monitoring corruption.

This last concern over political power raises the issue of subsidiarity. While regulating the use of AI by both business and government is an important good, society is not formed only by the market-state binary. Catholic social teaching, as part of its principle of subsidiarity, has encouraged a variety of social forms that exist beyond the market and state and yet are larger than the family.[26] These kinds of cooperative, nonprofit, yet nongovernmental organizations are threatened by AI in many instances, either though the decrease in the number and intensity of social ties due to the draw of social media and online shopping or to the concentration of power brought about by the capital-intensive nature of AI technology and data acquisition. The resources necessary to efficiently

---

[26] E.g., *Quadragesimo Anno*, §§ 79–80.

use AI threaten smaller organizations that lack these resources. **It is thus important for governments to explore how to support the continued existence of intermediary organizations as a way to ensure the distribution of power and social engagement in political society.** The importance of subsidiarity appears in government action in regard to AI. Not only do national governments and international organizations have a role to play, but regional and even city governments have also started regulating AI and banning implementations like facial recognition. Citizens and legislators at the lowest levels of government can shape the actions of transnational corporations and foster the conditions that allow for the emergence of institutions in civil society that bring a moral voice to the challenges of AI.[27] Broadening the reach of subsidiarity is essential to the productive and ethical implementation of AI.

Finally, misinformation and political polarization driven by AI have diminished social cohesion and trust in political society. Political actors are not innocent in this regard. Nearly all major politicians and parties have engaged in microtargeting of voter bases using data analytics, a practice surely at odds with the call of Catholic social teaching for participatory citizenship commensurate with the demands of human dignity. Moreover, far too many political actors engage in algorithmic-driven vilification of their opponents or use finely-sliced and/or questionable data to trumpet a point of view sharply at odds with basic reality. We have to be clear about how such practices damage the pursuit of a common good. Lies, Pope Francis has reminded us, manifest a refusal to believe that we belong to each other and, in doing so, put the lives of the vulnerable in jeopardy and lead to the very real danger of becoming a throwaway culture.[28] Until **political actors themselves embrace a renewed commitment to truth**

---

[27] Francis, "Address to the Pontifical Academy of Life."

[28] Francis, "Message for the 53rd World Communications Day: 'We Are Members One of Another' (Eph 4:25): From Social Network Communities to the Human Community," January 24, 2019, www.vatican.va/content/francesco/en/messages/communications/documents/papa-francesco_20190124_messaggio-comunicazioni-sociali.html.

and the common good, it is far from clear why anyone would expect regulatory changes or exhortations to solve the problems of misinformation or disinformation. Such changes will likely appear as merely coercive enforcements of a particular viewpoint by one or another political persuasion and thus be met with increased distrust.

Pope Francis has said that fraternity among all is the precondition for ensuring that a technology like AI is used in service to justice and peace.[29] Actors at all levels of government have many complex and practical tasks, and, of course, there are many important issues to argue over. But, in the time of AI, we cannot forget the primary importance for those in politics of the practice of such virtues as prudence, honesty, and charity. All the technical abilities of AI can never replace the demand for men and women of such character who govern and legislate and lead.

Working in an AI Economy

Despite the novelty of AI and the difficulty of predicting the specific changes it will bring to the workplace, Catholic principles provide a firm foundation for addressing the moral implications of a changing economy. For example, Catholic social teaching warned of the exploitation of workers and severe inequities brought on by labor long ago, back when nearly all labor was physical, and those warnings have not changed with the advent of business organizations driven by ideas and mental labor. The Catholic tradition will not stop challenging workplaces to consider how values such as dignity, the common good, and worker rights are an essential part of the workplace. This section describes opportunities to improve work in the age of AI from a Catholic perspective, even if the specifics remain mostly unknown.

Pope John Paul II described the dangers of technology supplanting the worker, "taking away all personal satisfaction and the incentive to creativity and responsibility, when it deprives many workers of their

---

[29] Francis, "Address to Participants in the 'Rome Call' Meeting."

previous employment, or when, through exalting the machine, it reduces man to the status of its slave."[30] An obvious way that the worker can be supplanted is through automation since, as Pope Francis notes, "The orientation of the economy has favored a kind of technological progress in which the costs of production are reduced by laying off workers and replacing them with machines."[31] Given the importance of work for personal growth and human activity, "it is essential that 'we continue to prioritize the goal of access to steady employment for everyone.'"[32]

The loss of human creativity and responsibility in work can occur more subtly through corporate surveillance of workers driven by AI.[33] As labor becomes more digital, much more of our work will leave a digital trail, and what is digital is far easier to record and track than what is analog. The times we begin and end work, our location, the messages we send to coworkers, and even what we are typing or whether we are sitting at our computer can be recorded digitally. Such surveillance serves as an easy path to control workers.

When evaluating corporate surveillance policies, it is crucial to keep in mind that the ultimate goal of most surveillance policies is accountability. Managers and business owners want to know that their employees are doing the work for which they are paid. In general, accountability at work is a positive thing, both for employers and employees. It is generally good for workers to have standards and expectations as they pursue their projects, and to understand how their work will be evaluated. And it is reasonable that managers want to understand how their employees spend their work hours.

But while accountability is a reasonable goal, many workplaces will make the false assumption that surveillance is the best or only route to

---

[30] *Laborem Exercens*, § 5.
[31] *Laudato Si'*, § 128.
[32] *Laudato Si'*, § 127, quoting *Caritas in Veritate*, § 32.
[33] Alex Pentland, *Social Physics: How Social Networks Can Make Us Smarter* (New York: Penguin Books, 2015).

accountability. In fact, in many contexts, surveillance can make workplaces toxic in two ways. First, it can lead to micromanagement, which offends against a human dignity that is connected with the ability to choose the strategy to achieve a goal through creativity and responsibility, even if the worker did not set the goal in the first place. The more surveillance there is, the less freedom workers have to approach work tasks in their own ways. The second problem is that there is a negative correlation between surveillance and trust, such that the more constant and intrusive the surveillance, the less the workers feel trusted, and in turn the less they will trust their workplaces.

While corporate surveillance approached prudently might produce some sensible policies that hold workers accountable, surveillance done poorly will have the effect of creating an environment that undermines the dignity of workers, creates conditions of mistrust between management and workers, and centralizes power. **Managers should find ways other than AI-driven surveillance to institute meaningful accountability**.

AI also affects workplace motivation. At the broadest level, motivations can be divided into extrinsic and intrinsic. Classic examples of extrinsic work motivations are "carrots and sticks." Those are obviously different motivations, but they are both extrinsic to the task at hand in the sense that the activity for which they motivate is irrelevant. In a workplace context, the easiest analogy is to compare the carrot to a wage, and the stick to the fear of getting fired, which are both extremely powerful motivators. Wages and layoffs directly concern human wellbeing, and the tradition of Catholic social teaching has been largely motivated by concern for exploitation of workers, working conditions, industry change, and wealth distribution, which all have direct implications for extrinsic motivations in the workplace.

But the story here is more complicated. Extrinsic motivations can be contrasted with intrinsic motivations.[34] In management literature and elsewhere, classic instances of intrinsic motivation include mastery (wanting to learn how to do things better), autonomy (wanting to accomplish a task in my own way), and purpose (wanting to make the world a better place).[35] The Catholic tradition describes intrinsic motivations using concepts of virtue and the common good. There are three things we must note about intrinsic motivations. First, while extrinsic motivators are powerful, intrinsic motivators are more so, driving people to work harder and with greater joy.[36] Conversely, extrinsic motivators can lead workers to focus on doing the bare minimum necessary to satisfy the externally imposed requirement. Second, intrinsic motivators are deeply tied to human dignity. A job with no intrinsic motivators at all will grind a person down over time because the job itself bears no satisfaction except as an instrument by which to satisfy or obtain the extrinsic motivator. Third, extrinsic and intrinsic motivations exist on a continuum and in context, such that we cannot in the abstract say "job X or industry Y is only extrinsically motivating, while job Z contains intrinsic motivators." By the same token, a given job can be differently motivating to different people. Any job or any task can be infused with intrinsic motivation for a given individual.[37]

---

[34] David M. Kreps, "Intrinsic Motivation and Extrinsic Incentives," *The American Economic Review* 87, no. 2, Papers and Proceedings of the Hundred and Fourth Annual Meeting of the American Economic Association (May 1997): 359–364.

[35] Daniel H. Pink, *Drive: The Surprising Truth About What Motivates Us* (New York: Riverhead Books, 2009).

[36] C.P. Cerasoli, J.M. Nicklin, and M.T. Ford, "Intrinsic Motivation and Extrinsic Incentives Jointly Predict Performance: A 40-Year Meta-Analysis," *Psychological Bulletin* 140, no. 4, (2014): 980–1008.

[37] A classic case study is hospital custodial staff who took pride in their work as essential to the success of the hospital and undertook it with a care for patients that reflected that shared end. See Amy Wrzesniewski and Jane E. Dutton, "Crafting a Job: Revisioning Employees as Active Crafters of Their Work," *Academy of Management Review* 26, no. 2 (2001): 179–201, doi.org/10.5465/amr.2001.4378011.

AI could expand the kinds of jobs or tasks that have intrinsic motivations. There are already examples of digital technology doing this. For example, when Microsoft introduced Excel spreadsheets, there was some panic in the field of accounting. Many accounting positions just moved numbers around, and with a digital spreadsheet to do all that automatically, the future need for accountants was in question. But because accountants were no longer needed to erase and recalculate numbers all day, they were freed to perform more interesting tasks, such as calculating and evaluating risk. There is no guarantee that AI technology will have this effect. We can also easily imagine a future in which AI saps intrinsic motivation due to either the tasks automated or its forms of implementation, such as intensified scheduling and surveillance. Moreover, in contexts where work is treated as a central source of a worker's dignity rather than a task that is dignified by the worker's personal pursuit of the good, intrinsic motivation can easily become a means of labor exploitation.[38] **AI should be used to increase intrinsic work motivations consistent with the inherent dignity of workers.** Such an approach honors the creativity of workers and empowers them to direct their work to the common good.

Finally, AI technologies might upset the balance of work with nonwork life. Economic pressures can blind people to the importance of a life full of family, friends, worship, nature, exploration, rest, hobbies, and leisure for individual and communal flourishing. Part of the success of labor unions and the tradition of Catholic social teaching was to ensure that workers were not exploited, in part by creating time and space for such activities. The many movements to establish boundaries to minimize the intrusions of work have been important and by many measures, successful. But recent digital technologies threaten to undermine that progress, and coming AI technologies might continue this trend. For example, emails

---

[38] Jonathan Malesic, *The End of Burnout: Why Work Drains Us and How to Build Better Lives* (Oakland: University of California Press, 2022). On the relation between work and human dignity, see especially *Laborem Exercens*, § 5–10.

can be sent around the clock, and meetings can be virtual, meaning that you can now be expected to work in the middle of family vacation. Scheduling software can create unpredictable shifts that use workers efficiently but undermine their ability to plan their personal lives. Virtual meetings and electronic messaging can be good insofar as they increase flexibility and allow workers more choice about when they work. But it is also possible to view these technologies as opportunities for employers to exploit workers and undermine the hard-fought victories of work/life balance. **AI should be used in ways that allow people to have a rich life outside of work.**

The effects of AI on work are open. Much depends on how AI applications and AI-incorporating workplaces are designed. AI could replace workers, submit them to control, crush their spirit, and undermine their private lives. Or it could serve to remove drudgery, facilitate creativity, and create more benefit for the common good. We ought to focus on ensuring that the latter kind of workplace comes into being.

Encountering the Other in an AI Community

As we have noted throughout, a focus on encounter and the quality of the relationships that human beings experience, among themselves and the whole creation, could foster discernment regarding the use of AI in people's lives, cultural settings, and social environments. A relational approach presupposes and promotes the participation and collaboration of everyone—particularly those who are left out, excluded, and marginalized—by contributing to addressing the social inequity, discrimination, and biases that are present in our world. AI technology could be at the service of this inclusive and comprehensive social agenda or could contribute to undermining or even threatening it. This section highlights themes for reflection in discerning how AI is affecting our relationships.

A focus on relationships implies that **technological advances should be at the service of all people, everywhere, and for the whole planet**, which are all subjects for encounter. Progress in developing AI systems should become a further opportunity that leads to searching for and promoting the common good of humankind and of the earth because the common good allows the ultimate realization of individual, social, and planetary capabilities. Hence, the common good aims at promoting relational and institutional dynamics within social contexts striving to achieve individual and collective flourishing by encompassing all social goods (spiritual, moral, relational, and material).

Individual and social identities are multilayered. They are embodied, culturally and historically situated, and shaped by experiences, events, dynamics, beliefs, values, and the contexts in which people live. Examining and discerning technological advances in light of a relational criterion allows human beings not only to use technology responsibly, but also to better understand their identities. The more human beings critically examine how they use technological advances, the more they manifest who they are and the more they preserve and continue to shape and enrich their own relational identities. In particular, a relational understanding of identity highlights how any person's identity relates to and even depends on other human beings. These relationships help us to be who we are and stress human interdependence. This interdependence varies according to our age, condition, and social location. While it exposes human vulnerability, it also fosters individual and social empowerment.

Our best interest is inseparable from the best interest of others. This demands care, particularly for those more vulnerable in families, communities, and society at large. AI could contribute to a renewal and expansion of how human beings understand and embrace their agency by contributing to a vision of social striving that promotes the common good. Moreover, AI could foster a deeper understanding of human relational identity, interrelatedness, and interdependence. AI, used well, has the potential to foster opportunities for strengthening and deepening the richness of what it means to be human.

We ought to analyze the use of AI and AI-embedded technologies in terms of how they foster or diminish relational virtues so that we strengthen fraternity, social friendship, and our relationship with the environment. Technology has enormous power not only to alter and control nature and our environment, but also change our behaviors, ways of thinking, and what we value. We should be mindful of the power of AI and AI-embedded technologies to interfere with genuine relationships by creating "the illusion of communication" and to provide us with "the appearance of sociability" while elevating the individual over community.[39] Because love demands that we move from preoccupation with ourselves toward others in the spirit of charity and solidarity, we ought to ask how we can use AI to achieve these ends and fulfill our purpose as children of God.

At a minimum, **we should safeguard against AI being used, intentionally or unintentionally, as a substitute for genuine relationships. AI should only be used to enrich our relationships with one another, our community, and with nature**. For example, the use of carebots, or robots deployed to provide basic living assistance, medical monitoring, and companionship with the elderly, should never be a substitute for the expert care of healthcare professionals nor relieve society or family members of their responsibility to care for and accompany the elderly throughout their natural life. However, using AI to assist those individuals who are physically or mentally impaired to communicate or connect with loved ones, caretakers, or the wider community is an acceptable use of technology as a tool to support our capacities or compensate for physical limitations. These concerns extend to other spheres that depend on relationships, such as the need for the interpersonal engagement of health care workers or teachers in medicine and education. Spheres of human encounter should not be undermined through their replacement by AI.

---

[39] *Fratelli Tutti*, § 43.

We also need to be cognizant of how AI and related technologies deplete natural resources and contribute to the degradation of the environment. **We should support policies that curtail such exploitative applications while seeking more sustainable ways of implementing these technologies.** Because the experience of nature and natural beauty is essential to our physical and spiritual wellbeing, we also ought to inquire into ways that AI and related technologies deepen or diminish our experience of awe and wonder engendered by the physical world. These technologies have great potential to expand our knowledge and appreciation of the natural world so that we can become better stewards of God's creation. Yet they also threaten to mediate our experience with nature so that our essential connection with the earth remains hidden.

Conclusion

The emergent use of AI throughout our world has the potential to upend many of the norms and expectations of our personal and social lives. It is important that we prepare both ourselves and our structures for these changes. But this is not the first technological revolution the Church has witnessed, and the long-standing tradition of Catholic thought can and should guide how we shape and navigate this new technological reality. Working within this tradition, Pope Francis's critique of the technocratic paradigm and call for a culture of encounter has given us specific guidance for addressing the pressing concerns of this current moment. The Church looks forward with joy and hope to continually witness to and celebrate the Gospel in every generation. Contemplating the gaze of the Samaritan can help to train our hearts and minds to best accomplish this unchanging goal no matter the turns and surprises along the way, including those of AI development. The scope of this gaze does not end at the AI technologies alone. Rather, this gaze reaches forward, to anticipate gifts and dangers. We do not simply wish to cultivate virtuous encounters with AI for the sake of their application alone, as interactions with AI are further ordered to higher goods. We emphasize that the encounters we wish to cultivate in an age of AI are ultimately ones of love toward our families, our neighbors, our homes, our world, and God. AI, along with all technological advancement, should seek to embed these relational encounters more deeply, rather than disrupt them. Moral evaluation in response to the current capabilities of AI and in anticipation of its possibilities is a truly human practice in service to what we love beyond our technological achievements. We strive to maintain an attentive and prudent gaze all along the journey to come, so that we are prepared to serve and to promote God's grace. Keeping in mind how AI can support or diminish virtuous relationality, **each of us should ask ourselves the following questions to ensure that we are integrating technology into our lives in a manner that enhances our relationships with others, with the world, and with God.**

- Do I feel energized or depleted after using AI-embedded technologies, such as social media and other apps?
- Do I often resort to technology in social situations instead of engaging with those around me?
- Do I use social media and similar technologies in ways that deepen my connection with loved ones?
- Do I use my smartphone, social media, and other AI-embedded technologies more than I would like?
- Am I able to spend time in nature or in meditation without being interrupted by handheld devices or other smart technology?
- Has my prayer life been enhanced by technology, or do I find myself neglecting this aspect of my life in favor of distracting myself with digital technology?
- How might AI curate or tailor news and information to reinforce my biases and narrow concerns? How might I expand my exposure to a wide array of information sources so that I am more aware of other perspectives to foster empathy with others, especially those on the peripheries?

Contributors

Nathan Colaner is an Associate Teaching Professor in the Department of Management at Seattle University, where his main research and teaching focus is on the ethics of artificial intelligence, especially as it relates to business. At Seattle University, he is also the Program Director of Business Analytics and the Managing Director of Ethics and Technology. His teaching revolves around institutional ethics, focusing on the ethical implications of organizations and an increasing reliance on digital technology. Outside of SU, he consults on AI ethics with businesses, government, military, other university ethics and technology centers, and religious societies to assess risk in implementing big data and AI solutions.

Jeremiah Coogan is Assistant Professor of New Testament at the Jesuit School of Theology. He received his PhD in Christianity and Judaism in Antiquity from the University of Notre Dame (2020). From 2020 to 2022, he was a Marie Skłodowska-Curie Fellow in the Faculty of Theology and Religion at the University of Oxford. As a scholar of the New Testament and early Christianity, Coogan focuses on early Christian theologies and practices related to books, knowledge, technology, and the body. His award-winning first book, *Eusebius the Evangelist* (2023), demonstrates how early Christians used emerging textual technologies to read Scripture and organize knowledge. Coogan's teaching spans the New Testament, early Christianity, and ancient Judaism, with a particular focus on Gospel literature and on the social history of early Christianity (including gender, enslavement, technology, labor, and empire). His pedagogy invites students to creative encounters with the New Testament in light of its manifold contexts, from the ancient Mediterranean to global reading communities today.

Contributors

Mariele Courtois joined the Theology Department at Benedictine College in Atchison, Kansas, as an Assistant Professor in 2022. Her research interests include biomedical ethics, technology ethics, disability theology, and the sacramentality of the hospital. She earned a PhD in Moral Theology and Ethics (2022) and Master of Philosophy in Theology and Religious Studies (2021) from the Catholic University of America. Her dissertation entitled "Biomedical Challenges to Identity and Parenthood: An Investigation into the Ethics of Genetic Technologies at the Beginning of Life" applies Edith Stein's understanding of individuality to ethical questions concerning genetic therapies and the relationship between disability and identity. While at CUA, she was a Graduate Scholar of the Center for Carmelite Studies. She also holds a Master of Theological Studies from the University of Notre Dame (2017) and a BS in Biology from Loyola Marymount University (2015). While at the University of Notre Dame, she was a Sorin Fellow for the de Nicola Center for Ethics and Culture. She is a member of The International Association for the Study of the Philosophy of Edith Stein.

Brian Cutter is an Associate Professor of Philosophy at the University of Notre Dame. Before starting at Notre Dame in 2016, he was a Bersoff Faculty Fellow at New York University. He received his PhD from the University of Texas at Austin in 2015. His research is primarily in the philosophy of mind, metaphysics, and philosophy of religion. Most of his work is aimed at making progress on perennial metaphysical questions about the mind and the place of human persons within the cosmic scheme. He has published articles in many top philosophy journals, including *Noûs, Mind, Philosophy and Phenomenological Research, Analysis, Philosophical Studies, Philosophers' Imprint, Australasian Journal of Philosophy, Philosophical Quarterly, Ergo, Analytic Philosophy, Oxford Studies in Philosophy of Religion, Faith and Philosophy,* and others.

Contributors

David E. DeCosse is the Director of Religious and Catholic Ethics and Director of Campus Ethics at the Markkula Center for Applied Ethics at Santa Clara University, where he is also Adjunct Associate Professor in the Religious Studies Department. DeCosse works in the area of Catholic social ethics. He is currently writing a book on the theology of conscience of Pope Francis. He is the author of *Created Freedom Under the Sign of the Cross: A Catholic Public Theology for the United States* (2022). In the last years, he has co-edited *Conscience and Catholic Education: Theology, Administration, and Teaching* (2022); *Conscience and Catholic Health Care: From Clinical Contexts to Government Mandates* (2017); and *Conscience and Catholicism: Rights, Responsibilities, and Institutional Responses* (2015). He has also written for publications ranging from *Theological Studies* to the *National Catholic Reporter*.

Justin Charles Gable, OP, is a Professor of Philosophy at the Dominican School of Philosophy and Theology in Berkeley, California. A native of southern California, Fr. Gable graduated from the University of San Francisco with a degree in philosophy, subsequently attending Fordham University in New York, where he received his MA and PhD in philosophy. He entered the Dominican Order in 2006 and was ordained a priest in 2014. Since 2014, he has been a professor at the Dominican School of Philosophy and Theology, becoming Chair of the Philosophy Department in 2022. From 2012 to 2016, Fr. Gable served as Vice-President of the American Maritain Association, and from 2019 to 2022 he served as Regent of Studies for the Western Dominican Province. His teaching and research interests include phenomenology, hermeneutics, philosophy of religion, and bioethics.

Matthew J. Gaudet is Director of Ethics Programs and Initiatives for the School of Engineering at Santa Clara University, where he is tasked with developing and managing a program of moral, philosophical, and theological formation for engineering students, preparing them to be conscious, reflective, and ethical as the future builders and maintainers of a technological society. Gaudet's research lies at the intersection of Catholic and philosophical ethics with the social sciences, especially the application of ethics to the topics of war and peace, the university, disability, and technology as well as the field of ethics education. His articles can be found in the *Journal of the Society of Christian Ethics*, the *Journal of Moral Theology, Teaching Ethics, Commonweal, America,* and the *National Catholic Reporter*. He has co-edited three special issues of the *Journal of Moral Theology*, including a 2022 issue on the topic of Artificial Intelligence.

Brian Patrick Green is the Director of Technology Ethics at the Markkula Center for Applied Ethics at Santa Clara University. His work focuses on AI and ethics, technology ethics in corporations, the ethics of space exploration and use, the ethics of technological manipulation of humans, the ethics of mitigation of and adaptation towards risky emerging technologies, and various aspects of the impact of technology and engineering on human life and society, including the relationship of technology and religion (particularly the Catholic Church). Green is author of the book *Space Ethics* (2021), co-author of the book *Ethics in the Age of Disruptive Technologies: An Operational Roadmap (The ITEC Handbook)* (2023), and co-author of the *Ethics in Technology Practice* resources (2018). He is co-editor of the book *Religious Transhumanism and Its Critics* (2022) and co-editor of a special issue of the *Journal of Moral Theology* on Artificial Intelligence (2022).

Noreen Herzfeld is the Nicholas and Bernice Reuter Professor of Science and Religion at St. John's University and The College of St. Benedict, where she teaches both computer science and theology. She is also a Principal Research Associate with the Science and Research Center (ZRS) Koper, Slovenia. She holds graduate degrees in Mathematics and Computer Science from The Pennsylvania State University and a doctorate in Theology from the Graduate Theological Union, Berkeley. Herzfeld is the author of *The Artifice of Intelligence: Divine and Human Relationship in a Robotic Age* (Fortress, 2023), *In Our Image: Artificial Intelligence and the Human Spirit* (Fortress, 2002), *Technology and Religion: Remaining Human in a Co-Created World* (Templeton, 2009), and *The Limits of Perfection in Technology, Religion, and Science* (Pandora, 2010) and editor of *Religion and the New Technologies* (MDPI, 2017) and *Religious and Cultural Implications of Technology-Mediated Relationships in a Post-Pandemic World* (Lexington, 2023).

James Kintz is an Assistant Professor of Philosophy at The Dominican School of Philosophy & Theology in Berkeley, California. He received his PhD in philosophy from Saint Louis University under the supervision of Eleonore Stump. His research focuses primarily on issues at the intersection of metaphysics and philosophy of mind, and he has published articles in journals such as *The British Journal for the History of Philosophy*, *The Review of Metaphysics*, and *Utilitas*. His current work explores the nature of personhood, the character of mutual awareness, and the cognitional theory and moral psychology of Thomas Aquinas.

Cory Andrew Labrecque is professor of bioethics and theological ethics, and the inaugural Chair of Educational Leadership in the Ethics of Life at the Faculty of Theology and Religious Studies at Université Laval in Quebec City, where he is vice-dean and director of graduate programs in theology. Labrecque's teaching and research examine how the Abrahamic religions—with a focus on the Roman Catholic tradition—approach ethical issues in medicine (especially related to aging and end of life), biotechnology, and the environment. He is the editor of La beauté, les arts, et le vieillissement (PUL, 2020) and « *Parle à la terre, et elle t'instruira* »: *les religions et l'écologie* (PUL, 2022). He is president-elect of the Canadian Bioethics Society, vice-president of the Comité national d'éthique sur le vieillissement (Quebec), and a corresponding member of the Pontifical Academy for Life.

Catherine Moon is a Postdoctoral Fellow at the Institute for Advanced Studies in Culture at the University of Virginia. She studies Edith Stein and the role of human experience in moral discernment and coming to know. Her present research at the IASC focuses on the role of religious experience to civil life in interreligious and postmodern secular contexts as well as the relationship between new technologies and the common good, particularly as it relates to education. She has previously taught courses in theology, philosophy, and ethics at Georgetown University, Mount St. Mary's University, and The Catholic University of America. She received her doctorate in Moral Theology and Ethics from The Catholic University of American in August of 2023. She also earned a Master in Theological Studies from Boston College in the School of Theology and Ministry as well a Bachelor in Liberal Arts from St. John's College Annapolis.

Anselm Ramelow, OP, is Professor of Philosophy at the Dominican School of Philosophy and Theology in Berkeley and a member of the Core Doctoral Faculty at the Graduate Theological Union. Fr. Ramelow also taught at the University of San Francisco and the Munich School of Philosophy and is a Senior Fellow at the Berkeley Institute. He obtained his doctorate under Robert Spaemann in Munich on Leibniz and the Spanish Jesuits (*Gott, Freiheit, Weltenwahl*, 1997) and did theological work on George Lindbeck and the question of a Thomist philosophy and theology of language (*Beyond Modernism—George Lindbeck and the Linguistic Turn in Theology*, 2005). He contributed articles to the *Historisches Wörterbuch der Philosophie* and essays on topics at the intersection of philosophy and theology, as well as a translation and commentary on part of Aquinas's *De veritate*. He continues to work on questions of free will, philosophy of religion (miracles, existence, and nature of God) and philosophical aesthetics.

Contributors

Paul Scherz is Associate Professor in the Department of Religious Studies at the University of Virginia. He is also a Visiting Fellow at the Institute for Advanced Studies in Culture UVa and an Advisory Fellow at the Grefenstette Center for Ethics in Science, Technology, and Law at Duquesne. Building on dual training in genetics and moral theology, his research examines the intersection of religious ethics with science, technology, and medicine. He also studies the influence of the Stoic tradition of virtue ethics on Christian ethics. He is the author of *Science and Christian Ethics* (2019) and co-editor with Joseph Davis of *The Evening of Life: The Challenges of Aging and Dying Well* (2020). His most recent book, *Tomorrow's Troubles: Risk, Anxiety, and Prudence in an Age of Algorithmic Governance* (2022), examines the role of quantitative risk analysis in contemporary culture and ethics. He is currently working on projects on AI ethics and the ethics of precision medicine.

John P. Slattery is the Director of the Carl G. Grefenstette Center for Ethics in Science, Technology, and Law at Duquesne University. Slattery holds degrees in computer science, theological studies, and the history and philosophy of science. He is the author of *Faith and Science at Notre Dame: John Zahm, Evolution, and the Catholic Church* (2019), the editor of *The T&T Clark Handbook of Christian Theology and the Modern Sciences* (2020), and a producer of the popular AAAS film series, *Science: The Wide Angle*. He has also published numerous essays and is currently researching the intersection of liberation theology and technology ethics, the history of intersections between science, technology and race, and the role of race and gender in historical discussions of theology and science.

Margarita Vega is Professor of Philosophy at the Dominican School of Philosophy and Theology in Berkeley, California. She has taught at the University of Valladolid in Spain and at the University of California, Berkeley. Professor Vega has published on Aristotle and the theory of metaphor, musical aesthetics, the social ontology of art, the mind-body problem, the definition of personhood, and the Chinese Room argument. She teaches courses on the philosophy of language, the philosophy of society, the philosophy of mind, metaphysics, theory of knowledge, philosophy of science, and philosophical anthropology.

Luis G. Vera is Associate Professor and Chair of the Theology Department at Mount St. Mary's University in Emmitsburg, Maryland. A native of Venezuela, Vera earned his BA from the University of Georgia and an MTS and doctorate from the University of Notre Dame. Vera's research brings Catholic social teaching and moral theology into engagement with technology ethics and media studies. He is especially interested in the various interactions between our cognitive habits and our tool use, as well as how these interactions can best help cultivate virtue, contemplation, and the love of neighbor. He has published or presented on topics such as augmented reality, digital surveillance, concealed-carry handgun use, medieval reading practices, and the role of memory in framing attention and media use. His current project explores the rhetorical patterns that can best contribute to the fruitful cultivation of memory and judgment in a digital age.

Andrea Vicini, SJ, is Chairperson, Michael P. Walsh Professor of Bioethics, and Professor of Theological Ethics in the Theology Department at Boston College. An MD pediatrician (University of Bologna), he is an alumnus of Boston College (STL and PhD) and holds an STD from the Pontifical Faculty of Theology of Southern Italy in Naples. He is co-chair of the international network Catholic Theological Ethics in the World Church. His research interests and publications include theological bioethics, global health, biotechnologies, and environmental issues. In 2015–2016, he had a research fellowship at the Center of Theological Inquiry (Princeton, NJ) on the societal implications of astrobiology. Recent publications include three co-edited volumes— *Reimagining the Moral Life: On Lisa Sowle Cahill's Contributions to*

Christian Ethics (2020), *Ethics of Global Public Health: Climate Change, Pollution, and the Health of the Poor* (2021), and *The Rising Global Cancer Pandemic: Health, Ethics, and Social Justice* (2022).

Warren von Eschenbach is a moral philosopher who earned his doctorate from The University of Texas at Austin, his master's degree from Marquette University, and his bachelor's degree from Trinity University (TX). He has written on artificial intelligence and trust and has published articles in *Philosophy & Technology, Journal of Global Ethics, The Journal of Value Inquiry, America Magazine,* and *Indigo Humanities Journal.* In addition, he is a contributing author to the book *Virtues in the Public Sphere: Citizenship, Civic Friendship, and Duty* (2019). Currently, he serves as the Vice Chancellor for Academic Affairs at the University of North Texas System. Previously, von Eschenbach was a faculty member and administrator for fourteen years in several roles in the Provost's Office at the University of Notre Dame, including as the inaugural Managing Director of the Notre Dame Technology Ethics Center.

Jordan Joseph Wales is an Associate Professor and the John and Helen Kuczmarski Chair in Theology at Hillsdale College. His scholarship focuses on early Christian understandings of the vision of God as well as contemporary questions relating to artificial intelligence. Currently writing a monograph on theology and AI, he is published in *Augustinian Studies, AI & Society,* and the *Journal of Moral Theology,* among others. He is a fellow of the Centre for Humanity and the Common Good at Regent College, University of British Columbia, as well as of the International Society for Science and Religion. He received his MTS and PhD in Theology from the University of Notre Dame after studying under a British Marshall Scholarship in the UK, where he received a Diploma in Theology from Oxford and a MSc in Cognitive Science and Natural Language from the University of Edinburgh. He is a recipient of a Graduate Research Fellowship from the National Science Foundation.

www.ingramcontent.com/pod-product-compliance
Lightning Source LLC
Chambersburg PA
CBHW071247230426
43668CB00011B/1619